THE ONLINE LEARNING HANDBOOK

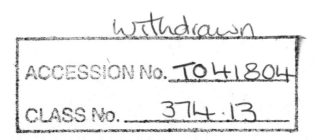

THE ONLINE LEARNING HANDBOOK

Developing and Using Web-Based Learning

ALAN JOLLIFFE, JONATHAN RITTER & DAVID STEVENS

KOGAN
PAGE

The authors would like to thank Mr Dennis Sale, Section Head, Educational and Staff Development Department, Singapore Polytechnic, for his contribution to Chapter 2, The Development Model.

First published in 2001

Kogan Page Limited
120 Pentonville Road
London
N1 9JN
UK

Stylus Publishing Inc.
22883 Quicksilver Drive
Sterling
VA 20166-2012
USA

The views expressed in this book are those of the authors, and are not necessarily the same as those of *The Times Higher Education Supplement.*

British Library Cataloguing in Publication Data

A CIP record for this book is available from the British Library.

ISBN 0 7494 3208 X

Typeset by Jean Cussons Typesetting, Diss, Norfolk
Printed and bound in Great Britain by Clays Ltd, St Ives plc

Contents

Foreword

The Times Higher Education Supplement is delighted to be associated with this essential guide for teachers in colleges and universities. Its aim is to help readers to keep up with rapid change and make the most of the Internet and the World Wide Web as aids to teaching and learning.

Over the last few years the impact of new technology has increased in every area of life, but none more than in the well-wired higher education community. Teaching and learning at the higher education level never did stand still but now the pressures from demanding students, quality auditors and fast changing techniques grow relentlessly.

This handbook offers numerous suggestions to improve communication between teachers and students, and to supplement traditional forms of teaching. It also explores the possibilities that new media offers for innovative ways of teaching and effective ways of learning. We hope it will prove a useful source of ideas, reference points and short cuts; that it will inspire readers to exploit and develop new technologies to their own benefit and that of students; and that it will help reduce the panic and increase the productivity.

Auriol Stevens
Editor, The Times Higher Education Supplement

Introduction

At the close of the 20th century, the Internet, and particularly the World Wide Web, has proven to be the most sophisticated communications network our civilization has ever known. Through its ease of use and low cost, the Web has become very effective at selling and distributing all kinds of things from stuffed toys to stocks to delivering pornography to anyone who cares to search for it. The Internet is also a provider of electronic mail, discussion forums, chat rooms and listserves, connecting people in ways they never thought or wanted to be possible. The Web is fast becoming as commonplace as the telephone, the radio and the television, and is well positioned to become the dominant means for individuals, companies and other organizations to distribute and exchange information.

Computer speed and storage capacity is doubling every half-year. As the world moves into the new millennium, 50 million households in the United States and similar numbers in Europe and Asia are connected to the Web and it is expected that by 2015 the entire 'developed' world will be online. What is by tomorrow's standards a winding pathway constrained by the electronic equivalent of a flagman walking in front of the moving vehicle, the Web of the future will be a multi-lane super-motorway, unrecognizable by today's standards. This digital revolution will bring together many, if not all, forms of communication including learning, thus creating a resource of unparalleled possibilities.

The real potential of the Web is as a tool that can be used in an infinite number of ways. For example, using the Web to deliver learning events has a number of advantages. By placing learning materials into a Web environment a great deal of both time and resources can be saved and an archive provided for learners who are unable to attend a learning session for whatever reason.

Using the Web as a learning delivery platform enables materials to be independent of application software and computer type. By using the Web as a learning system the designer can consider the diversity of the learners in terms of their experience, skill, reading level, overall ability and attitude by offering different explanations, remediation of various kinds and the opportunity to proceed at their own pace.

Resource and reference materials of all types can be made both accessible and searchable using indexing programs and utilities that allow all learners to have equal access. Supplementary information such as troubleshooting guides and how-to manuals can also be put into a Web distribution system. A variety of support features such as electronic bulletin boards and other discussion facilities can be set up and the Web can be used to distribute a variety of learner administrative information.

This book is about using the current potential of the Web to deliver learning materials to learners of all kinds, in all kinds of different places, at all kinds of different times. Before you can deliver the materials, however, they have to be designed, developed and put up on the Web so learners can use them. This book is about trying to cut through some of the hype and nonsense that surrounds Web-based learning and aims to help you create learning materials that learners will actually want to use and from which they might actually learn something! This book will not however make your long days any shorter, or your learning materials any easier to develop.

If you are somebody who in the course of your day has been given the task of developing new learning materials or redesigning old ones, or has just been charged with thinking about putting learning materials on to the Web, this is the book for you! It's simple and to the point, and is based on 18 systematic steps considered essential for making sure your Web-based learning materials are the best they can be. Each step is described in simple terms to help you better understand why it's needed and how that step is carried out.

The first four chapters provide you with the supporting knowledge. Chapter 5 begins the design and development process based on a systems approach, along with the integration of appropriate instructional design principles that give you the framework to create the learning materials. Inputs such as conceptual ideas and things learnt from the past, and outputs such as tutorials, formal learning events and general information topics and feedback from both formative and summative reviews will all provide you with an orderly framework to develop your learning materials. Simply using a systems approach, however, is not enough to develop Web-based learning materials successfully. Well-designed Web-based learning materials also use supporting knowledge and keep instructional design principles firmly in mind.

Each chapter includes a general discussion of the instructional design principles, followed where necessary with the appropriate materials design standards for the topic under discussion.

The digital learning revolution is upon us; use it well.

Chapter 1
Web-based learning

INTRODUCTION

The World Wide Web has great potential for use in the delivery of learning to a variety of people. However, as with many learning delivery tools, those involved in the design and development of the materials being delivered and the set up of the actual tool itself find themselves overindulging in the use of the many resources available to them in a Web environment and ignoring the basic principles of learning.

Any good Web-based learning has to be based on sound learning principles, not on the myriad of resources to be found on the Web or the number of animated icons that appear on a page. The use of the Web and its many resources does not necessarily equate to an effective learning environment.

In this chapter, Web-based learning is defined, and the advantages and disadvantages of using a Web-based learning delivery methodology are set out. Also described is the best use of Web-based learning.

THE INTERNET

With its growing popularity and ever-extending reach, the Internet now represents the greatest communications medium ever created. With an estimated 180 million users, and more than 8 million registered Web sites, the Internet's once-steady flow of information has turned into a formidable tidal wave.

From learners to homemakers to business executives, individuals from all backgrounds – and all parts of the world – are connecting to the Internet in exponentially increasing numbers. Combined with a dizzying proliferation of 'Net-enabled' devices, Internet connectivity has become both ubiquitous and relatively inexpensive.

Despite its popularity, however, the Internet, like television before it and radio before that, remains principally a mechanism for the exchange and distribution of information. But unlike its predecessors, the Internet offers far more possibilities for the bi-directional flow of information, making it extremely well suited for teaching and learning.

How the Internet works

The Internet is a vast, global collection of individually owned and operated computers and computer networks. No single organization can claim ownership of the Internet, although significant portions of the network are operated for profit by multinational telecommunication and networking companies. Computers connected to the Internet are called *host* computers, and each one has the capability to communicate with every other one. There are many ways to connect a computer to the Internet, including temporary dial-up connections and permanent or semi-permanent network connections.

In the home, most individuals connect to the Internet via a temporary dial-up telephone connection. To gain Internet access, subscribers will typically pay a fee to an Internet Service Provider (ISP), which acts as the 'on-ramp' for individual users, and maintains a network of computers permanently connected to the Internet (see Figure 1.1). Newer technologies, such as ADSL (asymmetric digital subscriber line) or cable connections to the Internet are becoming increasingly popular, and represent permanent or semi-permanent connections to the network. Once connected to the Internet, most users will use a Web browser to access a subset of the Internet, called the World Wide Web (WWW). The WWW is made possible by an ever-increasing number of Web servers on the Internet, which client computers access using a Web browser before making requests for Web pages.

Most of today's learning programs are delivered via the World Wide Web and involve using a Web browser to access the learning materials. The materials can be delivered over the Internet and/or over an internal network (in an organization) called an Intranet. Web-based learning is often referred to as online learning because the Web itself is a rich environment for building and delivering online courseware. Features such as e-mail, discussion forums, video conferencing and live lectures are all possible over the Web, and are some of the many components a learning facilitator can make use of in a Web-based learning event.

A Web-based learning environment is something that can be created and accessed using either the Internet or an Intranet. Such an environment is just like any other learning event in that it distributes information to learners. However, the Web can also perform other tasks related to communication, assessment and classroom management. Many of the tools that provide the functionality of Web-based learning use a variety of computer applications along with a graphic user interface that allows your learners to access and use the required learning materials.

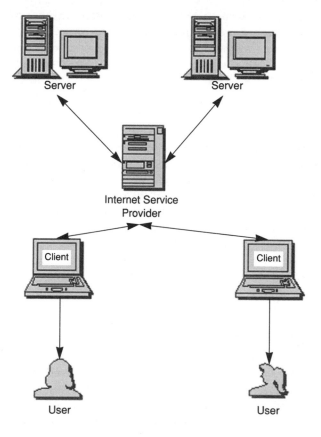

Figure 1.1 *How learners access the Internet*

Web-based learning can be used for a variety of learning tasks, and through the use of various kinds of software, learners are able to collaborate on projects and share information. A variety of specialized software technologies is also available that allows for the customization of applicants to the needs of an organization.

THE WEB-BASED LEARNING ENVIRONMENT

In a Web-based environment learning materials development involves setting up computers for learner use, preparing new learning materials and converting existing materials, creating quizzes, setting up classes and mailing lists, drawing or scanning pictures, digitizing video and developing audio files. In some cases the designer might also be involved in the setting up of a computer managed learning (CML) system to assist in tracking your learners through various learning events and the marking of quizzes and examinations.

After your learning materials have been developed and produced they are typically stored on one or more servers. The stored information can be in a variety of forms such as HTML pages, other application-based pages, audio files, graphics or video. These computers 'serve' as the distribution points for your learning materials. People wanting to access these materials can do so from their own desktop or laptop computers. Having learning materials stored on a server means that they can be searched, archived, indexed and converted easily and quickly. On many servers there is also a variety of applications that your learners need in order to complete the learning prescribed for them.

Client programs, or programs that are used by you and your learners, are those that ask other programs, such as those running in a Wide Area Network (WAN), to perform various tasks such as getting information or sending messages. These programs also provide the learners with the means of accessing the information that you have stored on local servers as well as accessing other network servers.

Client, server and support software

A large collection of software has been developed to help you design, develop and maintain the daily activity of Web-based learning. One way of grouping this software is as follows:

- *Support.* Software in this category generally has little or no direct connection outside your local area network. This is software your learners use to support their activity within the online classroom. Some examples include word processing, graphics programs and databases.
- *Client.* Your learners as they participate in a Web-based learning event do so via a computer and a collection of client software. This client software provides the interface between the learners and the learning event. Examples of client software include e-mail applications and other applications such as TopClass or Web CT where learners can come together and engage in various learning activities. In some virtual classroom environments 'live lectures' can be presented, learners complete their assignments at 'their desk' and group assignments can be completed in 'breakout rooms'. In this kind of virtual learning environment learners can work together (synchronous mode) or individually (asynchronous mode) at any time of the day.
- *Server.* Client software provides the interface that allows the learner to see and be involved in the learning event, but it does not provide a method for managing and distributing the information required to

allow a group of learners to communicate and share information. Management and distribution of information in a Web-based learning environment is the responsibility of server software.

Typically the computers that learners have on their desks provide both the support and client software, while the server software resides on one or two central computers. However, it is quite common for the developer of Web-based learning events to use one dedicated server, not accessible by the learner, as a means of storage during the development process and, when completed, to move the finished materials to a second server accessible by the learner. During the development stage your computer can contain all the necessary support needed to do the development work, including both client and server software.

Connections

For a Web-based learning event to work there must be a connection between the client and server software. Some variation in the types of connection is possible. The following list breaks the possible connections into three broad categories:

1. *Local Area Network* (LAN). Many businesses and educational organizations have some form of local area network.
2. *Home connections.* For most learners today, connecting from home means using a modem and a phone line. Although fast enough for most purposes, a typical modem can be quite slow for the retrieval of large documents or multimedia files. This problem has been partially overcome through the introduction of ISDN (Integrated Services Digital Network) lines and ADSL (Asymmetric Digital Subscriber Line) modems.
3. *Hybrid.* In a hybrid online classroom you might use CD ROM technology to distribute large amounts of basic information in a mass instructional mode along with an interface to a Web environment to provide information updates and communicate with your learners.

What can be done in a Web-based learning environment is limited only by the imagination of the designer and the available resources. For the most part the range of possibilities is almost endless. However, as advanced as technology has become, more work is needed to ensure the learning environment is fully conducive to the needs of the learner.

Most types of learning materials can be put, in whole or in part, into a Web-based environment. The ideal learning events for use on the Web are objective in nature and emphasize in-depth coverage and discussion. Web-based learning is suited to a learner-centred role, meaning that learning information is made available to learners to go through at their own pace; you provide the facilities that allow communication, thus encouraging them to take more control of their own learning. One of the most important things for you to understand about Web-based learning is that, unlike a face-to-face learning environment, the Web cannot 'teach' on its own, but merely acts as another form of learning delivery tool.

Text- and graphics-based Web-based learning

Text and graphics for online learning events should be designed so that your learners do not simply read off the computer screen, engaged only by the forward arrow. Any online learning event should contain hyperlinks to other materials for further study, or to charts and graphs that further illustrate the various learning points. Typically when you develop an online event, given today's technological restrictions, the event may contain a lower level of interactivity than a multimedia event that uses CD ROM technology or an event that uses a combination of computer-based training and online learning, but the online event does not necessarily contain a lower level of information.

Interactive Web-based learning

Interactivity at its best should be a simulation of the work situation and at a minimum you should include application exercises, drag and drop, column matching, testing and text entry. Designing this type of learning event helps bring learners into the materials, engage them in the content and allow them to practise the skills.

WEB-BASED LEARNING

Like all forms of learning, Web-based learning involves a myriad of methods and technologies, making it difficult to give it a precise definition. In broad terms, Web-based learning can be described as the delivery of and access to a co-ordinated collection of learning materials over an electronic medium using a Web server to deliver the materials, a Web browser to access them and the TCP/IP and HTTP protocols to mediate the exchange. TCP/IP is an abbreviation for Transmission Control Protocol/Internet Protocol, the suite of communications protocols used to connect host computers on the Internet. The TCP/IP protocol suite includes several protocols, the two main ones being TCP and IP.

HTTP is an abbreviation for HyperText Transfer Protocol, the underlying protocol used by the World Wide Web. HTTP defines how messages are formatted and transmitted, and what actions Web servers and Web browsers should take in response to various commands. For example, when you enter a Uniform Resource Locator (URL) in your browser, this sends an HTTP command to the Web server directing it to fetch and transmit the requested Web page. The URL is the standard convention of specifying the location of every resource on the Internet and within a Web application. A typical Web URL takes the form of http://www.website.com/a_page.htm.

While this definition of Web-based learning applies to a good portion of the learning programs available on the Internet today, it is by no means all-encompassing. For example, a learning program may use the Internet and TCP/IP as the delivery mechanism, but require a custom client application to gain access. Likewise, Web-based learning programs may include FTP (file transfer protocol) applications, video-on-demand services, intranet access, telephone use, CD ROM technology, print-based materials and a variety of other components that may or may not involve the use of the Internet, a Web browser and other conventional communications protocols.

Typically online and Web-based learning takes place in either an asynchronous or synchronous environment. An asynchronous environment is one where communication between learners and the facilitator is done via a computer forum of some description at different times. A synchronous communication environment, on the other hand, takes place in real time where those involved in the communication process are present all at the same time, but not necessarily in the same place. A video conference or a telephone call is an example of synchronous communication.

An asynchronous learning network (ALN) is a network of people who communicate at different times from different locations using the computer as a tool to manage that communication. A Web-based learning environment often uses some elements of ALN such as computer forums to assist the learners internalize the learning materials. However synchronous elements can also be included, such as video conferencing and discussion rooms.

Characteristics of Web-based learning

Like the growing number of applications available on the Internet today, Web-based learning events are becoming increasingly diverse, innovative and specialized. A university degree, for example, is attainable over the Web, as are entire libraries of information, lectures from prominent professors, live broadcasts of complicated medical procedures, virtual laboratories for conducting experiments and untold numbers of training and educational programs and resources (see Figure 1.2).

While Web-based learning can involve a diverse collection of methods and technologies, most co-ordinated programs include:

● learning materials made up of text, graphics and multimedia elements such as video, audio and animation;

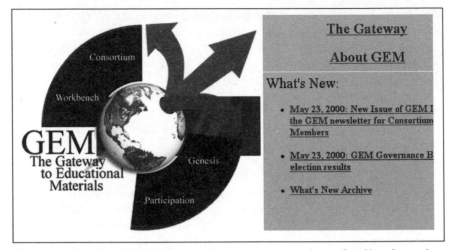

Figure 1.2   *The GEM site provides a large number of online learning events, http://gem.syr.edu*

(Permission sought)

- synchronous or asynchronous communications applications such as video conferencing, chat rooms, or discussion forums;
- the use of a Web browser;
- the storage, maintenance and administration of the materials on a Web server;
- the use of TCP/IP and HTTP protocols to facilitate the communication between the learner and the learning materials and/or the resources.

The World Wide Web by no means represents the most suitable environment for all types of learning programs. Several factors require consideration before embarking on a Web-based learning project, and the advantages and disadvantages of the intended approaches and objectives need to be examined very carefully.

There are a number of advantages and disadvantages to using the Web as a learning environment, which need to be contextualized to the situation. For example, one of the advantages of a Web-based learning environment is that it increases accessibility and promotes location independence. However, this is of little use if the learner does not have Internet access. The advantages and disadvantages also depend on the way the system is used. Web-based learning is only an advantage if existing distance learning materials are being replaced and the learners have Internet access. If a Web-based learning environment is developed for a particular group of learners, but you also intend to continue using the traditional face-to-face classroom-based learning model, then the time and effort involved in the development of the Web-based environment may not be an advantage.

Advantages of Web-based learning

There are many advantages to using Web-based learning, for example:

- It can be used to deliver learning at any time to virtually any place.
- It uses many of the elements of CD ROM-based learning, but adds an enhanced communication element.
- The learning materials are relatively easy to update.
- It can increase the number of interactions between the learners and the event facilitator.
- It allows learners to form both informal and formal Web-based learning communities.
- It allows the use of problem- and/or assignment-based learning.
- It can make use of resources already on the Internet.
- It can present real-time content using video conferencing, video streaming or discussion rooms.
- It has the ability to include multiple media such as text, graphics, audio, video and animation into the learning materials (see Figure 1.3).

Figure 1.3   *The first year French learning programme uses both online and CD ROM delivery, http://www.lamc.utexas.edu/fr/home.html*

- Information can be made available on the use of the materials by the learner, and facilitators can check learner progress.
- Learners for the most part are comfortable with a Web-based learning environment.
- It allows for a learner-centred delivery strategy that can take into account the many differences between learners.

Disadvantages of Web-based learning

The disadvantages of using Web-based learning have for the most part to do with the technical limitations associated with computers and the Internet itself. Over time these should become less of a problem. However, there are learning-related problems that will always exist. For example, not every learning event, particularly those in the 'soft' skills area, is suitable for Web-based delivery.

Some of the disadvantages to using Web-based learning include the following:

- Technical limitations cause many learning environments to resemble the early days of computer-based learning in that materials are static and interactivity is controlled by the forward arrow.
- The learning environment is relatively expensive to establish compared to other kinds of learning environments because specialist staff need to be hired and enhanced computer equipment needs to be purchased.
- The materials designer needs to have some knowledge of computer-based learning in order to design an effective learning environment.
- The limited bandwidth creates problems when downloading graphic-intense materials.
- Some learning environments require the learner to have a state-of-the-art computer and the most up-to-date browser.
- Training has to be provided for both facilitators and learners. Facilitators need to be able to develop, administer and facilitate the learning in a computer-related environment. Learners need to be 'trained' to understand fully and use the various resources provided for them.

Why use Web-based learning?

Using the Internet to deliver your learning event(s) has a number of advantages, for example:

- *Increased client base.* By placing the learning materials on to the Web the potential number of users is immediately increased.

- *Increased learner accessibility.* In a traditional distance learning environment a great deal of time is often needed for the learner to receive the learning materials and communicate with those providing the learning event. Using the Web the learner can access the materials as soon as they are placed on the server.
- *Ease of updating the learning materials.* Materials are very easy to update and learners can receive the new materials instantly.
- *Platform independence.* The Web environment allows the design and development of a learning event independent of software packages or computer platform. Typically, learning materials using a multimedia approach are designed using different application programs. This means that the learner's computer must contain a copy of that software in order to display the materials. The problem is that not all computer platforms are the same, not all Web browsers are the same and not all computers have the resources to make the presentation work effectively, all of which makes for a less than effective learning experience for the learner. Using the Web as a delivery platform along with an appropriate format for the learning event enables the materials to be independent of application software and computer type. However, you will still have to ensure that your learner's computer has a browser capable of displaying the materials as they were intended to be displayed.
- *Increased learner effectiveness.* In a face-to-face environment, an effective learning event is typically conducted in a lock step fashion where learners are considered to be homogeneous and the materials appropriate for all. Using a Web-based system, the diversity of the learners can be taken into account in terms of experience, skill, reading level, overall ability and attitude by offering different explanations, remediation of various kinds and the opportunity for the learners to proceed at their own pace.
- *Administrative support.* The Web can be set up to support a variety of features including electronic bulletin boards and other discussion room facilities to enable learners to keep up with changing learning materials. The Web can also be set up to distribute administrative information including test results, tutor lists, timetables, grades, announcements and other such resources.
- *Resource and reference.* Materials of all types can be placed online and made accessible. Information can be made searchable using indexing programs and utilities, allowing all learners to have equal access.
- *Increased learner expectations.* Tomorrow's learners will expect some type of Web-based support for the typical learning event.
- *Changing nature of knowledge.* Knowledge is increasing at a rapidly expanding rate and doubling approximately every three years. An astonishing 50 per cent of what the average learner has learnt in

school today will be obsolete in five years. This means that there is a need for lifelong learning, and Web-based learning is a convenient and cost-effective way of providing that learning.

- *Increased competition.* The business of learning is a multimillion-dollar enterprise and the advent of Internet-based learning means that the physical location of the learning institution is no longer of primary importance for the learner when enrolling in a learning event.

Design and development of Web-based learning

Web-based learning provides a way of delivering materials to learners that is often less expensive and more convenient than the typical alternatives. Because this type of learning is very new, distinctions between the various types of Web-based learning are still forming.

When you are developing a Web-based learning event and a 'system' in which to put that event, one of the most important factors for you to consider is holding the attention of your learners and engaging their minds long enough for learning to occur. Interactivity makes the difference between the system that simply presents information and one that helps learning take place. One of the first considerations in your design has to be the link between your planned learning event and any existing one. You will also need to review the specific learning needs of your learners and, along with the development of a graphic user interface (GUI), consider various hyperlinks to the learning materials you are going to put on your system. Along with this initial phase you will need to review the required learning materials and assess their viability based on delivery, treatment and various human-computer interface issues such as media elements and the use of such materials in a technology-based environment.

Learning materials

The use of a different medium for learning often has a significant influence on the learning that takes place, and the chosen design for Web-based learning must be appropriate for both the materials and your learners. It is important that you remember that Web-based learning has its own unique characteristics, which should significantly influence your design.

Web-based learning requirements

As you begin the design process you will need to review your current learning materials to identify the new materials that will need to be developed. This review should also clarify the knowledge and skills required by your learners and provide the baseline for the event information document. As you develop your basic specifications you will also need to identify the required learning objectives along with the standards of performance. This information should be documented in your event information document.

Web-based materials design

The materials design phase should be built on the information gathered along with any external constraints. During this phase you will need to develop a number of appropriate templates for use in the Web environment. These might include structural, presentation and adaptive templates and how-to tutorials.

A structured learning template simply presents the materials as a hierarchy of topics, one following the other. Here the learner works through the materials in a manner dictated by the designer. It has a standard start page that includes a navigation bar, which learners can use to move from one topic page to another, backward and forward.

A presentation learning template is designed to present information in a linear fashion. Presentations can include a slide show or a guided tour. The template should have a standard start page with a navigation bar that enables learners to return to the start of the materials at any time.

An adaptive learning template is one that picks the material to be displayed based on information about the learner. This template is designed so that the learner has no idea that there are other explanations available. The template should include a standard start page and navigation bar that enables learners to return to the start of the materials at any time.

A how-to learning template helps guide learners though the process of performing a specific task. The structure is usually linear, but some diversions to other templates such as a troubleshooting template can be built in along the way. This type of template can be combined with a reference structure to help learners look up unfamiliar terms.

At the same time as you are developing the templates you will also need to develop the required tutorial elements such as standard start pages, structure of elements pages, a consistent set of links and any recap and notes pages. As you write the design specifications you will need to consider your required strategies and treatments for the materials along with your assessment methodology.

The major differences between the designs of Web-based learning materials and paper or CD ROM-based learning lies in your understanding that your design needs to address four basic issues:

1. *Materials design.* Users of Web-based learning materials should not just look at the information you present to them; they need to interact with it in novel ways, which have no precedents elsewhere. Your materials design must include interaction metaphors, images and

concepts to convey function and meaning on the computer screen. In this way the design becomes an integral part of the learner's experience.

2. *Organizational design.* There are fundamental organizational reasons for subdividing any large body of information into its component parts. Any body of knowledge to be used in a Web environment must be designed so that the number of variables is kept to a minimum. This is done using a combination of graphic design and layout conventions along with the division of the information into its discrete units.

3. *Page design.* The spatial organization of graphics and text in a Web-based environment must help engage your learners in their learning; it must also direct your learners' attention, help them prioritize information and make their interactions more enjoyable and efficient. The Web page shares many similarities with pages in print publications, but because the Web page may be accessed directly, it should be designed to be more independent and not be an isolated fragment of information, divorced from the larger context through the lack of an essential link.

4. *Graphic design.* Optimizing the look and feel of a Web-based learning experience is important to the overall efficiency of the Web-based learning system. The use of a full screen graphic menu and background graphics, for example, could leave your learners sitting around waiting for graphics to load. To avoid this you will have to consider a design strategy that draws your learners into the materials with reasonable download times.

Typical components of Web-based learning

A typical Web-based learning environment can use all or some of the following elements:

- a learning event plan;
- learning materials presentation;
- learner assessment;
- Internet resources;
- instructional support;
- technical support.

Learning event plan

The learning event plan provides a description and a direction for the various learning activities, learner assessment details and a timeline for completion of the event by the learner.

Learning materials presentation

In this component the instructional materials are presented to the learner. This takes the place of a face-to-face presentation in a classroom environment. Typically these materials will be made up of text supported by a variety of other media to enhance the instructional message. This component can also include learner interactions such as learner-marked quizzes, open-ended questions, learner-developed summaries and the use of the Web as a research tool.

Learner assessment

Assessment methods used in this component will vary depending on the needs of the learner and the topic under study but basically there are three types of assessment – online quiz, written assignments to be completed offline and examinations.

The online assessment might use a computer-managed learning (CML) program that presents the learners with a series of diagnostic assessments. Feedback from these assessments helps the learners better understand and determine their progress through the learning event and at the same time allows the facilitator to track learners from event to event.

Written assignments are, for many learning events, a standard method of assessment. In the Web-based environment, assignments can be submitted as e-mail documents from the individual learner or from groups of learners working together on an assignment.

Examinations will still need to be held to determine learner progress. Exams can be conducted online using a secure computer-assisted testing software or they can be held in the traditional classroom setting.

Internet resources

Internet resources are available to assist the learner complete the learning event in a meaningful manner. These resources could include an online library and a list of relevant Web sites.

Instructional support

Support should include both electronic and facilitator support for the learner. Electronic support can be made up of a glossary of terms or a list of frequently asked questions (FAQs). Facilitator support can also include e-mail, creating and supporting a listserve (multiple e-mails) or involvement in a computer conference.

Technical support

Support here should include some form of technical help desk that will answer learners' technical questions regarding the learning event, the resources or the computer itself.

CONCLUSION

An online learning event does not just consist of a single type of Web page; rather it should consist of many components. The event must be more than just a page of text and graphics, because the learning principles demand a number of different components for the event to be effective. Determining the required components is an important part of the learning event design.

Web-based learning is growing in popularity but the materials developed must not let the technology drive the learning event development. The Web is only a delivery tool, not a method of instruction. Course development must be led by the same learning principles that are used in developing any learning event.

While there are advantages in using a Web-based learning event, it should be recognized that not all events are suitable for Web delivery. However, the Web can be used for different types of learner support, including enhancing and supporting face-to-face learning events.

Chapter 2
The development model

INTRODUCTION

The use of the Web is growing at an unprecedented rate. Estimates range from 6 to 20 per cent per month. In addition, the creation of Web servers, home pages and other resources is also expanding. All of which has huge potential for learning and training in many different ways.

Currently, for the most part the Web is just a vast collection of semi-structured 'stuff' that has little to do with learning. When properly developed, however, Web pages do have the potential to be more than just information storage. When well designed and well structured, Web pages can guide learners through a variety of experiences including activities that present information, afford practice and provide feedback to inform them of their strengths and weaknesses, and make suggestions for both forward and backward remediation. This chapter looks at a number of the models currently being considered for use in the design and development of Web-based learning materials.

Developing materials for learners' interaction at a location away from the provider is not a new idea and has been in practice in many parts of the world for a number of years. The reasons for learning at a distance are many and varied but are based primarily on the interests and needs of learners and the ability of learning event providers to put in place a communication infrastructure that allows them to provide both information and instruction.

In today's world not a great deal has changed with respect to learning at a distance. The learner still has a need to take advantage of various learning event offerings but now providers can offer information and communication beyond traditional methods, that allows learners to access the information they need with a maximum of flexibility to meet their individual needs. However, like the Web itself, a lot of the 'learning' materials are poorly developed and offer little beyond informal learning through browsing. Most learning materials appear to be developed with a view to interest and inform and are less concerned with learning. It is from this ambiguity that comes the need to consider a design/development strategy for Web-based learning.

There are two sides to the Web. The first is its use as a vehicle for a myriad of activities lumped under the banner of e-commerce. Its other side is as a vehicle for the distribution of resources, and it is in this regard that the Web has the advantage of flexibility and low cost. Given this, learning organizations of all kinds are placing their materials on the Web and making them readily available to learners. The fact that Web materials can be upgraded quickly and efficiently means that users always access the latest version of the materials, and the electronic nature of the medium can provide cost savings compared to other delivery alternatives.

Currently what is put up in the way of learning materials, however, is typically 'multimedia documents', and it is these materials that will need to evolve as software is redesigned to cater to the developer's needs and designers, both instructional and graphic, enhance their skills. For example, current instructional software is designed via collective feedback to provide learners with understanding and/or skill, whereas interactive software could provide a wider range of outcomes whereby designers could consider full modules of skill development as one of the main components of Web content. The Web is a distinct form of publication for informative materials distinguished by the way it is used. The question is: how is the information that is presented on the Web to be designed in an optimal way for learning?

Over the past 25 years, the model of choice for the design and development of learning materials has been a cognitive or systems approach. Typically such approaches incorporated fundamental elements of the instructional design process including analysis of the intended audience and the determining of learner goals and objectives. Instructional design refers to the process of learning materials development, and many instructional design models exist for use for different levels of instructional purpose. Generally speaking, however, the process is summarized into four general phases, those of information gathering, materials design, materials development and materials evaluation. One of the better-known models, and indeed the one underpinning much of the discussion in this book, is the Dick and Carey model (1978). This model describes all of the phases of a systematic, iterative process, which begins by identifying the instructional goals and ends with a summative evaluation.

It has been suggested that these so-called 'traditional' approaches to instructional design are not compatible with the ideas of the flexible learning process required for today's Web-based learning. The systems approach is being challenged by constructivist theories that describe the social context, roles and relationships of the learner as being central to learning. Non-linear development models by their very nature describe the learning process as dynamic and unpredictable, and ones in which learners can and do develop their own learning tasks.

For the most part, instructional design models have evolved through three iterations over the past 25 years. The first models were based on behaviourist ideas and concepts and were influential in the development of learning through 'teaching machines'. The second iteration introduced analysis, needs assessment and formative evaluation as major events in the design process. The third iteration was simply a refinement of what had gone before but it is in the latest iteration that more fundamental changes to the model are being advocated. Here the behaviourist viewpoint is being reworked and a constructivist approach to how people learn and what it means to learn has begun to take place.

The systematic design model was introduced into the learning setting with the intention of improving instruction in a variety of ways, for example active rather than passive learning, a learner-centred approach rather than a teacher- or trainer-centred approach, and measurable outcomes that met performance objectives was advocated. Currently, this approach is being criticized as 'top-down' and as a subject-matter expert approach to learning that is too linear and time-consuming to be practical in the 'real world'. It has also been argued that with the advent of the Web and the radical changes it has brought to learning and business, many, if not all, sectors of society are being transformed from an industrial age to an information age. This means that such things as standardization, top-down organization, centralized control, conformity and compliance are being replaced with customization, teams, diversity, initiative and personal autonomy and accountability.

Given the preceding, what new model or models might be considered for use in the world of Web-based learning? The approach, as noted above, that appears to be emerging is a constructivist one where learning is seen as a constructive process with the learner building an internal representation of knowledge.

DESIGN MODELS

Constructivism had its beginnings in 20th-century psychology and philosophy and the developmental perspectives of Piaget, Bruner and Vygotsky. From a constructivist viewpoint, knowledge and understanding are not acquired passively but in an active manner through personal experience and experiential activities. The key concept of constructivism is that the learner is active and seeking to make sense of the world. This means that learning needs to focus on problem-based scenarios, project-based learning, team-based learning, simulations and the use of technology resources. It also means that learning has to be based on authentic learning tasks that no longer occur in a linear fashion.

In a constructivist world, the decisions of learning take place in a series of iterative cycles.

The mental model

Mental models are the conceptual and operational representations that people develop as they interact with complex systems. Mental models are thought to consist of an awareness of the various components of a system and are assessed using a variety of methods including problem solving, troubleshooting performance, information retention over time, observation and user predictions regarding performance. Mental models appear to be more than structural maps of components; however, like knowledge itself, mental maps must be inferred from a performance of some sort.

Components of the mental model

- *Structural knowledge.* This is the knowledge of the structure of concepts in the knowledge domain and is measured through concept circles or maps and networks. However, these methods assume that structural knowledge can be modelled using symbols.
- *Performance knowledge.* In order to assess performance knowledge, learners have to perform problem-solving tasks to test their visual image.
- *Reflective knowledge.* Here the learner is able to show other learners how to perform a certain task. In this way the first learner must produce a list of 'commands', task descriptions and flowcharts to test his or her mental image.
- *Image of system.* This is the learner's model of reality and typically is assessed by having the learner articulate and visualize physical models or devices.
- *Metaphors.* As well as images, learners will often relate new systems to existing knowledge that allows them to describe or depict the image for others to 'see'.
- *Executive knowledge.* In order to solve problems it is essential for the learner to know when to activate and apply the necessary cognitive resources.

Designing and developing structured experiences based on the components of the mental model for the learner can be positively related to various case-based learning environments within a constructivist environment.

The cognitive apprenticeship model

Cognitive apprenticeship is based on various conditions for learning, for example: learning takes place within a context of meaningful, ongoing activities with a need for learners to receive immediate feedback on their success; other people can and do serve as models for imitative learning and provide structure to and connections between learners' experiences; the concept of learning being functional; and the idea that the need for and purpose for learning are often explicitly stated.

Traditional apprenticeships typically arrange opportunities for practice. Here the characteristics of learning include: the idea that work is the driving force, and the progressive mastering of tasks is appreciated for its immediate value in getting the work done; typical skills learnt start with easy tasks where mistakes are less costly; learning is focused on performance and involves the ability to do something rather than talk about it; and for the most part standards of performance are embedded in the actual work.

The precedents set in traditional learning methodologies provide a solid foundation for the use of cognitive apprenticeship in the development of both print and Web-based learning materials. The model tends to ignore the differences between education and training, and helps the learner to move into expert practice.

Cognitive management strategies include goal setting, strategic planning, monitoring, evaluation and revision. Learning strategies include knowing how to learn, such as exploring new fields, acquiring new knowledge on a subject and reworking knowledge already known.

IMPLICATIONS FOR A DIFFERENT APPROACH TO LEARNING MATERIALS DEVELOPMENT

The overall implications for learners and the use of a different approach to the design and development of learning materials have yet to be determined. At a time when the delivery of learning is undergoing such radical change it is difficult to see a new design model taking shape. Perhaps what needs to be considered as part of this transition is a review of current usage by the individual designer and the introduction of more flexibility into the current model to accommodate multiple goals and learning styles. The following list of design considerations can help introduce more flexibility into current design practice.

General development methodology:

- introduce more formative reviews into the design process;
- develop a fast-track methodology using just those steps in the process that are needed to complete the given learning materials;
- include all end users as part of the design team.

Needs assessment:

- consider solutions such as job aids, just-in-time learning and performance support systems as part of the overall approach;
- make use of market-oriented needs assessment strategies in addition to a standard gap analysis;
- do not be driven by easily measured learning outcomes.

Goal/task analysis:

- distinguish between 'educational' and training goals;
- use objectives to guide design without insisting on operational performance that may constrain the learner's performance;
- allow for the multiple layering of objectives around various learning experiences;
- don't try to capture content in a goal or task analysis;
- allow for instruction and additional learning goals to emerge during instruction;
- allow for multiple levels of expertise when assessing the learner;
- give priority to problem solving;
- look for information-rich ways to represent materials and assess performance;
- define content in as many ways as possible.

Instructional strategy development:

- determine which are instructional goals and which are learner goals and support learners in pursuing those goals;
- allow for multiple goals for different learners;
- determine and better develop the interdependency between content and methodology;
- cover content in as much depth as possible;
- encourage learning to learn, and provide guided control to the learner;
- design instructional strategies that use authentic problems in collaborative, meaningful learning environments;
- consider designing the actual learning environments and not just selecting instructional strategies;
- extend learners' responsibility for their own learning, make learning meaningful and promote active knowledge construction;
- consider strategies that provide for multiple perspectives for learning.

Media selection:

- consider media very early in the design process;
- develop materials that are sensitive to the learner's media sophistication.

Learner assessment:

- incorporate assessment into the learning materials as much as possible;
- assess the learner in as authentic a context as possible;
- evaluate both processes and products.

Some caution regarding the preceding is noted, however. The possible risks of introducing such design considerations could result in more costly instruction, a greater need for instructional resources and information management, less coverage of materials, less demonstration of skill mastery and chaos if poorly implemented.

A MODEL OF LEARNING AND THINKING

No matter what model is used for the design and development of Web-based learning materials the challenge is to engage the learner with knowledge in ways that lead to learning higher cognitive skills. Ultimately Web-based learning will be judged by its ability to engage the learner and develop the ability to think.

In order to identify the ways in which Web-based learning can meet the challenge, it is essential to have a clear conception of what types of learning can be developed and how these contribute to effective thinking. There is no shortage of models and theories of learning and thinking. Indeed, it could be argued that the various perspectives and terminology confuse rather than aid learning materials development. Furthermore, learners are influenced by a whole range of social and situational factors that pervade their everyday lives. Developers of Web-based learning materials should recognize, whether operating from a constructivist or objectivist perspective, that learning is not just a simple product of some given development input.

Typical materials development models are broad learning frameworks and as such can only be judged in terms of the opportunities they offer for learners to achieve meaningful learning, which in this context is defined as learning that:

- is perceived to be useful by learners;
- enables effective real-world application;
- provides a sound basis for future learning;
- promotes self-esteem and confidence.

All learning involves the acquiring of some knowledge, though the extent of this varies depending on what is to be learnt. Learning a language, for example, requires much knowledge acquisition. However, even in skill-based activities there is still important knowledge to be acquired for effective performance. The key mental process involved in knowledge acquisition is memory.

The mere acquisition of knowledge in itself is often not sufficient for effective learning. Learners need to make sense of what they have learnt and know when, where and how to use knowledge. Understanding the knowledge acquired is, therefore, fundamental to effective learning in most cases. Understanding involves more than memory; it requires learners to think about what they are learning and make sense of it in terms of real-life applications. Without understanding, much of what is learnt through memorization is of little use and is likely to be soon forgotten. The key process in understanding is thinking.

Learning is often carried out for the practical purpose of developing competence, be it work- or recreation-related. Learning in these situations involves actually doing the activities, and improvement in performance requires practice over time. The need to do the activity applies to all areas of human performance, not solely physical skill acquisition.

In real learning situations, these aspects of learning do not occur as separate processes, but are dynamic and mutually support the overall learning process. For example, if learning is to be competent, learning materials need to use knowledge dynamically, progressively and thought-fully in a practical way. Knowledge only becomes practically useful in application. Equally, thinking without knowledge or application is of no practical use and doing without knowledge or thinking is, in the most extreme case, random behaviour.

In basic terms learners need to be able to think well, as thinking plays a crucial cognitive role in developing meaningful learning. Furthermore, if the goal is to develop highly competent performance, an effective and dynamic balance between knowledge acquisition, thinking and doing must be developed.

The term thinking, in the most general sense, can be used to refer to any goal-directed mental activity. For example, day-dreaming, trying to remember a road name and looking for novel solutions to a problem can all be classed as acts of thinking. However, in the context of learning, the designers and developers of learning materials are more interested in certain specific types of mental operations being developed by the learner. These are often expressed under such broad classifications as critical thinking and creative thinking. The problem is to determine what exactly is to be included as thinking when developing a Web-based learning event.

Types of thinking

Thinking can be usefully conceived in terms of six interrelated types of thinking, as shown in Figure 2.1.

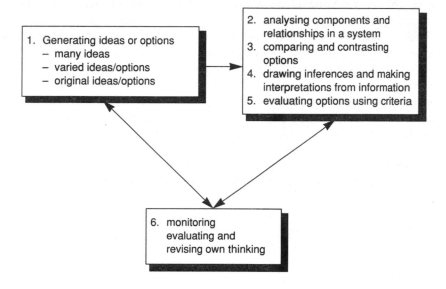

Figure 2.1 *Types of thinking*

Creative thinking is essentially contained in type 1, the generating of many, varied and original ideas or options. Creative thinking is easy to conceptualize, but most difficult to facilitate and assess. The key components of critical thinking are typically types 2–5, supported by type 6, which is generally referred to as 'metacognition'. However, while it is conceptually useful to consider thinking in terms of broad component types, actual thinking is a dynamic activity using different types of simultaneous thinking. Good thinking can be seen as the effective, orchestrated use of any or all of these types of thinking to achieve a given objective. Central to the overall management of good thinking is the ability to monitor, evaluate and revise one's own thinking – type 6, the metacognitive aspect. Problem solving typically involves all these types of thinking to varying degrees of complexity, depending on the nature of the problem. The more complicated and open-ended the problem, the greater the organization, range and complexity of thinking needed.

In considering how best to promote specific types of thinking in a Web-based environment the key stages of the development cycle need to be followed systematically, and two questions critically addressed at each stage. First, what are the limitations of this mode of delivery and in what ways can this be compensated? Second, what are the possibilities for enhancement at each stage and what other features need to be incorporated?

Learning objectives identify what a learner should be able to do as a result of a performance. In order to promote thinking, it is essential to incorporate learning outcomes that, where possible, emphasize real-world applications. For this reason, the materials focus then moves away from memorization to actual performance and the types of thinking that lead to the development of competence.

Consider, for example, the following learning outcomes:

- Analyse the impact of pollution on water quality.
- Compare and contrast specific retaining structures.
- Evaluate food packaging techniques to advise on use for specified food products.
- Generate new design options for marketing a health food product.
- Predict the outcomes of specified legal scenarios.

In all the above cases, learners would need to use some or all of the types of thinking identified earlier in order to effectively meet these learning objectives.

In designing Web-based learning materials, it is important to identify what learners are expected to be able to do at the end of the learning event. An important initial consideration is whether the objectives are in fact realistic, given the nature of the learning environment to be provided. For example, it may be unrealistic for learners to acquire certain psychomotor skills. Similarly, the development of good thinking skills in a particular subject area usually involves experience of problem solving and decision making in real-world situations. If these are to be part of the learning objectives, it will be necessary to build other learning contexts into the overall event learning plan.

As for any learning event, the objectives define what is to be learnt and therefore what is to be assessed. They also largely dictate the methods of delivery. In terms of identifying the types of thinking that are to be promoted, the following two-step methodology may be useful.

Step 1 is to identify the specific types of thinking that need to be incorporated in the learning objectives and determine what learners need to be able to do in a real-world context. In doing this, it is necessary to identify some of the types of thinking that will need to be promoted and assessed in the course of the learning event. For example, if the event involves learners looking at different options and making choices, this will require them to compare and contrast options. To do this they have to be able to identify the similarities across options, determine the differences between options and consider the significance and implications of both similarities and differences in a range of applications.

However, some of the things identified will involve specific tasks or activities. For example, in a building management programme, it may be that learners are expected to be able to prepare a tender report. In cases where a specific product outcome has been identified for the event that involves more than simply memorizing information, specific types of thinking skills can be identified by asking the following question: how would a highly competent person think when doing this task in the real world? In order to arrive at an answer to the question, the developer of the learning event must:

1. analyse the learning environment;
2. compare and contrast the environment and identify similarities and differences;
3. make inferences and interpretations from the available information;
4. generate a range of options of what to do;
5. evaluate the options against criteria;
6. develop the materials accordingly.

In performing these mental operations, there is likely to be metacognitive activity on how well the specific types of thinking are being done and integrated.

Step 2 of the two-step methodology is to develop the learning outcomes to incorporate the types of thinking to be promoted in the learning event. In terms of writing objectives to incorporate types of thinking, it is necessary to choose between two equally valid and perfectly combinable options. The first is writing the objectives to emphasize the type(s) of thinking, for example analysing the components of a simple circuit or comparing and contrasting food packaging tests. The second is writing the objectives to focus on the products of the thinking, for example, creating a simple circuit or selecting a food packaging test for a range of products.

It is also important to consider knowledge not simply as a collection of facts and concepts to be presented but as raw material that will engage the learner in thinking and doing. It is essential to have learners think well because thinking plays the crucial cognitive role in organizing and linking between knowledge and doing. Quite simply, good thinking makes this link effective. Thinking without content to consider is erroneous and, equally, knowledge is only made meaningful through thought.

It is in this area that Web-based learning can offer such rich opportunities, and it is possible to provide more diverse content material as well as encourage the learner to seek new and relevant material.

However, the Web-based environment's offering of so much access to information can present as many problems in terms of effective learning as it does opportunities. While it is always nice if learners achieve beyond the range and level of the learning objectives identified in a learning event, it must be remembered that these are always the baseline from which the effectiveness of the event is evaluated. As a consequence, decisions about what content to include in a Web-based event must still follow certain essential established principles relating to materials development. Most importantly, the knowledge specifically made available in a learning event must:

- clearly underpin and facilitate the learning outcomes of the programme;
- focus on the concepts and principles essential for providing understanding of the topic;
- have appropriate structure and sequence to facilitate learning;
- sufficiently link to learners' prior knowledge and experience.

However, as new knowledge is always emerging, the Web-based environment makes possible easier access to information than a traditional event. The opportunities to keep content knowledge updated and dynamic are a major defining feature of Web-based learning. Providing good structure to key content knowledge and at the same time exploiting the freedom of the Web will be a challenge for Web-based learning materials developers.

Developing thinking skills in a Web-based learning environment will constitute one of the biggest challenges in the development of Web-based learning. Design models have moved a long way towards understanding the important components of learning essential for promoting thinking and meaningful learning. Most apparent is the recognition that thinking is an active process, which requires a learning design that is interactive and collaborative.

The important role of the facilitator in promoting thinking in a Web-based environment cannot be minimized. As there will be less face-to-face contact than in the traditional classroom or, indeed, only virtual contact, the ability to provide input that encourages specific types of thinking to promote effective learning will be especially important. In a real-world classroom there is more time along with visceral cues to guide the communication process. Online, the communication demands are very different. The interpretation of the written word and the ability to use it effectively becomes heightened.

In a Web-based environment it will be necessary for the facilitator to provide learners with guidance on the types of thinking necessary for successful completion of certain aspects of the programme. However, making learners aware of the types of thinking and what such thinking entails, while important, will not in itself ensure that they are doing their thinking effectively. What is absolutely essential is to provide learners with learning tasks that clearly require them to employ specific types of thinking.

CONCLUSION

This chapter has reviewed a number of design models and suggested some design changes to the current development model to help the designer develop better Web-based learning materials. The chapter concluded with a discussion of a thinking model for Web-based learning materials development and the various considerations that have to be made in order to incorporate thinking into a Web-based learning event.

Chapter 3
Learning at a distance

INTRODUCTION

In today's technology-driven environment, the Web is increasingly being used to deliver learning materials to learners at a 'distance' who might never actually attend a class in a face-to-face environment. This chapter reviews a number of issues with respect to distance learning and presents an overview of the development and delivery of Web-based learning materials to the distance learner.

DISTANCE LEARNING

In order to design and develop an effective Web-based learning event, it is first necessary to review the fundamentals of distance learning. In the traditional distance learning environment, the learners are geographically distant from the facilitator and work independently through a variety of learning materials. Support is provided in various forms and in some cases learners meet for tutorials and study schools.

In today's typical distance learning environment, not a great deal has changed, at least in terms of the model from the original. The learner is still geographically distant from the facilitator, still works independently through the learning materials and support is still provided through the mail – except now it's electronic mail, discussion forums or other electronic means of communication.

The major change, of course, is the way the learning is delivered to the learner – now delivery is through a vast electronic network, and the learners and facilitator communicate via asynchronous and synchronous networks. However, in some cases it may still be appropriate to use traditional methods of support such as the telephone, tutorials and intensive study schools.

WEB-BASED LEARNING AND DISTANCE LEARNING

There are two basic ways of using Web-based learning events. The first is where learners receive a major component of the instructional materials from the Web, and study independently. In this case learners need the support of a facilitator and other supportive methods outlined in this chapter. The second method is where the Web is used for learner support. In this case learners still learn in a traditional environment but Web materials are used to complement the instruction. Learners can use the Web to read course notices, background notes and prerequisite materials. In other situations learners can complete projects and case studies collaboratively and complete electronic assessments. In this case the need for electronic supportive measures may not be as great as in the case of the distant learner.

SUCCESSFUL DISTANCE LEARNING EVENTS

The desirable components of a distance learning event can be categorized as follows:

- text-based learning materials;
- intensive study schools and tutorials;
- instructional support;
- the organization;
- assessment tasks;
- learning event design;
- materials development teams.

Text-based learning materials

One of the key features of Web-based distance learning materials is that they should be 'user friendly' and written at the appropriate reading level for learners.

In the development of Web-based learning materials the administration, counselling, event facilitation, learner enrolment and evaluation are only important as far as they support the individualized learning of the learner. Furthermore, the approach of the organization in preparing learning materials and providing support should be designed to build a positive approach between the learner and the supporting system. For example:

- Learners respond better if they relate well to their facilitators.
- Learners relate better to the facilitator if there is a well-developed two-way communication backed up by effective learning materials.

- If learners gain intellectual pleasure from learning they are motivated to achieve their learning goals.
- A conversational style of language promotes good relations between the facilitator and learners, as it is easier to understand and remember.

To create a friendly atmosphere between the facilitator and learners there should be regular communication between them. The facilitator should use learners' preferred names and use the appropriate tone when communicating with them. All communication should be short and to the point, but not unfriendly. Also, all communication from the facilitator should be positive and supportive.

One of the more common ways of developing text-based content is to develop the materials into a story. This is very much dependent on the subject matter, of course, but with a story it is possible to hold the attention of learners. Making the story engaging encourages learners to ask themselves relevant questions. The story should present the topic in clear readable language and be written so as to invite an exchange of views and be judgemental about the topic. Where possible the learners should also be emotionally involved with the materials to help them develop a personal interest in the subject matter. Including relevant links in a Web-based learning event is one way to do this, so learners have the choice of accessing additional information.

Text can be made conversational by writing in plain terms. Write as you speak, using words with which your learners are familiar and which are appropriate for their reading level. Write in the active voice using personal pronouns such as 'I' and 'you'. Keep sentences short, simple and to the point. Avoid the use of clichés and slang. If you use technical terms, make sure you define them. A good way to check if your text is conversational is to read it out aloud.

Web-based materials can also include audio files so learners can listen to the text as well as read it. However, while this may be desirable, it can be technically challenging as audio files can be quite large and can take a long time to download. Given this, it may be just as effective to use audio to outline or overview the important points in the learning materials. This might include the introduction, the summary and important concepts through the materials. Audio can also be very effectively used to explain a complex diagram, rather than descriptive text. Along with audio, video can also be introduced to explain a process or procedure.

As a learning event designer, you need to be concerned with the amount of bandwidth available for the delivery of audio or video files. The size of such files can easily grow to a point of impracticality, making them extremely slow or impossible to download. To help resolve this problem, a popular technique is to stream the files to your learners. This technique allows an application called a media player to begin playing the media clips immediately, instead of waiting for the entire file to be downloaded. However, even when streaming is used, bandwidth continues to be an issue, as streamed content created to stream over a network using a 28.8 kilobit per second (kbps) bandwidth cannot stream at more than 28.8 kbps. This means that no more than 28,800 bits of information are travelling across the network each second. A learner cannot receive content streamed at a higher bandwidth than the network connection supports. Therefore, you must consider the bandwidth limitations of your learners, and develop materials to a standard that your target audience can support.

When designing your Web-based learning materials you should:

- design in channels for communication between the facilitator and learners;
- design in channels for communication between learners;
- encourage the facilitator to communicate with the learners in a friendly manner;
- develop text at the appropriate reading level for learners;
- use personal pronouns;
- make the reading level appropriate;
- use familiar words;
- use simple sentences;
- use the active voice;
- present information as a story if appropriate;
- use audio and/or video files as a means of personalizing the information;
- use audio and/or video files appropriate to the network bandwidth.

Intensive study schools and tutorials

Intensive study schools and tutorials allow learners and facilitators to interact with each other, helping both parties better understand how different learning issues affect others, and clarifying any areas of misunderstanding. Facilitators can use case studies and localized examples to make the event more relevant and interesting. Tutorials and intensive study schools also partly help overcome the problem of isolation, which learners may feel as a result of studying alone.

In a Web-based learning event there may still be a place for tutorials and the intensive study school, but many of their functions are being replaced by either synchronous or asynchronous communication. However, synchronous communication can be problematic.

Instructional support

Distance learners can be supported in many ways apart from the learning materials themselves. Instructional support is defined as any assistance provided in interpreting and understanding the learning materials including interactions associated with assignments. Instructional support is essential for successful learning because no matter how effective the learning materials are, learners will still need individual advice and assistance. Typically the facilitator is the main agent of instructional support that learners interface with.

The facilitator

The role of the facilitator and other aspects of instructional support are discussed in detail in Chapter 16, but perhaps it is relevant to look at how a Web-based learning event can be supported by the facilitator.

Facilitators have many functions. Firstly, they need to answer learners' e-mails containing questions about the learning event content or administrative matters. They need to inform learners of any changes to the learning event. If a discussion forum is used, the facilitator will have to moderate it or appoint someone to moderate. If facilitators allow learners to telephone them, they will have to answer the learners' questions. If a computer-managed learning system is used, they will have to monitor the learners' progress and take corrective action if their progress is not satisfactory and they will have to mark certain kinds of assignments.

The facilitator can communicate with learners in many ways, other than computer-mediated communication (CMC), and can still use telephone support. Some of the common ways of communicating with learners include asynchronous communication such as e-mails, listserves and discussion forums:

● *E-mail.* Electronic mail can be used by the facilitator and for learner-to-learner communication. E-mail is cost-efficient, fast and convenient. It can be used to make learning event announcements and to inform learners of any common problems and how to overcome them. Group e-mail can also be used to contact all learners simultaneously. The ability to attach files to e-mail also means that facilitators can distribute course materials. However, they must be careful not to overload learners' mailboxes. Since e-mails can be saved and referred to later, they become a resource for learning event information. Learners can ask questions by e-mail, and although the facilitator's response may not be immediate it may take only a matter of hours for the answer to be returned. E-mail allows for communication between learners, and therefore collaboration, so that they can work together on projects and assignments. Learners can also communicate with people outside those involved with the learning event to assist them with their study. There is one caution with e-mail: it is not a good idea to let learners e-mail you without some sort of guidelines, as otherwise you will become flooded with e-mails and have impatient learners waiting for an answer. Chapter 16 gives you suggestions on guidelines for facilitating a Web-learning event by e-mail.

- *Listserves.* A listserve is an e-mail list that allows any of the users registered on the list to e-mail a specific listserve address, after which the e-mail is forwarded to everyone on the list. Listserves are not suitable for transmitting course information, but they are useful for the discussion of topics relevant to the learning event. The problem with the use of listserves is that messages can be overlooked as they are part of your regular mail.
- *Discussion forums.* Discussion forums or bulletin boards are often built into a Web-based learning event and allow the facilitator to post learning event information or announcements, changes to the learning event or deadlines for assignments. They also can be used by learners to post questions about the learning event, which the facilitator and other learners can answer. This is more efficient than the learner e-mailing the facilitator directly as it allows other learners to answer the question more quickly than the facilitator. It also allows other learners to read the question, which may be similar to one they were going to ask. Discussion forums can also be used by the facilitator to open a discussion on a relevant topic; learners are encouraged to reply and the facilitator moderates the discussion.

When designing your Web-based learning event you should:

- incorporate an active role for the facilitator;
- include communication channels for the facilitator to communicate with learners;
- encourage learners to communicate with others outside the learning event;
- develop regular communication sessions between the facilitator and learners;
- include a mechanism for learners to ask questions, such as a discussion forum;
- develop discussion topics in which learners must participate;
- design activities that allow learners to work collaboratively.

Asynchronous communication allows greater interaction between facilitators and learners and between learners themselves. Learners can hold discussions using discussion forums and work collaboratively using e-mail. Using these methods it may not be necessary to conduct intensive study schools and face-to-face tutorials.

Effective facilitation is crucial to the success of the learning event. No matter how effective the learning materials are, if the instructional support is poor the learners' progress will be poor.

The organization

As well as needing facilitator support, a distance learning event also needs efficient administration; learning materials need to be available on time; enrolment needs to be efficient; and instructional support needs to be well organized.

Organizations delivering Web-based learning events must be responsive to requests from learners. These may be for technical support or questions about the enrolment procedure, but whatever the request learners must feel that the organization is supporting them. The organization needs to be flexible towards learners, for example by allowing them some flexibility in assignment submission dates. The more learners feel they can customize the learning event to their own particular study pattern the more likely they are to complete the learning event.

The learners should be considered as clients of the organization and treated accordingly. Organization staff should have a positive and helpful attitude and keep learners informed of any changes in the learning event by e-mail or course notice board. When the organization has any communication with learners, it should always be friendly in tone and non-confrontational. One essential area in which the organization needs to be efficient is technical support. If and when learners are having technical problems they must be dealt with as soon as possible, as learners may not be able to access the learning materials, which creates a negative motivational effect.

When delivering a Web-based learning event the organization should:

- be responsive to learner's requests;
- be as flexible as possible;
- be supportive;
- have a positive and helpful approach to learners;
- have a client-centred approach;
- keep learners informed;
- use a friendly tone in all communication;
- be corrective rather than confrontational;
- provide ongoing technical support.

Assessment tasks

In the traditional model of distance learning, the usual methods of learner assessments are assignments and examinations. In the entire event, learners may have only one examination. The diagnostic use of the examination is usually minimal and only relevant if the learner does not meet the set standard and has to repeat the topic. The facilitator typically marks assignments in the traditional environment 'by hand' and the turn-around time can be very long.

A Web-based learning event, on the other hand, allows the facilitator to provide rapid feedback to the learner via e-mail, along with feedback from other learners if the assignment is posted on a discussion forum to get other opinions. In a Web-based learning environment a number of assessment tools and programs are available, helping both facilitators and learners track their progress. One of the most effective is computer-managed learning (CML), where learners are presented with regular assessments that can be repeated until mastery of the topic is achieved.

When designing your Web-based learning event, you should provide:

- assessments that are balanced and consistent throughout the learning event;
- assessments that are as relevant to the learner's situation as possible;
- rapid feedback to learners regarding their assignments;
- some form of computer-managed learning that allows learners to obtain immediate feedback on their assessments.

Learning event design

Learning event design not only covers the 'design' of the event, it should also include its delivery and philosophy. Event design must be applied to the learning materials, communication methods, assessment tasks and learner interaction with the learning materials. The learning event must also impart relevant knowledge and skills to learners. When delivering a distance learning event, local cultures and environment must also be taken into account. A relatively simple task such as a Web-based learning event can be quickly adapted to suit local conditions.

When designing a Web-based learning event you must also ensure that you are using delivery methods that match the resources learners have available. It is essential in a Web-based environment that learners have appropriate computer and Internet access. Consider the following to ensure your course delivery methods match the resources the learners have available:

- If you are unable to determine your learners' Web browser types, then you will need to develop your learning materials for cross-browser compatibility.
- The optimal screen resolution for the learning materials should match the typical resolution used by your target audience.

- If you are using browser plug-ins, then you must ensure they can be downloaded and easily installed.
- If you are using any special viewers to display certain file types, then you must ensure learners have access to the viewers.
- If you are using multimedia files, then you must ensure learners have the appropriate players to play them.

Materials development teams

One of the most effective methods for developing the text-based content for the distance learning event is to use a team of people rather than an individual writer. While the individual may write the initial draft, the other members of the team comment and edit the materials. The result is the development of far more effective learning materials than could be produced by the individual writer. A typical team might include a project manager, one or two subject-matter experts, an instructional designer, multimedia designers, a Web application programmer, and a Web server administrator.

CONCLUSION

A Web-based learning event should include relevant and well-designed learning materials; interaction between learners and facilitator; instructional support for the learner; along with balanced and consistent assessment. You should also include learning tasks that require learners to collaborate with people outside their normal realm of study.

Chapter 4
Web-based learner support

INTRODUCTION

In the last chapter, we discussed how the Web could be used to deliver and support a learning event. The Web and Internet technologies can also be used to support traditional learners who are studying at a learning institution or some other organization. This method of using the Web is called Web-based learning support or Web-based performance support. This chapter discusses how Web-based learning can be used to support a learning event that is conducted in a traditional face-to-face environment. Some of the methods are more appropriate to distance learning events, but can still be used to support a face-to-face environment. Here the designer must determine which methods are the most appropriate, taking into account learners' characteristics, the topic under study and the learning environment.

TYPES OF WEB-BASED LEARNING SUPPORT

There are many different types of Web-based learning support and they can be classified as fully Webbed learning events and Web-based learning support. Fully Webbed events are those where the learners and facilitator are physically separated and learners access their learning materials via the Web.

Web-based learning support is where most of the activities are conducted in a face-to-face mode and some portion of the event is put on the Web. This could simply be an electronic notice board available to learners to inform them of any changes to their learning event or it could be a resource page giving the learners a list of relevant links. Web-based learning support can also involve e-mail, chat lines, discussion forums and video/audio computer conferencing.

Computer-mediated communication (CMC)

Learners can communicate in several ways with facilitators and fellow learners in the online environment. The term for communicating via the online environment is computer-mediated communication, where messages or data can be both sent and received via the computer. These include asynchronous methods, such as e-mail, listserves, and discussion forums or threaded discussions, and synchronous methods, such as Internet relay chats, real-time audio, application sharing or whiteboards, and video conferencing.

Computer-mediated communication is an important component of Web-based learning, as it allows for both communication and collaborative learning, which in turn can lead to deeper processing of information and create a sense of learning community. The University of New Mexico lists learning events that show how computer-mediated communication can be used in the online environment (see Figure 4.1).

TEACHING WITH the INTERNET
Examples of Delivery/Strategies

Method/Strategy	Example	Method/Strategy	Example
Content – Full Text	Philosophy Text	*Simulation*	Virtual FlyLab Water
Notes	Philosophers	*Case Study*	A Winter Storm
Complex Lab	Anatomy Frog Dissection	*Presentation*	Study of Wind NASA Projects
Collaboration	Group Projects	*Group Discussion*	About Listservs
Role Playing	MOO/MUD	*Application*	MegaMath
Drill – Practice	Math Drill	*Experiential*	Newton's Apple

Figure 4.1 *Examples of learning events using computer-mediated communication, http://www.enmu.edu/~kinleye/teach/Inetch.html*

(Reproduced with permission of Ed Kinley, Director of Information Technology, New Mexico University)

WEB-BASED LEARNING SUPPORT

There are four basic categories of Web-based learning support:

1. online materials – distributing learning materials;
2. computer-based training – drill and practice, simulations, computer-managed learning;
3. asynchronous communication – non-real-time interaction by people using the computer;
4. synchronous communication – real-time interactions by people using the computer.

Online materials

The facilitator distributes learning materials using the Web and learners retrieve the information from their computers. Learners can also retrieve information from many other sources on the Web. This is one of the major advantages of Web-based learning.

Web resources can include:

- databases;
- journals;
- software libraries;
- special interest groups;
- other learning events.

Specially designed materials can include:

- notice boards;
- frequently asked questions;
- past examination papers;
- prerequisite materials;
- learning event participant materials;
- presentation programs.

Existing material

A vast amount of information exists on the Web. Yet, finding the relevant information can be a daunting task. In this case, an annotated index of links containing notes about what the site contains and its relevancy can be invaluable to learners. These links must be periodically checked, however, to ensure they are still active.

Databases

Databases, including those put up by governments, libraries and educational institutions, are a good source of materials. The Yale Style Guide is

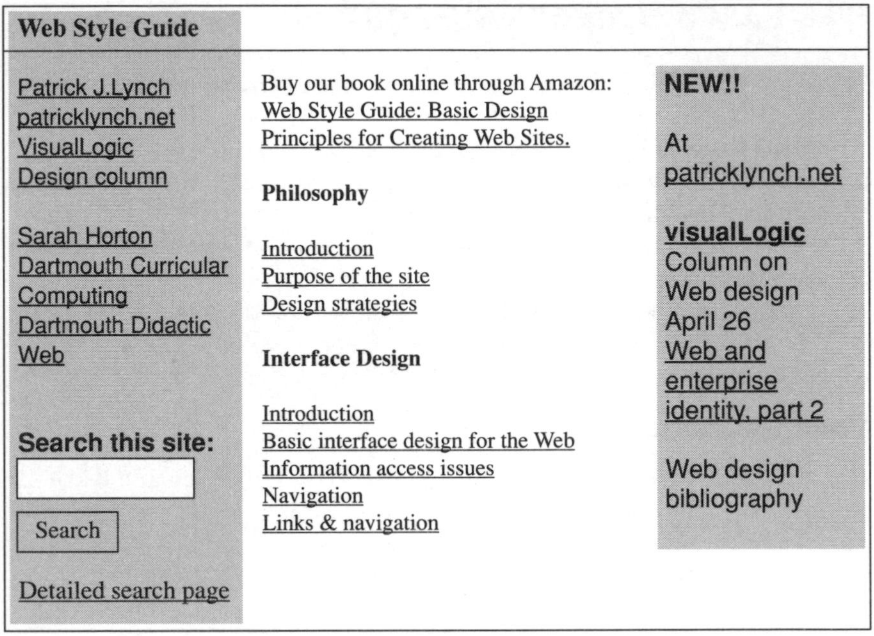

Web Style Guide		
Patrick J.Lynch patricklynch.net VisualLogic Design column Sarah Horton Dartmouth Curricular Computing Dartmouth Didactic Web **Search this site:** [_____] [Search] Detailed search page	Buy our book online through Amazon: Web Style Guide: Basic Design Principles for Creating Web Sites. **Philosophy** Introduction Purpose of the site Design strategies **Interface Design** Introduction Basic interface design for the Web Information access issues Navigation Links & navigation	**NEW!!** At patricklynch.net **visualLogic** Column on Web design April 26 Web and enterprise identity, part 2 Web design bibliography

Figure 4.2   *The Yale Style Guide,*
http://info.med.yale.edu/cairn/manual/

(Copyright Lynch & Horton, 1997, Yale University)

a good example; it contains extensive information on graphic interface, Web sites, electronic page layout, graphics, multimedia and animation design (see Figure 4.2).

Journals

There are many professional journals available on the Web. Facilitators can include online journals as an integral component of their learning materials with full knowledge that they will be regularly updated and the links will remain active. Online journals are a good source of information for helping learners to complete projects, assignments and other research work. A good example is the Asynchronous Learning Network (http://www.aln.org/), which contains the Asynchronous Learning Network journal. The site also contains discussion forums on all aspects of asynchronous learning, some free courses and a notice board that gives details of conferences and online learning events (see Figure 4.3).

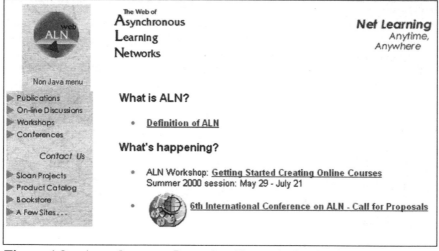

Figure 4.3   *Asynchronous Learning Network site, http://www.aln.org/*

Software libraries

Software libraries contain programs that the learners may download to their own computers. However, some sites require specific viewers and plug-ins before learners can view the site. There is a range of software available from the Lycos download site on education, which includes downloads for pre-school, grade school, high school and adults (see Figure 4.4). It also includes materials for e-books, references, computer how-to, teaching tools, mathematics and engineering.

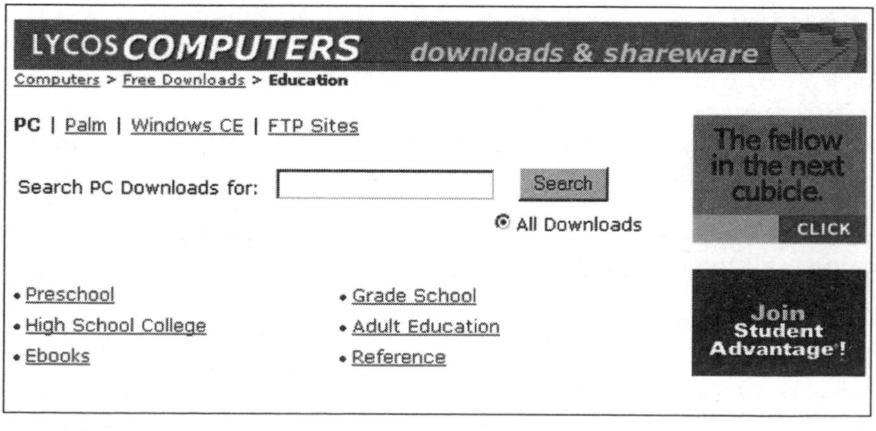

Figure 4.4   *Lycos site,*
http://www.lycos.com/computers/downloads/education.html

(Permission sought)

Interest groups

There are many special interest groups that communicate via the Internet, the largest one being newsgroups. Such groups discuss – using forums, e-mail and listserves – a vast array of subjects, some of which may be relevant to your learning event. Usenet is a good example of an online interest group, where there are hundreds of discussion forums on many different topics discussed. Here learners can read the discussion forum and once registered can post questions and replies. Tile.net provides lists, and a description of the topics discussed (see Figure 4.5).

TILE.NET/NEWS
The Complete Reference to Usenet Newsgroups

Listed by Newsgroup Hierarchy

- aaa – aaa
- ab – Alberta, Canada
- abg – abg
- acadia – Acadia University in Wolfville, Nova Scotia
- acs – OSU ACS Campus

Figure 4.5   *Tile.net, http://tile.net/news/*

Other learning events

There are many self-contained online learning events available that can be accessed at no cost. The World Lecture Hall, for example, has over 700 learning events available, many of which are self-contained and can be completed without the assistance of a facilitator (see Figure 4.6).

Hannum's Web-based instruction site, available from North Carolina University, is a good reference for the development of Web-based learning materials (see Figure 4.7).

Material specifically prepared for a learning event – distributed materials

The notice board

The notice board is an information and resource listing site for learners that serves a similar function to making announcements to a group in a face-to-face environment. It typically contains the following types of information:

- facilitator name(s) and e-mail addresses;
- learning event objectives;

- lecture date and topic covered;
- lecture readings;
- assignment deadlines;
- announcements regarding changes to the learning event;
- administrative details.

The notice board serves as an advanced organizer for both learners and the facilitator.

World
http://www.utexas.edu/world/lecture/

Lecture Hall

Search World Lecture Hall: *(Accepts AND, OR, NOT, and*)*

| | Submit | Submit |

What's New   Add listing   Update listing

The World Lecture Hall (WLH) contains links to pages created by faculty worldwide who are using the Web to deliver university-level academic language. Please see our policies and commendations, send comments, and visit our database-driven developmental Web site.

Figure 4.6 *World Lecture Hall Site,*
http://www.utexas.edu/world/lecture/

(Reproduced with permission of The University of Texas at Austin)

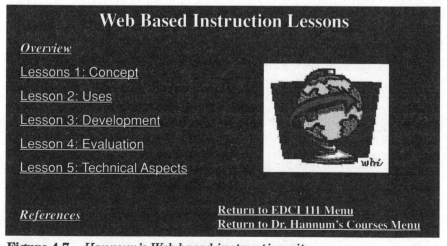

Web Based Instruction Lessons

Overview

Lessons 1: Concept

Lesson 2: Uses

Lesson 3: Development

Lesson 4: Evaluation

Lesson 5: Technical Aspects

References   Return to EDCI 111 Menu
          Return to Dr. Hannum's Courses Menu

Figure 4.7 *Hannum's Web-based instruction site,*
http://www.soe.unc.edu/edci111/8-98/index_wbi2.htm

Frequently asked questions

Frequently asked questions answer those questions learners commonly ask about the learning event they are studying. An appropriate list of frequently asked questions can be extracted from a previous learning event's free-flow discussion forum. Once the questions are chosen, facilitators must ensure they are fully answered to satisfy the needs of the learners.

Prerequisite materials

Prerequisite materials are those topics learners are expected to know before they begin the learning event. Usually a facilitator begins the learning event with an overview or advanced organizer that reviews concepts from the previous learning event. Learners who know the topic can work through the topic quickly or not at all, while others can work through the topic at their own pace. Having the prerequisite material available on the Web means learners can upgrade their knowledge to ensure they can cope with the learning event they are current studying.

Learning event participant materials

Having participant materials available on the Web can have advantages over having their printed counterparts (see Figure 4.8). For example:

- learners can access the learning event participant materials from anywhere they can access the Internet;
- materials can be updated easily;
- photographs and graphics can be included;
- audio, video and animation files can be included;
- links to relevant Web sites can be provided;
- quizzes can be included.

Presentation programs

Electronic presentations are particularly effective in showing complex diagrams and other such illustrations. Both video and audio can also be added to augment the presentation (see Figure 4.9). Presentations can be used afterwards for revision purposes.

Computer-based training

Computer-managed learning assessments are relative easy to design and develop. Most instructional management tools have a computer-managed learning component that allows the facilitator to set electronic assessments. These can be marked by the computer and give the learner immediate feedback. Using an assessment strategy where learners are required to complete electronic assignments is an effective use of Web-based learning support. Any type of test question can be included in an

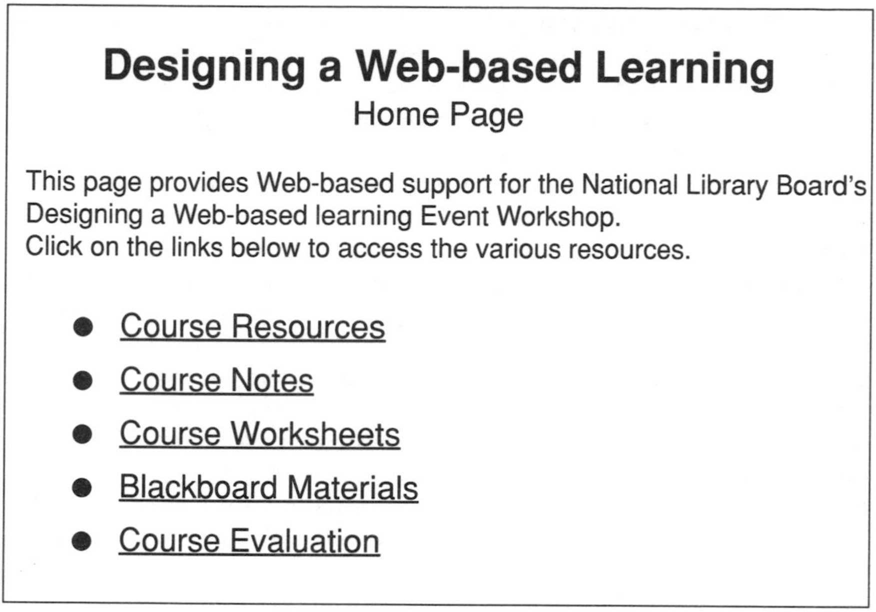

Designing a Web-based Learning
Home Page
This page provides Web-based support for the National Library Board's Designing a Web-based learning Event Workshop.
Click on the links below to access the various resources.
Course Resources
Course Notes
Course Worksheets
Blackboard Materials
Course Evaluation

Figure 4.8 *Example of a course notes page*

(Copyright Inquiring Minds, 2000)

Designing a Web-based Learning Event March 2000
Course Goal
Who am I?
Course Objectives 1
Course Objectives 2
Course Objectives 3
Time Table Day 1
Time Table Day 2
'Course Resources'
Defining Terms 1
Slide 11
Designing a Web-based
Learning Event March 20

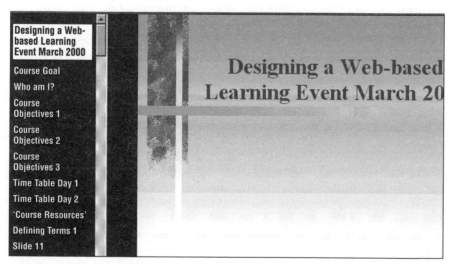

Figure 4.9 *Example of an electronic presentation program on the Web*

electronic assessment; however, the most effective are objective-type questions such as multiple choice, true and false, short answer and matching.

Computer-managed learning benefits learners by:

- providing them with immediate feedback on tests and quizzes;
- allowing them to work at their own pace;
- being non-judgemental;
- providing the opportunity to complete assessments when and where they please.

Computer-managed learning benefits facilitators by:

- giving them a greater opportunity to personalize the learning event and recognize learners' prior learning;
- allowing them to engage in more productive interactions with the learners;
- allowing the inclusion of sound, video and animation files as part of the assessment questions;
- providing valid and reliable testing procedures;
- using a record-keeping system;
- enabling the early identification of learner difficulties.

The Learning Manager (TLM) is both a computer-managed learning application and an instructional management tool (see Figure 4.10). Using the learning manager, you can place learning materials on the Web and monitor the progress of the learners using the assessment component. The Learning Manager can deliver online tests and provide learners with feedback. Using this type of management tool the facilitator can monitor learner progress and assist them when needed.

Asynchronous communication

Asynchronous communication involves people interacting at different times. Computer conferencing or discussion forums are often used to facilitate asynchronous communication. Using tools such as e-mail, list-serves and threaded discussion forums, asynchronous communication can be conducted between the facilitator and learners, and between learners.

There are a number of learning activities that can be developed using asynchronous communication, for example:

- moderator-led discussions;
- presentations;
- free-flow discussions;

- peer reviews;
- debates;
- learner-led discussions;
- individual case studys;
- team case studys;
- individual journals;
- group projects;
- external discussions;
- buzz groups;
- brainstorming;
- role playing;
- seminars;
- simulations.

These learning activities are, for the most part, typically designed around the discussion forum as the method of communication. However, e-mail and listserves can also be used. The use of e-mail as a method of communication is discussed in Chapter 16.

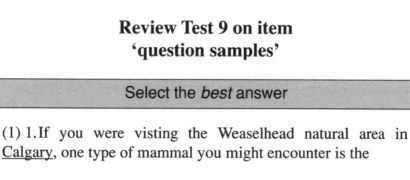

Figure 4.10 *Typical TLM test question page,*
http://www.wineducation.com/TLM.htm

(Reproduced with permission of The Learning Manager™, a registered trademark of The Learning Manager Corporation)

Discussion forums

Discussion forums have a unique role in a learning event in that they allow asynchronous discussions between learners and the facilitator and among the learners themselves. For learners, the discussion forum is valuable because it allows them to express themselves in a less formal way than in assignments, but their postings can be more thoughtful than answers given in the classroom. There are many ways a discussion forum can be used to support and enhance learning events.

Most instructional management tools have discussion forums as one of their components. The advantages of using discussion forums include being relatively easy to implement, and ease of tracking read and unread messages. Some discussion forums can be set up so that the facilitator and/or learners are notified when there are new messages. Discussion forums usually have sorting and searching features that are helpful when there are large collections of messages, including links and attached files. Two of the commonest forums are the introduction, which contains intro-duction information about the learning, and the free-flow discussion forum, where the learner can ask any questions about the learning event. There are numerous ways you can use discussion forums to assist your learning event.

An example of a discussion forum can be seen at the Asynchronous Learning Network site (see Figure 4.11).

Free-flow discussion forum

In any learning event learners will have questions, but they may not ask them in the face-to-face presentations because of time constraints or simply because they are too shy to ask. A discussion forum associated with each learning event is an effective way of allowing learners to ask questions. Discussion forums have the advantage of allowing learners to formulate their questions without time constraints. A new thread should be developed for each topic, where learners can ask questions about that particular topic. The facilitator can answer each question in detail, knowing that if other learners have the same questions the work will not have to be repeated. Hopefully, learners will try to answer one another's questions creating a more collaborative learning environment.

Once the learning event is completed, facilitators can use the informa-tion in the discussion forum to produce a list of frequently asked ques-tions, which can become a permanent component of the learning event. Learners should be encouraged to use the forum, but if they don't ask questions, a facilitator may wish to consider logging in as an anonymous learner and asking questions to stimulate and encourage other learners to ask questions. When facilitators do this, they should try to post messages that will provoke a response from other learners.

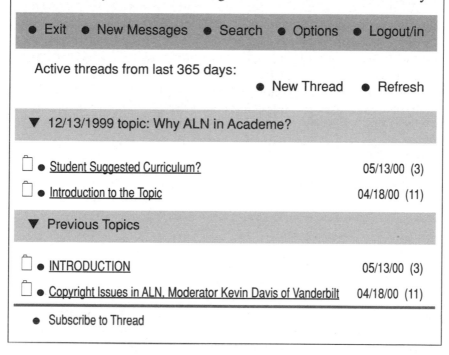

Welcome to ALNTalk, a free web-based conference covering various topics in the arena of education. Sponsored Sloan Foundation and the Center for Asynchronous Learning Networks at Vanderbilt University.

● Exit ● New Messages ● Search ● Options ● Logout/in

Active threads from last 365 days:
● New Thread ● Refresh

▼ 12/13/1999 topic: Why ALN in Academe?

● Student Suggested Curriculum?   05/13/00 (3)

● Introduction to the Topic   04/18/00 (11)

▼ Previous Topics

● INTRODUCTION   05/13/00 (3)

● Copyright Issues in ALN, Moderator Kevin Davis of Vanderbilt   04/18/00 (11)

● Subscribe to Thread

Figure 4.11   *Asynchronous Learning Network*

Peer review discussion forum

Peer review involves learners commenting on other learners' assignments. These comments can be used to revise the original assignments. Peer reviews have a number of advantages, including a sense of ownership so that learners are more committed to the outcome or final product, and the development of a range of transferable skills that are valuable during other learning events. Peer review helps learners become more independent because they don't rely totally on the facilitator for feedback. Learners can post their assignments on the discussion forum either directly or as an attached file. When using a peer review forum the facilitator should provide clear guidelines for review and explain to learners how to comment on assignments.

Moderator-led discussion forum

A moderator-led discussion involves the facilitator posting a question or statement on a discussion forum and encouraging learners to respond.

Moderators must give careful consideration to what questions or statements they post in order to start the discussion. Learners will need specific tasks to help give them some direction. Asking learners to discuss freely is of little use, as they need specific guidance. Forums should be timed so they complement topics covered in the learning materials, and should be seen as an integral part of the learning event and set for a specific time as part of the event. Learners appreciate comments by facilitators, so it is important that they comment on as many postings as possible. Responding to forums can be time-consuming, so facilitators must set realistic goals both for themselves and for the learners. More information on moderating a discussion forum is provided in Chapter 16.

Presentation discussion forum

The presentation discussion forum is normally used when the presenter cannot physically give the presentation to the learners. The facilitator posts articles, a study guide, various presentations, links to other materials that the learners study and can ask questions about.

Debate discussion forum

A debate is a structured discussion during which two sides of an issue are presented by two individuals or groups within a set time frame. In a debate discussion forum, two teams of learners are formed and they prepare a list of pros or cons on a topic given to them by the facilitator. The topic and background to the discussion are posted on the forum and the two teams present their views to the other learners. After expressing their views, the facilitator summarizes the debate and discusses its relationship to the learning materials. In this kind of forum facilitators must provide clear guidelines and perhaps appoint a moderator if they do not wish to moderate the forum themselves.

Learner-led discussion forum

A learner-led discussion involves a learner or a group of learners posting a question, statement or summary of readings on the discussion forum and encouraging other learners to respond. It is similar to a moderator-led discussion, but here the learners are the moderators. It allows learners to articulate their ideas and assists other learners in understanding the learning materials. Learners typically need assistance in moderating the discussion and developing the type of questions or statements needed to start. It is useful if the facilitator joins in as an anonymous learner to ask relevant questions not asked by others. Again, the facilitator will need to guide the learner on how to moderate the discussion.

Individual case study discussion forum

A case study is a discussion of a prepared case situation that helps learners understand and practise problem solving and decision making. In an individual case study, the learners create a 'case' that incorporates explanations and ideas from the learning materials. The 'case' is placed on the discussion forum and the other learners analyse it according to the theories presented in the learning materials. One of the best ways to determine if learners understand a case is to ask them to summarize it in some form. Other support materials for the case may include drawings, blueprints, reports, instruction manuals, memos, letters and multimedia files. These may not be posted on the discussion forum itself, but be made available through a link. The learner or learners who created the case then become the moderators of the discussion. Here the facilitator should provide a list of cases from which the learners can choose, and participate in the discussion as an anonymous learner.

Team case study discussion forum

In the team case, learners are divided into teams and presented with a case by the facilitator or one of the learners. The teams then analyse the case in terms of the ideas and theories presented in the learning materials. This allows each team to develop its own response. The results of the analysis of the case are then placed on the discussion forum and the participants discuss the results.

Individual journal discussion forum

In an individual journal discussion forum, all learners are assigned a 'thread' or portion of the materials and asked for comments. In this kind of forum the facilitator can also ask learners to respond to specific questions and provide model answers. Typically, when this happens it is only the facilitator who reads this part of the discussion, as it may be used as part of the learners' final assessments. Learners receive some feedback on their comments from the facilitator either regularly or at the completion of the learning event.

Group project discussion forum

The group project discussion allows learners to work together on group presentations, projects, assignments and case study preparation. The forum allows them to analyse problems, co-ordinate individual and group work, and review one another's work. It also helps learners to understand the dynamics of collaboration and to be more effective in completing tasks.

External discussion forum

There are many public discussion forums already available that can be relevant to your learning event. For example, Usenet newsgroups have discussion forums on a wide range of topics, and learners should be encouraged to join these forums to synthesize their ideas and more importantly discuss relevant topics with people outside their normal sphere of influence.

Buzz group discussion forum

In a buzz group discussion forum, a small number of learners are given a problem or an issue to discuss without the assistance of the facilitator. Here they discuss the issue among themselves and when finished release the results to the other members of the forum and answer their questions or comments.

Brainstorming discussion forum

In the brainstorming discussion forum, the facilitator posts a problem and learners suggest solutions. Members of the group are not expected to comment on the solutions given by other learners. Once the discussion is complete, the facilitator can moderate a discussion on the advantages and disadvantages of each solution.

Role-play discussion

Role-plays are designed to partially replicate the real world. Learners put themselves in dramatic situations and act out the scenes. In this case, the facilitator will need to explain the goal(s) of the role play and assign roles to the participants. Learners study their roles and define their characteristics and behaviour. The role-play then goes online in the discussion forum. After the role-play, the group analyses what has happened and makes comments in the discussion forum. Some examples of effective role-plays include court trials and board meetings.

Seminar discussion forum

In seminar forums, small groups of learners prepare a paper or presentation on a topic selected by the facilitator or by themselves. The learners prepare for the seminar using a discussion forum to which other learners do not have access, after which a presentation is made to the larger group for discussion and analysis. The facilitator plays a less predominant role than in group discussions, and attempts to co-ordinate, facilitate and make comments on the presentations.

Simulation discussion forum

A simulation is an attempt to create the illusion of reality, where reality cannot be used because of various constraints, such as time, cost, danger, complexity and location. Simulation forums are often used in conjunction with games. A major weakness in simulations or games is that they do not reflect the real world because they are time-limited and the learners playing roles are known to the other participants. In the discussion forum environment, the communication for the game can be structured. For example, all the learners are assigned pseudonyms, so that none of the learners know who the other members are. The learners would then be assigned roles in a small business and asked for their reactions as and when the facilitator releases information to them. The simulation can be played over a few hours, days or even months.

Synchronous communication

Synchronous communication involves people interacting in real time. An online 'lecture' or a telephone conversation is an example of synchronous communication. Using the Internet, people can communicate synchronously using Internet relay chat, real-time audio, application sharing or whiteboards, and computer video conferencing. However, these tools are difficult to use for large numbers of learners because of co-ordination problems and the stability of technology using a low bandwidth. There may be a need to use synchronous computer communication in fully Webbed learning events, but this need is reduced when facilitators are meeting learners on a regular basis.

CONCLUSION

There are many ways in which Web-based learning support is used to assist learners studying in a face-to-face environment. Providing course-specific learning materials online is one way of doing this, as is providing learners with a series of links to existing resources. Computer-managed learning is also an effective method because the learner can be 'tracked' through their various assignments. Potentially, one of the most effective methods of improving learning is to use group-based learning with discussion forums as this will help encourage collaboration between learners. The type of Web-based learning support given to the learners is dependent on the designer and the available technology.

Chapter 5

Eighteen steps for building a Web-based learning event

INTRODUCTION

Developing materials for a Web-based learning event differs little from developing any other type of learning event, as the Web is only a delivery tool. The traditional systems approach model for designing instruction such as the one developed by Dick and Carey (1978) is effective in ensuring that all the various parts of a typical learning event work together towards a well-defined goal – that of producing effective instruction. This chapter briefly describes each of the steps to be carried out if you are to design an effective Web-based learning event.

INSTRUCTIONAL DESIGN MODEL

The 'traditional' systems approach model as developed by Walter Dick and Lou Carey was heavily influenced by the work of other instructional designers in the field and is behaviourally orientated. It emphasizes the identification of the skills learners need to learn and the collection of data from learners to revise instruction.

In describing their model Dick and Carey note that:

the model includes nine steps or procedures that are used to design instruction. This set of procedures is referred to as a systems approach because it is made up of interacting components each having its own input and output, which together produce predetermined products. A system also collects information about its effectiveness so that the final product can be modified until it reaches the desired quality level... The systems approach model is not a curriculum design model. In order to design a curriculum many more steps would be required.

(Dick and Carey, 1978)

Figure 5.1 shows the nine steps of the Dick and Carey model, together with the 'Revise instruction' step, each of which are described below.

Identify instructional goals

The first step in the systematic development of learning materials is to identify the goals of the learning event. These goals outline what you want the learners to be able to do at the completion of the learning event, and are determined from the needs assessment or from your practical experience of conducting similar learning events.

Conduct instructional analysis

Once the instructional goals have been determined the next step is to identify the subskills the learners must acquire as they work towards the instructional goals. Here you identify the rules, concepts and information the learners need to know. If it is a procedural task, then you identify each of the steps involved.

Identify entry behaviours

Once you have identified the content and the specific skills of your learning event you must determine what knowledge and skills the learners need before they begin the learning event. Factors that need to be taken into account here include general characteristics, such as age, interests, preferred learning style, occupation, socio-economic group and level of computer literacy, as these will have a bearing on the design of the learning event.

Develop performance objectives

Performance objectives are the specific learning outcomes determined for the learning event and written in performance terms. They should include the performance learners must attain, a standard of achievement and the conditions under which the performance is carried out. Objectives are developed from the instructional goals, instructional analysis and the identified entry behaviour of the learners.

Develop learner assessment

In this step, the learner assessment plan is developed. Here you will develop various assessments to help determine whether the learners have met the performance objectives.

Develop the instructional strategy

The instructional strategy describes how learners are going to achieve the performance objectives. For an overview of these strategies, see the section on 'Developing materials' later in this chapter.

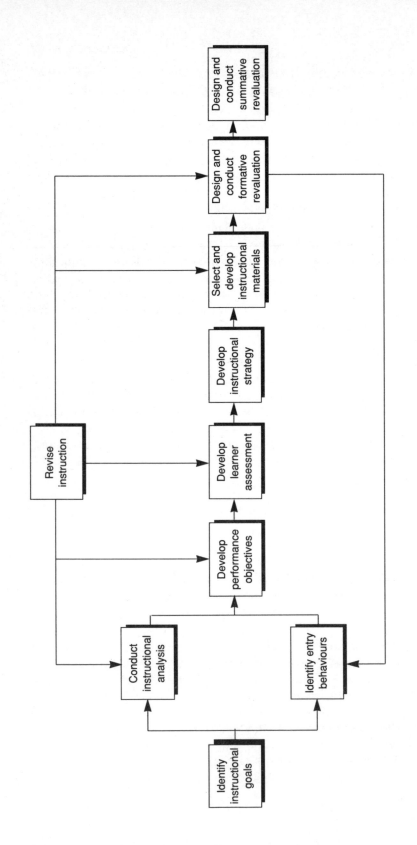

Figure 5.1 *The Dick and Carey model*

Select and develop instructional materials

In this step instructional materials are developed and selected, based on the appropriate resources. If delivery is to be totally Web-based, then you must decide if you can use existing Web-based resources or if new resources will need to be developed. In either case, you will have to apply resource selection criteria to ensure you are using or developing the appropriate type of resource.

Design and conduct formative evaluation

Once the learning materials are completed you must put them through a series of evaluations to determine how well they perform with respect to their stated goals and objectives. You can have subject-matter experts to go through the material on a one-to-one basis and you can have small groups of learners work through the material and obtain their feedback on the content and design. Each evaluation will provide you with different kinds of information to help improve the materials.

Design and conduct summative evaluation

In a summative evaluation, a field trial can be conducted with actual learners working through in real time to determine if the learning materials are truly effective. Based on the results of the field trial, the learning materials may have to be revised.

Revise instruction

The information gathered from the formative evaluation is used to determine where learners had problems achieving the stated performance objectives and is used to revise the various facets of the learning event.

WHY ARE THERE 18 STEPS TO DEVELOPING A WEB-BASED LEARNING EVENT?

Dick and Carey used a nine-step approach to developing instructional materials. In this book, an 18-step approach is suggested, as the development of a Web-based learning event is actually the development of a curriculum. The nine steps of the Dick and Carey model are included, some of which are broken into smaller steps to make the process more systematic. Some of the steps are specific to the development of a Web-based learning event, such as reviewing Web-based learning resources. The '18 steps' is a generalized model for development, to provide guidance when designing Web-based learning events.

Web-based design model

As described in the first part of this chapter, the development model used as the basis or foundation for the design of the Web-based learning materials described in this book is a systems model that has been described by the model developer as requiring additional steps to make it appropriate for the development of learning materials. What are those additional steps and how are they determined?

Typically the design and development of effective instruction revolves around the four basic fundamental steps of gathering information, developing materials, producing materials and evaluating materials, where evaluation includes checking the materials themselves and reviewing both the delivery methodology and the design quality of the event. These basic steps are alluded to in Dick and Carey's description of their systems model when they describe it as a series of interacting components that produces predetermined products and collects information about itself, so the final product can be modified until it reaches the desired quality level.

It can be argued that Dick and Carey themselves expand the four basic design and development steps into the nine steps outlined in the first part of this chapter (see Figure 5.2).

However, for the model to evolve into an actual methodology for the development of Web-based learning materials, an additional series of steps based on the four underlying principles and directly linked to the model for the development of learning materials has to be determined. These additional steps are outlined in Figure 5.3 (on page 64). It is these steps that are reviewed in the remainder of this chapter and described in detail throughout the rest of this book.

There is no magic in the actual number of steps. As the process evolved and the steps were determined, the final count in this case was 18. It may be that you will find some steps unnecessary in the work you are doing and will want to eliminate them, or conversely and more likely, you may want to add additional steps that are appropriate to your needs and your organization. The point is that the suggested model is flexible enough to be able to work for you and aid you in the design of effective Web-based learning events.

DEVELOPING WEB-BASED LEARNING

The following part of the chapter outlines each of the steps for the development of Web-based learning materials. To make it easy to see where each of the steps fits in terms of the development cycle's four fundamental steps of gathering information, developing materials, producing materials and evaluating materials, the steps are grouped into the four basic steps for developing learning materials.

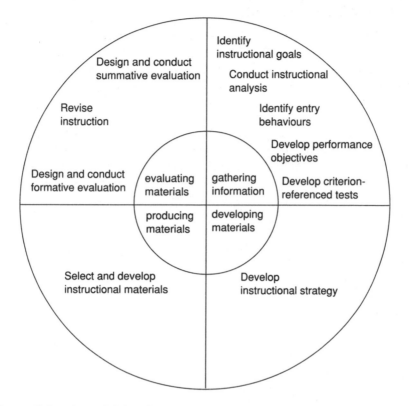

Figure 5.2 *A model for the development of learning materials*

Gathering information

The gathering information stage in any learning materials development project can include the administration of a demand survey, the carrying out of a needs analysis and the setting down of general development specifications for the learning event.

Step 1: Prepare the Web event information document (WID)

Preparing the Web information document is generally the first step in developing any learning event. This document is designed to record the basic information regarding the learning materials you are going to develop. The document is used in a number of different ways such as providing a basis for determining the feasibility of a Web-based learning event, providing a consistent development methodology and providing a basis for planning the project. The document is designed to be used by anyone given the task of developing Web-based learning materials.

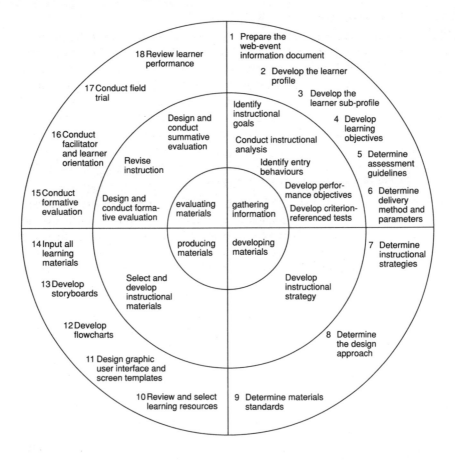

Figure 5.3 *Eighteen steps for developing Web-based learning materials*

The WID is a planning document and is the basis for the development of the learning event. The information put into the documentation can change as you further investigate the requirements of both the learners and the organization.

Step 2: Develop the learner profile

The learner profile is a block diagram that outlines the topics that must be learnt in order for the learner to complete the learning event successfully. Typically a profile is developed with a small group of subject-matter experts who determine and order the topics that should be studied. Each topic then provides the basis for the general learning objectives (GLOs) for the event. Specific learning objectives (SLOs) are determined from the sub-profile.

Step 3: Develop the learner sub-profile

The sub-profile is an extension of the learner profile and provides greater detail regarding what the learner has to achieve and the standards required. Specific learning objectives are developed during this step and should include as a minimum a statement of learner performance. Conditions of performance and standards can also be included as part of the objective as required by the organization. The same team of subject-matter experts that developed the learner profile usually develops the sub-profile.

Step 4: Develop learning objectives

Both the general and specific learning objectives developed from the profile and sub-profile describe the performance requirements of the learners. Objectives help learners know where they are going and how they are going to get there. They also tell facilitators how they will know when learners have arrived at or met the stated objectives. The objectives should include:

- performance – what learners are expected to do;
- conditions – the important conditions under which the performance is to occur;
- standards – the minimum criteria that learners must meet in order for the performance to be acceptable.

Step 5: Determine assessment guidelines

Using both the general and specific learning objectives as a basis for development, this step involves the development of an assessment methodology or plan. What kind of instruments are going to be used, when will they be administrated and what kind of rating or marking system is going to be applied?

Many of your determinations at this stage will be largely dependent on the features and operation of your assessment software. If you are using a popular, established package, it will probably contain a feature set for building and delivering online assessments. You can therefore establish guidelines for including graphics, videos or audio clips with your questions, as well as guidelines for other Web-based question techniques such as drag and drop, tag placement, fill-in-the-blanks and even full text input.

Smaller, less featured assessment packages may limit you to multiple choice, true/false or check-all-that-apply type of questions, which will affect your guidelines for setting questions and your assessment guidelines.

Regardless of the software, you will need to determine how learners will 'submit' their assessment materials to the system or course facilitator, and how the assessment materials will be marked. Normally, learners will simply link to an assessment page from the courseware itself, complete the test or quiz, and click a 'submit' button to send their answers to either the facilitator or the system itself. Depending on your guidelines, the assessment can then be:

● auto-marked, giving the learner immediate feedback results;
● auto-marked, with the results sent only to the facilitator, who will convey the results to the learner;
● sent to the facilitator for manual marking;
● marked using a combination of all three techniques.

Finally, your assessment guidelines may need to include some type of security or identity verification scheme. How can you be sure, for example, that the learners who submit a test are really the people they claim to be? In an unsupervised Internet or intranet environment, this is essentially impossible to do. The only way to be entirely certain of the identity of your learners is to check their identities manually before they take an assessment. If you require this level of security, you will need to establish a supervised, computer-based testing environment.

If security is of paramount concern for your online assessments, you may want to consider employing an encryption scheme, such as Secure Socket Layer (SSL), which will ensure that any questions your system sends out over the Internet are encrypted, and cannot be 'sniffed' or tampered with in any way.

In addition to electronic assessments you may include written assignments to assess the higher-order objectives and/or the overall learning outcomes of your learning event. To set an assignment you must first determine the purpose of the assignment and what you intend to test. Second you must determine how you are going to test the objective and the type of question you are going to use. Finally you will need to set assessment guidelines to ensure learners know what they must include in their assignments. For the facilitator, a marking guide should be prepared to ensure all assessment of learners' work is fair, consistent and valid.

Step 6: Determine delivery method and parameters

Before you develop your design approach and instructional strategies you should first determine if the learning event is suitable for online delivery. Once suitability is determined, the delivery methodology and parameters for the event can be finalized. To give your decision a framework, the questions you should ask yourself are presented under the following headings:

● The learning event: content and design.

- Learning event facilitators.
- The organization supporting the event.
- The learners.

The learning event: content

Is the learning event one that has been delivered before?

Developing new learning materials is a major task involving their design, development, delivery and evaluation to ensure their effectiveness. For this reason, you may wish to consider using existing materials, preferably ones that have been delivered and, more importantly, evaluated a number of times before. In this way, when they are redesigned for the Web, you can gain a measure of proven effectiveness.

Are motor skills a major component of the learning event?

Developing Web-based learning materials to help develop and assess psychomotor skills can be time consuming, costly and difficult. In which case you may want to consider delivering the theory portion using the Web, and support this by using face-to-face laboratory sessions. However, it is really a matter of how much theory is included in the total material, and whether it is substantial enough to be delivered in a Web-based environment when learners still have to attend laboratory sessions.

Are socialization and the changing of learner attitudes important components of the learning event?

If socialization and the changing of learner attitudes are important components of the learning event, then Web-based learning may not be appropriate. Some aspects of social work, certain sales techniques and many aspects of counselling are difficult to design, learn and facilitate in a Web-based environment. Changing people's attitudes is best done in a face-to-face environment.

Do the learning materials need to be updated on a regular basis?

If parts of the learning event need to be updated regularly, then Web-based learning probably is suitable. The ease of updating Web-based material is one of its major advantages.

Are there existing relevant resources on the Web?

If there is already a large amount of subject matter and other information relevant to your event presently available on the Web, then it is probably suitable for Web-based delivery. In which case your learning event could take the form of a learning resource guide used to direct learners to the relevant materials and provide links between them.

Is self-pacing an important aspect of the learning event?

If, due to the diverse nature of the learners, self-pacing is an important aspect of the learning event, or your aim is to give the learners more control over their learning, then Web-based delivery may be a good choice. Web-based learning is a good environment for self-paced learning because multimedia and well-defined hyperlinks can be used to help learners better control their learning.

Is the delivery of multimedia essential to your learning event?

If multimedia is essential to your learning event, then Web-based learning may not be suitable. One of the advantages of the Web is that text, graphics, photographs, audio and video can be integrated and used to instructional advantage. One of the major disadvantages however is delivering these materials to the learner.

Do you have existing computer-based resources that can be converted to Web-based materials?

If you have relevant word-processing and electronic-presentation files, they can be converted relatively easily for use on the Web. Existing graphic and video files can also be converted. If this is indeed the case, your learning event may be suitable for Web-based delivery.

The learning event: design

Are large numbers of learners involved?

Preparing well-developed Web-based learning materials takes a great deal of time, uses substantial resources and can be quite costly. Therefore, if the number of learners is small, then it is probably not financially appropriate to develop Web-based learning materials. However, if there are large numbers of learners involved, then the development of Web-based learning could provide a viable return on investment.

Will small groups of learners be involved in the event during different time periods?

For a variety of reasons, different groups of learners may be involved, or want to be involved with, the learning event during different time periods. If this is the case, you are going to have to build flexibility into the event to suit a variety of different schedules. Here the use of a Web-based delivery methodology is probably a good choice, provided the total numbers of learners is relatively large.

Does collaborative learning form an important component of the learning event?

Collaborative learning is one of the fundamental goals of learning at a distance. In a Web-based environment, learners can collaborate using a variety of different tools, including chat rooms, Usenet, e-mail, bulletin boards and various types of computer forums. If one of the aims is to encourage collaborative learning, then Web-based delivery may be an appropriate approach.

Is consistency in learning needed?

Often, even though the facilitator of a classroom-based learning event is using a guide designed specifically for that event, what is actually delivered to the learner can be quite different from the approved syllabus. If consistency of information delivered is important to you, then you may want to consider a Web-based learning methodology.

Do you want to use computer-managed learning?

If you require detailed tracking of your learners' progress, then you may want to consider using a computer-managed learning (CML) program. CML is a management tool designed to assist facilitators and learning administrators with the problems of tracking learners' progress. Many CML programs are available for the Web environment, and some can be used to both build and deliver learning materials.

Is continuity in learning required?

Continuity in learning can be a problem in the 'traditional' learning at a distance environment, given that both facilitator(s) and learners can be scattered over a wide geographical area. This is less of a problem in a Web environment because both facilitators and learners are location independent. However, there is still the problem of time difference. If continuity in learning is required, then it may be appropriate to use a Web-based delivery methodology for your learning event.

Are enough skilled staff available to develop the learning materials?

Designing and developing Web-based materials requires people with course development skills, instructional design skills and technical expertise in computing. It is important that you understand that Web-based learning is technology dependent, and requires multi-faceted support during the materials design stage and later during the delivery stage. If this is unsustainable, your learners will not receive quality learning. Having the right people to design and support the learning is critical to the success of the event. If you have such people available, or you are prepared to employ them, then Web-based learning is feasible.

Learning event facilitators

Do the teaching staff need to have computers and Internet access?

With Web-based learning, developers and tutors must have the appropriate access to computers and the Internet. Modem access speeds should be at the very least 28.8 Kb/s. More appropriate speeds are 56.6 Kb/s or broadband connections, such as ASDL or cable modem access. Without 'high speed' access, Web-based learning may not be an appropriate delivery method.

Are the learning event facilitators supportive of Web-based learning?

Support for those involved in Web-based learning is essential to the success of the learning event. The use of a new delivery methodology can bring about fear of change and a desire to retain the status quo. In many cases, facilitators feel they do not have the skills and knowledge to cope with the new methodology. Training of facilitators then becomes an important part of the implementation of Web-based learning and is critical to its overall success.

The organization supporting the event

Is the organization supportive of Web-based learning?

Even if facilitators are supportive of Web-based delivery, the support of the organization is essential to effectively implement Web-based learning. The organization has a number of important functions to carry out, for example, it will probably need to allocate some type of funding for Web-based learning, and arrange for the participation of its staff, who may or may not be entirely enthusiastic about the project. Without the required organizational support, a great deal of time and effort may be squandered.

Is encouraging and developing lifelong learning one of the goals of the organization?

It has long been realized that learning does not end when a person leaves school, college or university. Learning needs to continue throughout a person's life to ensure the appropriate skills for that time period have been learnt. This means that a person needs to be trained, retrained and have their knowledge and skills updated on a regular basis. Many organizations have implemented a lifelong learning plan as one of the primary goals for their staff. If this is the case in your organization, then Web-based delivery may be an appropriate method to support this initiative.

Will Web-based learning give your organization a competitive edge?

Marketing lifelong learning is a very competitive business, with many organizations competing for learners both locally and internationally. Organizations that use a Web-based delivery methodology for their learning events are often better able to serve their clients because of the flexibility of their delivery options. If your organization sees the delivery of Web-based learning events as giving them a competitive edge, then it is probably an appropriate delivery method.

The learners

Do learners need to have computer and Internet access?

Web-based learning requires learners to have both computer and Internet access. Without such access, Web-based learning is not possible. It is also worth remembering that, as well as access to the Web, learners must have a suitable computer and the appropriate software to access the learning event. If both current and potential learners have access to computers and the Internet, then Web-based learning may be a viable delivery method.

Are Internet connection costs a factor?

Learners who access the Internet from home typically do so from a dial-up connection, for which they pay a monthly fee. Costs are usually determined by the number of hours spent online, and these costs can be high if your materials require hours of access or download time. If Internet access is relatively inexpensive, and the learning event requires relatively few online hours, then Web-based delivery is a distinct possibility.

What if learner motivation is low?

Web-based learning requires considerably more motivation and application on the part of the learner than other kinds of learning events. This means that, since Web-based instruction is learner-centered and learners can control the pace of their learning, they have to make decisions about when and where to study. If learner motivation is low, these type of decisions can be off-putting. If this is the case, Web-based delivery may not be an appropriate choice. In contrast, if learner motivation is high and the materials can be designed to take advantage of this, then Web-based delivery may be feasible.

Is remedial learning needed?

It is rare that all learners have the same entry level skills. Web-based delivery makes it easier to deliver remedial learning to those who require it. Combining Web-based delivery with a computer-managed learning strategy, for example, allows you to administer and track learner progress and provide remediation. Based on individual learner test results, remedial learning tracks can be developed to ensure all learners are given the same opportunity to meet the event goals and objectives. If remediation is needed, a Web-based delivery methodology combined with computer-managed learning may be appropriate.

Do learners want to learn at a location away from the organization?

Even if learners are geographically close to the learning organization, they may not want to study there if work or family commitments make it difficult or inappropriate. Given the nature of a Web-based learning environment, learners may want to study at a time and place suitable for them. If this is the case, then Web-based learning may be appropriate.

Selection table

To help you determine whether your learning event is suitable for Web-based learning, the following selection table can be used. Answering the questions regarding the content of your proposed learning event, the facilitators you plan to use, the organization and your learners, can help you decide whether the learning event is suitable for Web-based delivery.

Selection checklist

Is your learning event suitable for Web-based learning?

Content
Is the learning event one that has been delivered many times before?   ☐

Are motor skills a major component of the learning event? ☐

Are socialization and the changing of learner attitudes
important components of the learning event? ☐

Do the instructional materials need to be updated on a
regular basis? ☐

Are there existing relevant resources on the Web? ☐

Is self-pacing an important aspect of the learning event? ☐

Is the delivery of multimedia essential to your learning
event? ☐

Do you have existing resources that can be converted to
Web-based materials? ☐

Design
Are large numbers of learners involved? ☐

Will small groups of learners be involved in the event
during different time periods? ☐

Do small numbers of learners become available over
different time periods? ☐

Does collaborative learning form an important component
of the learning event? ☐

Is consistency in learning needed? ☐

Do you want to use computer-managed learning (CML)? ☐

Is continuity in learning required? ☐

Are enough skilled staff available to develop the learning
materials? ☐

Learning event facilitators
Do the teaching staff have computers and Internet access? ☐

Are the learning event facilitators supportive of Web-based
learning? ☐

The organization
Is the organization supportive of Web-based learning? ☐

Is encouraging and developing lifelong learning one of the
goals of the organization? ☐

Will Web-based learning give your organization a
competitive edge? ☐

The learners

Do the learners have both computer and Internet access?   ☐

Are Internet connectivity costs a factor?   ☐

Is learner motivation low?   ☐

Is remedial learning needed?   ☐

Do learners want to learn at a location away from the
organization?   ☐

It is important to understand that one single overriding factor may make your learning event unsuitable for Web-based delivery. For example, if Internet connection is very expensive this may override everything else. Your delivery methodology includes determining how you are going to deliver the actual learning event. For example, is it going to be exclusively Web-based or is it going to be a combination of classroom, self-directed and Web-based learning? You will also need to consider how much learner support, both online and offline, will be needed by your proposed delivery method. Your delivery parameters are the guidelines that govern the type of Web-based media that your servers are capable of delivering and that your learners' computers and Internet connections can realistically support.

To help determine your methodology and parameters, you need to consider the following:

- Is your learning event going to be delivered over the Web, by an intranet, via a CD ROM/Internet hybrid, or by a combination of media?
- Will your learners be accessing your courseware via dial-up modems, by ADSL or cable modems, over your company or campus LAN, or by a combination of access methods?
- Are your Web or media servers capable of supporting such technologies as streaming audio or video?
- Do you have server software capable of delivering your desired learning materials?
- Will you be saturating the bandwidth on your company or campus LAN if you choose to include large amounts of audio or video materials?
- Can you specify certain software requirements, such as type of required Web browser? Or will your learning event be browser-neutral?
- What are the (average) specifications of your learners' computers?
- Are your delivery parameters likely to change in the near future? Are upgrades planned for your software, server hardware, LAN or Internet connection?

The type of media you plan to include in your courseware, especially with regard to the use of audio or video, will vary depending on your delivery parameters. For this reason, you may want to set out a number of basic hardware and software criteria that your target audience must adhere to if they intend to be actively involved in the learning event.

At this stage you will also need to consider if you need to use an instructional management system or develop your own learning event software. An instructional management system is an authoring program that allows you to create your own Web-based learning event. These programs allow you to select the media to include and the level of interactivity. Instructional management programs have their advantages, however the one major disadvantage is the cost of the program. If you do decide to use an instructional management program you should evaluate it in terms of the service provided by the vendor, its platform, software, ease of use and development, computer-managed learning component, vendor support provided and cost of licensing fees.

Developing materials

This stage is made up of just three steps: determining the learning strategies, the design approach and the materials development standards. Each of these steps is fundamental to the selection and development of your materials in the producing materials stage.

Step 7: Determine instructional strategies

In this step you have to determine how learners will learn from the materials being presented. To meet the learning objectives, learners are presented with information, interact with certain aspects of the materials and complete various activities. They also need to complete assessments and communicate with others including the learning event facilitator(s).

The instructional strategy describes how learners are going to achieve the performance objectives. There are five parts that make up an overall instructional strategy. These are:

1. Pre-instructional activities that involve gaining the learners' attention and introducing the learning event. Here objectives are stated and attempts made to recall learners' prior knowledge.
2. Information presentation. Here content is sequenced and structured in a manner that is suitable for the learners. The appropriate amount of information is contained in the unit of instruction and other individual elements.
3. Practice. Activities that allow learners to apply the knowledge they have learnt. Feedback should be given regarding their performance on each activity.

4. Assessment of learning outcomes. Here, the achievement of learners is measured to determine what has been gained from studying the learning event. This should include both formative and summative assessments, along with pre-, post- and embedded-tests.
5. Follow-up and remediation. Additional learning activities are provided for learners who have not achieved the objectives in the form of remediation and enrichment.

Step 8: Determine the design approach

In this step you have to determine the 'tools' needed to allow or help learners complete the various activities set up as part of the learning materials. For example, minimum requirements for a typical Web-delivered event might include:

- browser software;
- a media player;
- a 'whiteboard' or notepad for learner notes;
- an electronic assessment application;
- bulletin board access;
- an e-mail address.

The types of tools you choose are dependent on the delivery parameters you determined in step 6. For example, a delivery model using just the Web or a Web/CD ROM combination will greatly influence your choice of software.

If you decide to use an instructional management system a number of components will be built into the software. These could include:

- *Notice board.* In this section announcements, updates and reminders are shown.
- *Course information.* In this section general information about the learning event is given, including the learning event overview, objectives, prerequisites and the time and dates for the various activities.
- *Facilitator information.* This section contains information about the learning event facilitators and how to contact them.
- *Materials presentation area.* This section contains most of the instructional information such as the learning materials, Web-based resources and other related materials.
- *Assessment area.* This section contains the learning event assignments, tests, quizzes and surveys.
- *Communication.* This section contains the communication tools such as discussion forums, chat rooms and e-mail addresses.
- *Links.* This section contains external hyperlinks to related Web-based materials which are different to those provided in the materials presentation area.

- *Learner tools.* This section contains the various 'tools' learners require such as a calendar, the means to check assignments, manage home pages and edit their profiles.

There are many different types of instructional management programs available, all with different options. It is important to evaluate them, so that you can determine which one best meets your needs.

Step 9: Determine materials standards

Whether you are one person developing a short Web-based learning event or a member of a large team developing a range of Web-based events and related courses, the project will require documented technical and instructional guidelines. These guidelines serve as a reference during the development of the learning materials and will provide you with the details regarding which items should be included in the various parts of your learning event. The guidelines are generally in the form of a manual or design document, which is distributed to the development team. While it is important to clarify the guidelines as precisely as possible, remember that techniques and methodologies can change over the life of the project, which means that the guidelines must be flexible enough to change as needed for the overall good of the project.

To ensure that the learning event is technically feasible and sound, a set of criteria and standards will have to be established that define the chosen technology platform. These guidelines can be broken into content and layout guidelines, and process guidelines.

Content and layout guidelines

These guidelines govern the parameters and standards by which the content of the learning materials is produced and presented. Content and layout guidelines include user interface and style considerations such as font type, size, colour and effects, hyperlink colours, roll-over properties and more. Content and layout guidelines also define colour themes and motifs, and placement of navigational controls, along with guidelines for producing audio, video, images and other multimedia elements.

Process guidelines

Process guidelines govern the practices and processes by which the materials are built and maintained. These guidelines cover required software, programming methodologies, coding procedures, file naming conventions, bandwidth considerations, quality control standards, security concerns and more. Process guidelines help to ensure that all developers follow the same or similar conventions when building the components of a larger system.

If you are delivering your courseware over the Web, you need to be conscious of the many different types of computers, operating systems and Web browsers used to access it. For example, you have no way of knowing if your learners are using Internet Explorer or Netscape Navigator as their Web browser. This means that you either establish user requirements or develop materials that are entirely cross-platform compatible. However, given the many problems and difficulties of developing learning materials with cross-platform compatibility, establishing user requirements offers you the best choice.

Instructional guidelines

Along with content and layout guidelines you will also need a set of instructional guidelines to ensure the learning materials meet acceptable standards. These are the standards that may be set by your organization or may be derived from those set by institutions of learning. Such guidelines may include those set to ensure that learning objectives are written to include at least a recognizable performance statement, or that orienting devices are built into the materials to guard against learners being lost in cyberspace. The guidelines might also include requirements for test item design, test bank development and item pool size.

The overall aim of the guidelines is to ensure the learning event is consistent, user friendly and developed in such a way that learners can actually learn something!

Producing materials

In this phase the instructional materials are developed and keyed into your chosen Web delivery platform.

Step 10: Review and select learning resources

Good instructional materials take considerable skill and expertise to produce. Therefore in order to be cost- and time-efficient you may wish to consider using instructional materials already produced. Typically these materials come in two formats: either print-based materials that can be easily converted to Web-based documents or materials that already exist in an electronic format, such as text, audio, video and animation files.

The following criteria can be used to help you determine if the resource is suitable:

● Identify the type of resource. For example, a video file may not be suitable unless it has been converted to a streaming format.
● Relate the content of the resource to the needs of the learning event and review the resource against the appropriate learning objectives.
● Determine the pace of the materials in the resource; does it fit with your existing materials?

- Judge how current the materials are.
- Assess the resource for both comprehension and readability, and compare it to the abilities of your learners.
- Determine what copyrights are attached to the materials.

Among the major resources you will use in your Web-based learning events are other Web sites, so these should be evaluated and selected in a systematic manner. The following criteria can be used to help you determine if the Web site is suitable for your Web-based learning event:

- *Access information.* What is the name of the site and at what speed are you accessing it?
- *Technical aspects.* Is the site stable and do the pages download in a reasonable time?
- *Learning outcomes.* Does the site cover the objectives the learner needs to achieve?
- *Information presentation.* Is the information broken down into manageable chunks and are the materials logically sequenced?
- *Multiple media.* Does the multimedia enhance the message?
- *Design.* How does the screen design effectiveness measure up to the design/development standards?
- *Authenticity.* Have the authors and site developers been clearly identified?
- *Navigation.* Is the site easy to navigate?
- *Links.* Are the links clearly identified and logically grouped?

Step 11: Develop graphical user interface and screen templates

The graphical user interface (GUI) contains all the various elements that are 'seen by' your learners and with which they will interact as they progress through the learning event. The GUI includes elements, such as navigation buttons that are used on every screen of the learning material, as well as elements that are specific to certain topics.

A good approach to developing your GUI is to first determine which elements are required on every page or screen of the learning event. These will probably include such common elements as navigation buttons, banners, headers and/or footers, and links to the main sections of your material. Once the common elements have been determined, you can begin to develop the 'look and feel' of the GUI, by determining where elements should be placed on the screen, whether they should be bitmap graphics or text, and how they should operate. You will also want at this stage to begin making decisions about font use, roll-overs, colour motifs, backgrounds and general use of graphics.

In general, your GUI should be uncluttered, uniform in layout and operation, and intuitive. The interface should not get in the way of your learning materials, but rather to facilitate access to your learning content.

Once the GUI and the screen layout are completed, you can begin to develop the various templates you need. Typically the number and kinds of templates are determined from the flowchart(s) and can include:

- advanced organizer – where the learning event overview is presented;
- information presentation – where the learning materials are presented;
- assignment – where learner assignments are outlined;
- assessment pages – where a topic quiz, test or examination is presented;
- resource pages – hyperlinks to other Web sites;
- main and sub menu pages.

If you are using an instructional management tool then some templates may already be developed, so you only have to decide which ones you are going to use in your learning event.

Step 12: Develop flowcharts

In this step you produce a flowchart or flowcharts, which show in a graphical format the structure of the learning materials you are going to put on to the Web. A flowchart is a map of the place where your journey begins and ends. Like any good map a flowchart will show you the routes between the various places you will visit on your journey and how you can travel quickly from one place to another using alternative routes. A flowchart will change based on the nature of the project, the material under development and the people doing the development.

Step 13: Develop storyboards

When developing your Web-based learning materials you will need the storyboard to help ensure the learning materials are developed to the correct specifications. If you are developing the learning event your-self, without the assistance of a programmer, then the storyboard can probably afford to be a little less detailed. If you are using a programmer you will need to include more detail so as to communicate your requirements regarding each screen. A storyboard is developed and written directly from the flowchart. There are many different formats for storyboards, and they will vary according to the type of learning event being produced. An example of a storyboard is shown in Figure 5.4.

Screen Number:	Screen Type:	Next:		Previous:	Back:	Link:
Topic Title:		Screen Title:	Section:			

Notes	Text	Graphics	Audio	Video

Figure 5.4   *An example of a typical storyboard*

The components of this storyboard include:

- screen number – the number of the screen based on its position in the flowchart;
- screen type – a description of the kind of screen such as presentation, assessment, main menu, glossary and the like;
- next – the number of the next screen;
- previous – the number of the previous screen;
- back – the screen the learner will return to when the back button is activated;

- link – the screen or screens, Web sites and/or other resources to which this screen is linked;
- notes – any notes to the programmer written by the developer to tell the programmer what is needed on the screen;
- text – the actual text that appears on the screen;
- graphic(s) – a concept for the graphic, chart or illustration that will appear on the screen. This part of the storyboard can also include the name and location of previously developed graphics that can be used in this location;
- audio – the script for the audio that will accompany the screen, which can also include the name and location of previously developed audio files that can be used in this location;
- video – the name and location of previously developed video files suitable for use in this location.

Depending on the complexity of the learning event you may need to produce separate audio, video and animation storyboards.

Step 14: Input all learning materials

In this step the text is placed into the various templates using your storyboard as a guide. The text materials are created, keyed in, edited, proofread, formatted, assembled, tested and eventually published. The non-text components of the learning event such as graphics, audio, video and animation files must also be completed and placed into the templates. At this stage the instructional designer or, if it is a large project, the instructional design team will need to monitor the development of learning materials to ensure they all meet the required specifications.

Evaluating materials

During this stage in the proceedings a formative or ongoing review is planned, facilitators and learners are oriented and a field trial is conducted.

Step 15: Conduct formative evaluation

A formative evaluation is the step where the concepts, metaphors, ideas, graphics and the myriad of other things that go into the learning event are put together into a 'beta' version and reviewed by the various members of the team involved in the project. The review team might include the client, instructional designer, subject-matter expert(s) and programmer, and will determine if the event is meeting the needs of all concerned and meeting the specifications set for the design.

Once the review is complete any changes are incorporated into the event prior to its initial implementation. A second formative evaluation is sometimes planned to take place after the event has been revised.

Step 16: Conduct facilitator and learner orientation

Staff need to be orientated regarding the facilitation of a Web-based learning event. Typically facilitators need to know how to:

- conduct the learning event;
- determine the requirements of learners;
- assist learners in achieving the learning objectives;
- moderate the discussion forum;
- comment on learners' work.

Research has shown that even experienced classroom facilitators require assistance to be effective Web-based facilitators.

Learners also need to know how to access the learning event, sign in and use the event to their advantage. They need to know how to solve problems and who to contact if they cannot overcome the problem. They also need assistance and guidance regarding studying in a self-study environment as opposed to a facilitator-led environment.

Step 17: Conduct field trial

A field trial should be conducted in real time with a small number of the target audience 'working through' the learning materials. Facilitators should also be in place to assist learners as and when needed.

Step 18: Review learner performance

The field trial should be evaluated to determine what, if any, changes are needed to the learning materials. A summative evaluation will determine:

- the ability of the Web system to support the learner;
- the learning gains;
- the effectiveness of the learning environment;
- the effectiveness of the support offered to the learner;
- how the Web-based environment compares with the traditional environment.

Based on the finding of the evaluation, changes may be needed to the learning materials and the support measures.

CONCLUSION

In this chapter each of the many steps involved in the design, development, implementation and evaluation of Web-based learning materials have been outlined. The steps are explained in a linear manner, but it must be emphasized that the cycle is iterative in nature with each step being dependent on many others. Each step must constantly be revisited as the learning event develops. Each of these steps is explained in greater detail throughout the remainder of this book.

Chapter 6
Getting started

INTRODUCTION

The initial design and development phase of learning materials for use in a Web-based learning environment is, for the most part, no different to the design and development of materials for use in any other learning environment. Typically when you start any Web-based learning materials development project you are going to have to ask yourself and others a lot of questions to help you determine the focus, priorities and guidelines for your learning materials. Once that is done you then have to determine the actual details of the materials themselves. This is the analysis portion of your work and covers the first three steps in the design and development process of Web-based learning materials. Once you have asked all the relevant questions and, at least for the moment, received what you hope are 'good' answers, then you have to put together a skills profile of the competencies learners must exhibit when they have successfully completed the learning event.

This chapter is about designing and developing your Web-based learning materials, which includes asking the right analysis questions and preparing a Web learning event document.

STARTING THE PROJECT

The assumption is made here that you have at least a basic idea of the extent of the learning materials you are going to have to develop. Many details still have to be worked out, of course, but overall you have a basic plan and you are ready to start putting the plan into place.

A typical Web-based learning materials project usually takes place in four distinct stages, as detailed in Chapter 5. Briefly, these stages are:

1. *Gathering information.* The gathering of information helps you determine the focus, priorities and guidelines for the learning

materials. Also included in this phase of the work is determining the details of the materials, the aims, the objectives, the sequence of the materials and how you might present them to the learner. In most materials development projects the first part of the work includes determining the assessment guidelines, the delivery methodology and the delivery parameters so the learning event can be appropriately delivered to the learner. This phase of the work makes up steps 1 to 6.

2. *Developing materials.* This phase of the work includes just three tasks: determining learning strategies, determining a design approach and developing the standards you want your materials to be based on. This phase of the work covers steps 7, 8 and 9.

3. *Producing materials.* In this third phase of the work, the actual learning materials are put together and placed into the learning event structure. The work starts with the selection of existing resources followed by the design of the graphic user interface (GUI) and the screen templates along with the development of flowcharts and storyboards. This phase of the work ends with the inputting of the learning materials into the screen templates. This phase of the work covers steps 10 to 14.

4. *Evaluating materials.* This final phase is concerned with evaluating the materials on an ongoing basis using a formative review procedure, conducting both facilitator and learner orientation to the learning event, conducting a field trial to ensure the event works as it was meant to work and reviewing learner performance. The final phase covers steps 15 to 18.

In the first phase of the project you need to document the answers to all the questions you need to ask for each of the subsequent stages. Documentation is important for the continuity of the project and the materials being produced. Good documentation ensures a record of events needed for an audit trail of overall progress in the project, client and subject-matter expert (SME) review, material changes and revisions, and implementation procedures.

PRO FORMA DOCUMENTATION

This chapter discusses the issues surrounding the completion of the Web-based learning event information document (WID). This document, along with the skills profile and sub-profile, is discussed in Chapter 7. Together these documents make up the data-gathering tools you need to collect all the information for designing and developing your Web-based learning materials and to support the actions you take as you develop those materials. The documents assist you in gathering the information you need for both documentation purposes and the subsequent summative evaluation of the learning materials. Summative evaluation is important, as it allows others to review what has been developed and to comment on its authenticity and accuracy. The aim of the WID is to assist you in gathering learning event data, and to ensure the skills profile is correctly focused and other important details are well documented.

Gathering and formatting any learning event documentation should be done to suit the needs of the project. What's important is that it's done in a systematic manner; its format is secondary.

PREPARING THE WID

The WID described here is designed to record the basic information regarding the learning materials you are going to develop. This document can be used as:

- a basis for determining the feasibility of a Web-based learning event;
- a memory aid during the development of the learning materials;
- a basis for a project audit trail;
- a consistent development methodology for different kinds of learning materials;
- a basis for planning the materials development project;
- a basis for determining overall project costs.

The WID is designed to be used by anyone given the task of putting together Web-based learning materials. An example of a typical WID is included at the end of this chapter, as Figure 6.1.

Basic information

The first question you have to ask is straightforward: what is the working title of the learning event? Most people have a title in mind so this should be an easy question to answer.

Purpose

The next section of the WID is the purpose section and asks the question: why is there a need to develop this learning event? Articulating a rationale for the learning event is, surprisingly, one of the most difficult questions you will have to deal with. Whether you are completing the WID in an interview situation or completing it yourself you will have to allow time for the rationale to be formulated. In an interview situation, you may need to work with the interviewees to help them formulate the rationale and put it in writing. When the rationale is completed it will help you to put in writing the learning event goals and the general learning objectives as well as in focusing the development of the skills profile.

You may find that the rationale will be a compromise worked out between what is needed by learners and what is needed by others involved in the project. Whatever the outcome, however, discussion will have taken place, opinions have been aired and positions taken. For many materials development projects this is a healthy process and will help you better prepare for potential problems.

Audience

The next questions deal with the audience, those people you are developing the materials for and who are often forgotten in the rush to get the materials ready. However as you consider whom the event is really for and the fact that with a Web-based environment the potential audience is world-wide, the answers you come up with may significantly alter the direction and content of the materials you end up developing. You may also wish to consider a secondary audience, as the possibility of a wider audience may help increase budget allocation and the subsequent addition of other enhancements that were not part of the original plan.

In considering the audience for the learning event, take into account such things as:

- age;
- level of education;
- reading level (ability);
- the learner's motivation for using the Web as a learning medium;
- cultural background;
- previous Web-based learning experiences;
- attitude toward Web-based learning;
- type of computer, software and Internet/Web access;
- the learner's knowledge and ability to cope with the learning materials.

The more you can describe your audience, the more likely you are to develop relevant learning materials. Who are they? How old are they? What kind of learning experiences have they had? Have these experiences been Web-based? These questions can be asked of all learners from the young to the not so young, at all levels of learning. If they are young adults or older, you might want to find out if they work and, if so, what kind of work they do. If they are young learners, you might want to determine their aspirations for the future. Answers to these and other similar questions will help you determine the kind of learning experiences you need to design.

Consider putting together a simple electronic questionnaire to find out more about the learners who are going to be in your virtual classroom. Ask them questions about their likes and dislikes in terms of learning materials and electronic learning. Find out about the kind of computers they have and the kind of Internet connection they use. Try to determine what location they will be accessing the learning materials from. Ask them if they surf the net and the kind of sites they access most frequently.

If they are young learners, ask them about their favourite subject in school; if they are older learners ask about college and university experiences and the like. Remember, however, to take into account that some of your learners may not have had a secondary education experience, so design your questionnaire accordingly. What you are trying to find out is something about their preferred learning style and the materials they like best. Also remember that learners of all ages make choices about their learning, and if they have made the decision to sit in on your learning event they will want to learn something and they will want their money's worth. Take into consideration that it's far easier to walk out of the virtual classroom door in a Web-based learning environment than it is to walk out of a real door.

If you use a questionnaire to gather your information, be it on- or offline, try to keep it as short as possible and make sure that you keep the questions simple. Use a Likert scale or some other form of rating system to quantify reaction. Likert scales are easy to construct and usually have four or five choices that express different degrees of agreement or disagreement and yield ordinal measurements. If you put your questionnaire online, make sure that it is easy to answer and make sure that respondents have the opportunity to change an answer as and when they think fit. Also keep in mind that the typical level of respondents to any questionnaire is only about 30 per cent.

If you want to use open-ended questions, you have the choice of asking respondents in a face-to-face interview, or posting the questionnaire to the respondents' e-mail or to a discussion forum. The problem you face if you post the questionnaire is one of time for reading and understanding all the responses and replying to particular respondents if you feel it is warranted.

Outcomes

The next part of the WID deals with the goals and objectives of the learning materials. The writing of both goals and objectives suggests measurement of some kind. However, trying to measure something that is not clearly defined is very difficult and it's hard to know what materials should be developed. As the developer you will require a fairly precise set of goals and objectives for your own guidance as well as determining what has to be achieved by the learner. Goals are broad statements of intent that provide you with the overall direction of the learning event. You also need to take into consideration that learning event goals often include both assumptions and values that are going to be conveyed in the materials.

Objectives at this stage of the project are simply general learning objectives (GLOs) that provide you with a methodology to reach the desired goals. Useful objectives help you answer the following questions:

- What should learners be able to do with the skills and knowledge they have learnt?
- Under what conditions should learners be able to do the tasks that they have learnt?
- How well must the performance of learners be carried out? What are the standards that learners must achieve?

Notice how the emphasis here is on learners, not anything or anyone else.

Objectives are, of course, useful in the design of all your learning materials including those designed for use in a Web-based environment, as they tell learners where they are going, how they are going to get there and how the facilitator of the event will know when they have arrived. A useful objective is one that allows the facilitator to make the largest number of decisions relevant to its achievement and measurement. Well-written objectives will help you determine:

- material content;
- materials delivery methodologies;
- types of learning strategies;
- learner assessment methodology;
- evaluation procedures.

The key to writing a meaningful objective is its measurability. A well-written objective contains a statement of learner performance regarding achievement of the competencies set in the skills profile, for example: 'Using appropriate word processing software, prepare a standard business letter. The letter should comprise three paragraphs with no spelling or typographical errors and be completed in 20 minutes or less.'

GLOs are developed based on the rationale for the learning event and the overall information-gathering exercise. At this stage in the process the GLOs, like the event itself, will be subject to much scrutiny and possible change during the upcoming profile session. However, that does not mean they can be ignored. (For a full discussion of objectives, see Chapter 8.)

Analysis

In this section of the WID, the questions focus on an analysis of how the various parts of the learning event will fit together.

What topics are going to be included in the learning event?

You should be able to determine at least a part-answer to this question from the information you have been given to date. Your answer can also include a short, general description of the learning event. Remember that it will be subject to change.

Will this learning event need to fit with the other existing events in the programme or course of study?

This question is obviously more complex than the previous one but you should be able to answer it, generally speaking, based on discussions you should have held with your client. ('Client' here can be either your organization, if you are an employee; another department or division within the organization, for which you are developing materials; or an external client: you may be an independent consultant or you may work for a large organization putting together learning materials for a wider audience.) However, to answer this question correctly you need to determine if a total programme has been developed for learners, and where and how the learning event you are developing fits into that programme. The question is an important one, as it will help you make some decisions regarding content, and planning any pre- and co-requisites that may be required. It will also help you determine if you are going to have to repeat or overlap any of the materials.

List the pre- or co-requisites needed by the learner

What you are trying to discover here is the entry behaviours needed by learners for the learning event. The question you need to ask yourself or others is: what do learners need to know in order to learn each of the skills that will be taught during this learning event? As Dick and Carey (1978) note in their discussion of the systematic design of instruction, the fundamental question you have to consider centres around content. Is specific content being delivered to learners or is the target audience being taught something? If it is specific content you are delivering, then the audience has to match itself with those pre- and co-requisites. However, if your rationale is to deliver something to a specific audience, then the learning event must be modified until it meets the entry behaviours of the learners.

How many hours of study will be included in the event?

Typically organizations describe a learning event in terms of its perceived number of hours or days. Being presented with a time for the length of the event when you do not know what is going to be included in it just adds another dimension to the challenge of Web-based learning materials development. Note the time you have been given in your documentation materials and remember that you have been given a very important and valuable piece of information that you will need when you start developing your project timeline.

Once you reach the profile stage you will get a fairly definitive idea of what materials need to be developed; then you can compare it with the time frame you have been given and determine if the two are compatible. If they are not, you can start negotiating an increase in time or a reduction in the amount of learning materials.

As part of the information document you are developing, you will need to get a good idea of the topics being considered for delivery to learners. If there is not sufficient room on the page, simply add a separate sheet. This list will help you better focus your profile session and better determine what learning materials will have to be developed. No matter if you are completing the WID during an interview with an SME or completing it yourself, you will need to ensure that the list is based on *the needs of the particular job or life skill learners need to learn* not on materials that it would be nice for them to know.

It is important that you list just the main 'need-to-know' topics as they are understood at the time of completing the WID. The next phase of the getting-started process is the development of the skills profile, which is what determines the 'need-to-know' content.

How is the event going to be delivered to the learner?

Determining how the materials are to be delivered is a very important question, as it will affect your considerations for human resources, your time allocation and your budget.

In a Web-based learning event you can deliver the materials in a number of ways. First, you may wish to consider delivery of the entire event over the Web, or just partial delivery so that the Web becomes a resource for some other kind of learning event. If you are part of a large organization that has its own internal network or intranet, you may be asked to deliver the materials over that network. Using the Internet or an intranet has its advantages such as allowing you to quickly make changes to the materials. However, bandwidth limitations can make the transfer of certain kinds of media files very slow.

You can consider a local area network (LAN) as a delivery vehicle. Nowadays, most mid-size to large universities and organizations have constructed sophisticated LANs that are well suited for the delivery of Web-based learning materials. In most cases, learners will use a Web browser to access materials across the LAN, retrieving them from a dedicated Web server.

You can also deliver your learning materials using CD ROM technology. Here, the contents of the CDs are copied to a network or a Web server and made available to learners either via a network or by accessing the materials using a Web browser. Alternatively, you may choose to have your learners access the CDs directly, and load them into a CD ROM jukebox, which can typically hold anywhere from 10 to several hundred CDs at one time.

The final delivery option you may wish to consider is the so-called CD ROM/Web hybrid solution. In this case, some of the learning materials are stored on a Web server for learner access, and some of the materials (for the same learning event) are accessed directly from a CD ROM sitting in the drive of the learner's workstation. This method is typically used when you want to incorporate large amounts of audio or video into a learning event but the network does not have the bandwidth to support it.

Design

Following the analysis is the design portion of the WID.

What kind of learning materials are going to be appropriate for the learner?

It is important that you plan how your learning materials are to be developed. If, for example, you are going to have one or more people helping you develop materials, it is imperative that you know exactly what you want from them and how those materials are to be developed. You will also have to make decisions regarding the graphic user interface and the various template screens.

What should be the readability level of the materials?

Readability is all of those elements in Web-based learning materials that affect the ability of learners to understand them, learn from them, interact with them and find them interesting. As part of the development of your learning materials, a readability index needs to be applied to ensure the materials are being developed to the correct level for your audience.

What instructional strategies are going to be used?

Here it is important for you to consider your instructional strategy and how learners are going to achieve the learning outcomes. A number of delivery strategies can be used in a Web environment, including a presentation format, presentation and practice tutorial, interactive demonstration tutorial, skill-modelling tutorial, guided exploration tutorial or simulation. However, there are a number of criteria to consider as you review the various delivery strategies:

● If I use this strategy will the learners be learning at a simple knowledge level, an application level or a synthesis level? What is best for them?

● What are the needs of the learners?
● How well do the learners understand the instructional strategy I'm considering? Are they going to be confused?
● What constraints am I facing with regard to group size and the learning environment?
● What role do I expect the learners to play in the materials and am I also expected to play a role?

Notice how the emphasis here is on learners, not on the technology, the event facilitator or the organization under whose banner the event is being developed. Just learners!

How are the materials going to be formatted?

Here you have to give some thought to how the Web screens will look, what 'things' you will put on the screen, what kind of font you will use and its size, along with a number of other items. Your decision here will also affect the software used to build the various screens. Remember that your formatting decisions will have to be made in the context of the maturity level of the learners and the topic of the materials. The real answer to the question will come later on, but it's something you at least need to be aware of now!

Once the design questions have been answered you can move on to the development questions.

Development

This portion of the WID is focused on the graphic user interface, screen templates and copyright issues.

Here you are going to have to consider the graphic user interface (GUI) and the various screen templates you will want to use. The GUI identifies the learning event for the learners and provides them with a unique interface between themselves and the materials developed for the event.

You are also going to have to consider various kinds of screen templates. Template screens help give learners visual clues as to where they are in the learning event and help them quickly understand how the materials are structured by helping them form a mental map. Template screens can include topic menus, introduction and topic summary screens, materials discussion screens, learner assessment screens, event information screens, materials presentation screens, additional resource screens and an advanced organizer screen.

What are the copyright issues that need to be addressed?

Today you have to assume that all the materials you want to use for your

Web-based learning event will have some form of copyright encumbrance attached to them. This means that you have to set up a methodology to keep track of the materials being used and their source. Certain materials such as cartoons, comic strips and video clips of sports events command high fees and you need to be aware of those fees and the worth of using such materials when you may be able to develop your own or, with a slight modification to your storyboard and no serious loss to the quality of the learning event, not use them at all.

What other materials will be needed to enhance the learning event with respect to learning?

Assuming that you have given due consideration to the question of instructional strategies and made some decisions about delivery, this question asks you to go one step further and reflect on what other things you might need to do to enhance that delivery, or help deliver the learning materials to the learners. Whatever they are, use the same criteria that you used for determining your instructional strategies to help you in your selection.

What other materials exist that can be used for this learning event?

The final question in this section of the WID deals with getting and reviewing any existing materials available to support the new materials you are developing. Completing this review will help others overcome the perception that you are 'reinventing the wheel'. One of the major sources of information is the Web itself. To use the Web successfully you need a systematic search facility. Attach a list of support materials if necessary and add to it as needed. Carry out a review of similar topic materials to determine how suitable they might be for use with current materials. Finally, remember that you need to obtain copyright permission for all the materials being prepared for inclusion or adaptation in your learning materials.

Assessment and evaluation

This portion of the WID focuses you on developing a methodology to measure learner achievement. As part of the design and development process, you will have to complete a formative or ongoing review of the project. Ask yourself and/or others how assessment and evaluation fit into the overall project and what, if any, special consideration needs to be given to these issues.

Typically learner assessments are developed to help you diagnose, prescribe and grade learners. Diagnostic assessment such as pre-tests provides information about learning needs prior to the event taking place. Prescriptive assessments such as written assignments, collaborative projects and other assignments are very much like diagnostic decisions except that they take place during the event rather than before it. Grading follows instruction and tells you how well learners have achieved the goals and objectives of the learning event. Learner assessment must also provide you with conclusions to help you determine if learners are able to apply what has been learnt to new situations. Finally, the evaluation of instruction, the learning environment, the facilitation of the learning materials and delivery is carried out across learners rather than on individuals, and it is their collective performance, good or bad, that provides its basis.

How will learner achievement be determined?

To help you answer this question you will need to consider a computer-managed learning (CML) or some other form of electronic assessment package to track and assess learners. If you decide that CML is indeed needed then you will have to review your technical specifications to make sure it can be properly supported and you also have to consider if it can be justified in terms of the number of learners and properly supported from both a computer and user perspective.

How will the ongoing appropriateness and overall effectiveness of the learning materials be determined?

Ongoing materials appropriateness during development is typically determined using a formative evaluation procedure where learning materials are systematically examined to ensure they are meeting the goals and objectives set for the event and the overall standards set out for the project. Typically you need to set up a minimum of two formative evaluations during the life of the project, in addition to the other milestones being set: the first after the design approach has been determined and the second after the initial input of the learning materials into your screen templates.

Material improvement is also based on a summative evaluation that should take place prior to the materials being delivered for the first time. One of the most effective summative evaluation methodologies is the field trial. That being said, however, the field trial is much neglected in the development of a learning event, with time and budget constraints being the reasons most often cited. However factors such as the materials being a 'once only' delivery event and the notion that material revisions can be carried out as delivery takes place also contribute to neglect in this area. The field trial is, of course, the time you get to make sure all the various parts of the event are working the way they were designed to work. Questions that need to be asked at this time include:

● Are the materials being delivered correctly?

● Is the learning environment right?
● Is the facilitation process what was planned and expected?

Make sure the field trial is set up to answer these questions.

When you review the learning event scheduling, consider the concept of just-in-time (JIT) learning where the opportunity for learners to gain knowledge of a particular topic is offered just prior to that knowledge being needed. For example, if a learning event has been designed to train administrators to develop a budget and present it for review prior to the start of the financial year, then you may wish to consider offering the learning event to coincide with that need.

You also have to consider getting feedback from learners regarding their reaction to the event. A typical reaction survey or 'happiness index' simply asks the participants how they liked the materials. However, this kind of index only measures the 'entertrainment' (sic) value of a learning event, and the results are sometimes difficult to apply, as the suggestions are often self-cancelling. It is important that you determine what needs to be evaluated and design the methodology so you can collect the information you need.

Resources

In the resources section of the WID the focus is on people, time and costs.

What are the constraints of the project regarding time, money, people and equipment?

The major items you are asked to consider at the start of any Web-based learning materials development project are time, available financial resources, the people and the equipment you need to do the job. It is essential that you spend time making sure that all of these items are properly in place, as they are crucial to the overall success of the project. Here you need to consider each of the following:

● How much time do I have to complete the project?
● What funds are being allocated to the project?
● Who can I get to help me do the job?
● What equipment will be needed?

Perhaps the most difficult problems surrounding the development of Web-based learning materials are: 1) convincing those who assigned you the task that it can't be done in a matter of weeks; 2) convincing people that a substantial amount of money will be needed up front for the preparation of the materials; 3) convincing people that you are going to need help to do the job; and 4) convincing those responsible for assigning you the materials development team that the team members may need time away from their regular duties and/or some form of compensation for the extra hours they are going to put in. Don't forget too that if you are part of a large organization and have been assigned to the project for the materials development phase of the work, you are also going to need time away from your regular duties.

Up to now there are no consistent rules of thumb that can be used to determine required development time for Web-based learning materials as there are with print-based and other materials. One such guideline currently in use suggests that you allow 2.5 hours of development time per minute of completed learning event. However, if your materials include the use of audio, video, animation and electronic quizzes, time factors will increase significantly and could reach as much as five hours of development time per minute of completed learning event.

Michael Greer in his work, *ID Project Management: Tools and techniques for instructional design developers* (1992), provides a number of fundamental rules of thumb for consideration:

- Audio scripts require about 1.3 pages of script for each minute of audio and two pages of script for each minute of video. An experienced writer can write one page of audio script in one hour and one page of video script in 1.5 hours.
- Introductions and summaries for audio, video or interactive segments require about half a page of introduction and half a page of summary. An experienced designer can write an introduction and/or summary in about one hour.
- Learner exercises typically require up to five pages of materials. Experienced designers can develop such exercises at a rate of one page per hour. Finally, learner quiz questions usually need at least 30 minutes of professional development time per question, meaning that a 25-question test is going to take a minimum of 12.5 hours to develop, while a 50-question test will take up to 25 hours to develop. You also need to remember that some test questions do not 'work' the first time they are used and have to be revised, increasing the time factor even more.

What people are going to be needed to complete the project?

It is important to remember when you are involved in the design and development of learning materials that there are many 'experts' and you will be faced with trying to balance the various tasks necessary in developing the materials and to ensure that those working with you are working on the tasks most appropriate for them. These tasks are many and varied and can include providing information for the development of the profile, validating the profile, developing the learning materials, validating them and developing ancillary materials. It is in your best interest

Table 6.1 *People's roles in a Web-based materials development project*

Person	Role
Project Manager	The person with overall responsibility to ensure that all project elements are in place and of the highest quality, delivered on time and within budget.
Instructional Designer	The person who provides ideas and possible solutions to complex learning or information delivery problems.
Subject-Matter Expert	A content expert used as a consultant during the design and production process to ensure the accuracy of factual materials.
Content Developer	The creator/developer of the subject matter to be contained in the product (in many Web-based learning materials development projects this role is incorporated with the role of instructional designer).
Multimedia Designer or Graphic Artist	The creator/developer of the charts, graphs, illustrations and graphics contained in the product.
Web Application Programmer	The person responsible for making sure all the facets of a Web-based learning event work to the satisfaction of the learners, all the team members, the event facilitator, the evaluation team and the organization.
Media Producer	The creator/developer of other resources needed for the learning event to be a success (in many Web-based materials development projects this role is incorporated with the role of multimedia designer).
Editor	The person responsible for ensuring the learning materials are grammatically correct, consistently formatted and generally conform to the standards and specifications set for the project (in many Web-based learning materials development projects this role is incorporated with the role of instructional designer).
Web Master/ Administrator	The person responsible for making sure all facets of Web-based learning event consistently work to the satisfaction of learners, the event facilitator and the organization.

Table 6.2 *Typical responsibilities of a learning materials development team*

Person	Definition
Project Manager Manager	Liaise with the client to agree on scope, budget and timeline.
	Negotiate with the client, SME, content developer and instructional designer with respect to overall aims and rationale to support production.

	Ensure that milestones are met.
	Maintain budget limitations.
	Make final decisions where conflicts arise with regard to content, quality and time scheduling.
	Formally approve the proposal, prototype, design documents and working versions.
	Note and negotiate major content changes with the client.
Instructional Designer	Liaise with the project manager and SME on a regular basis.
	Provide a comprehensive set of learning objectives to meet the overall aims of the project.
	Identify and analyse individual learning points and suggest feasible actions and solutions to meet product goals.
	Identify and develop standards for the analysis, design, development, implementation, evaluation and validation of the learning event.
	Identify the various elements needed to develop a graphic user interface that meets product goals.
	Identify the various elements needed to develop a screen layout that meets product goals.
	Identify the various elements needed to develop a series of screen templates that meet product goals.
Subject-Matter Expert (SME)	Liaise with the instructional designer on a regular basis during the design process.
	Check all materials for accuracy.
	Formally approve design documents at predetermined stages prior to development.
	Provide and/or suggest suitable resources and sources of information.
	Provide regular feedback to the content developer.
Content Developer	Liaise with the project manager.
	Produce an outline plan in conjunction with other team members and client.
	Liaise with the instructional designer and SME on a regular basis during the design process.
	Produce full design documentation in an appropriate format.
	Produce appropriate flowcharts and storyboards for use by the programmer and others in the design and development team.

	Analyse and translate content and treatment to produce flowcharts, storyboards and other design documents.
	Incorporate, note and communicate minor content changes at the request of the client, SME or instructional designer.
	Note and negotiate major content changes with the client, SME and instructional designer.
Multimedia Designer or Graphic Artist	Liaise with the instructional designer on a regular basis.
	Suggest graphic and multimedia-based solutions to the instructional designer, content developer and SME sufficient to meet product needs.
	Provide a comprehensive set of charts, graphics, illustrations, graphics and other multimedia that accurately reflect and depict the content of the event.
	Design a graphic user interface and screen layouts based on the initial design concepts as outlined by the instructional designer.
	Design a series of screen templates based on the initial design concepts as outlined by the instructional designer.
Web Application Programmer	Liaise with the instructional designer and content developer on a regular basis.
	Suggest feasible, computer-based actions and solutions to ensure the learning event meets all identified goals.
	Provide comprehensive hardware and software solutions to ensure the learning event meets all identified goals.
	Set up the various facets of the learning event to ensure all identified goals of the project are met.
Media Producer	Liaise with the instructional designer, SME and content developer on a regular basis.
	Suggest audio, video and animated solutions to the instructional designer, SME and content developer sufficient to meet product needs.
	Provide a comprehensive set of audio, video and animation-based resources that accurately reflect and depict the content of the event.
Editor	Liaise with the instructional designer, SME and content developer on a regular basis.
	Review and revise all learning materials for consistency of format.
	Review and revise all learning materials for grammatical errors.
	Review and revise all learning materials for grammatical consistency.

Web Master/ Administrator	Liaise with the instructional designer, project manager and programmer on a regular basis.
	Suggest feasible actions and solutions with respect to the set-up and administration of the Web site to ensure it meets project goals.
	Provide comprehensive Web-based solutions to ensure Web site administration meets the goals of the project.

to make sure that those listed in the WID are the most appropriate people for that part of the development process.

When you consider the people you actually need, consider their abilities, their commitment to a project, their availability and of course their expertise. You will have to develop timelines for them along with realistic milestones and you have to keep them on target and ensure the work they do is done correctly the first time. You also have to be prepared to find others to do the work if things go wrong.

Table 6.1 outlines the kinds of people and expertise you need to get a Web-based materials development project completed.

Table 6.2 indicates typical responsibilities of a learning materials development team.

What are the cost implications for the project?

A number of the questions posed in the WID ask you to consider items that could have high cost implications. You should now go back over each of your answers to those questions and determine, as far as possible, the cost for each of the decisions made. For example, if it was determined that screens are to be developed using a particular software, will you have to hire someone to do it or can it be done by a member of your team? If you have made certain technical decisions regarding delivery, can those decisions be supported with sufficient funds? If you have made certain decisions regarding the development of other support materials, have you got the expertise to do it or do you have to get it elsewhere at a higher cost? Given the length of the project, has the team got sufficient time to complete it or will things be stalled two months from the end? Also consider what costs, if any, you are facing with respect to copyright.

Some of these costs are, of course, impossible to determine at this stage. But you need to be prepared. Consider a worst-case scenario, develop a budget and ensure that you have all the various contingencies covered.

The preceding is designed to help you better understand where and how to start a learning materials development project. Take the time to go through this process as soon as possible after you have been assigned to the project and use the answers as part of your planning process. Develop as much documentation as you can to help you be a more informed decision-maker.

What other resources will be needed?

It is important that you determine all the resources you need before you actually need them. Previously you considered time along with human and financial constraints but you also need to consider a number of other things. For example, is the physical space in which you now work large enough and are the computers and computing power you have adequate enough to do the job?

Remember that even the most mundane of computer applications can take up large chunks of hard disk space and any sophisticated materials development work is going to need huge amounts of disk space. Do you have the facilities to make back-up copies of your work? Do you have access to reference materials and all the various consumable items you will need over the life of the project? Do you have Internet access as and when needed? Quite often in the design and development of Web-based learning materials three servers are set up to accommodate the development process. The first holds all the materials under development and is used strictly for development purposes. The second is set up for testing and field trial(s) and the third is a repository for the learning event(s) currently being delivered to learners. Work out a plan for what you need.

Technical issues

The final section of the WID concerns itself with technical issues. Typically one of two models is followed depending on who the service provider is and who the participants are. The first model is more typical of a 'business' model where the provider of the learning event lists the technical requirements that potential learners have to comply with in order to participate in the course. If it's a 'school'-based model where the provider is a school or college, the organization often tries to determine what technical hardware and software are being used by learners and to ensure that the learning event under development does not exceed those technical capabilities.

What type of computer will be needed?

If you're designing learning materials strictly for Web browser access, then the computer platform is something of a non-issue, as most popular Web browsers are available for the Macintosh, Windows and UNIX operating systems. However, if your learning event includes more than just simple Web pages, you will probably need to decide on a single target platform and develop your materials accordingly. For example, your event may include downloadable binary or executable files that only work on the Windows platform, or it may include a video conferencing component that requires users to run client software that is operating system specific.

If your organization wants to determine the typical computer configuration of potential users, surveys are a good way to gather this information. Once all the data has been collected and tabulated, decisions can be made as to the fundamental design of your learning materials.

What type of Internet connection will be needed?

If you're developing your learning event strictly for access over your company or campus LAN, then modem considerations are a non-issue. Otherwise, it is advisable to keep in mind that the majority of Web users today are still connecting to the Internet with modems capable of supporting either 28.8 kbps or 56.6 kbps baud rates. You can of course specify that your participants require cable or ADSL connections, but your design considerations should normally be focused at the low end of the scale.

Software

Software considerations for the learning event fall into two categories: 1) the software needed to build and host the event; and 2) the software needed by learners to access the event. If your target audience is large and your needs are comprehensive, then you are probably best to consider building and hosting your learning event with an established courseware management system. Most large-scale systems can support dozens of courses, allow learners to sign on to the learning event, track them through each phase of their learning and provide event facilitators and administrators with extensive reporting capabilities. Alternatively, you may choose easy-to-use HTML editing tools to build a single-course Web site made up of simple Web pages. These types of events can be hosted by a commercial Internet Service Provider or loaded on to a company or campus Web server.

The software required by your learners can range from a free Web browser to expensive and sophisticated client-side programs needed to access complex server-side applications. This will be your decision to make, based on your knowledge and experience of your chosen tools and your potential audience.

Which browser will be needed?

While there are a number of free Web browsers available, most people access the Web using either Microsoft's Internet Explorer or Netscape's Navigator. From a development perspective, you need to be aware of the (sometimes glaring) differences in the way these two browsers will display your learning materials. While both offer support for the HTML 4.0 standard, they can differ drastically in the way they render your Web pages, display fonts, position tables, support dynamic HTML and more. They also do not offer equal support for such technologies as XML,

ActiveX, Java and VBScript, so you need to determine how important or critical these technologies are to your learning event. Browser plug-ins are also an issue, as they can sometimes behave very differently when used with different browsers.

If you have no way of determining learners' chosen Web browsers, or you wish to develop cross-browser learning materials, then you must test your learning event extensively against the most common browsers. This typically means trading functionality for compatibility, but will result in less complaints and better overall reach. The overall design of your learning materials will largely affect your decision to target a single or multiple browser learning audience.

What plug-ins will be needed?

While browser plug-ins can sometimes greatly extend the capabilities of today's Web browsers, they can also be problematic for some Web users. They often require technical considerations beyond the capabilities of learners and their computers, and in many cases do not work successfully. While certain plug-ins, such as Adobe's Acrobat Reader or Macromedia's Flash, have proven to be very useful and reliable, the same cannot be said for many others. If you choose to build learning materials that are dependent on a browser plug-in, you must test its operation extensively to ensure it will operate on a variety of different computer platforms and will not impede learners' access to the materials.

Finally you should list the software you will need to complete the project.

Finalizing the WID

If you completed the WID during an interview with an SME you will have to write it up ensuring that the goal(s) and GLO statements are measurable and appropriate for use in the development of the learning materials. Next you need to have it validated by the person or persons you interviewed. If you completed it yourself, have it reviewed by your colleagues to ensure the materials are correct.

CONCLUSION

This chapter reviewed the development of the Web-based learning event information document. When complete, the WID forms the basis for carrying out the profile session and helps you better determine the techniques for delivering the learning materials to learners. The WID is an important addition to your project documentation and can provide the basis for the many decisions you and others have to make regarding the overall development of the learning materials.

Figure 6.1 shows an example of a WID. The format used is not important; what matters is the questions asked and how the answers to those questions are used in the next stage of the project.

Figure 6.1   *An example of a WID*

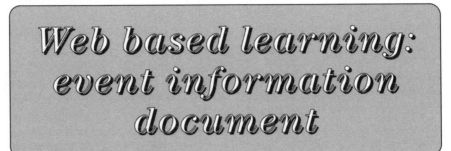

Learning event working title:

Purpose

Rationale: Why is there a need to develop this learning event?
Why is there a need to deliver it using a Web-based
methodology?

Audience

Name the principal audience:

What is the size of the audience?

Name the secondary audience:

Outcomes: Goals

What are the learning outcomes of this event?

Objectives

What must the learners do to achieve the learning goals?

Analysis

What topics are going to be included in the learning event?
Attach a separate page if needed.

Will this learning event need to fit with the other existing events in
the programme or course study?

List the pre- and co-requisites needed by the learner?

How many hours of study will be included in the event?

How is the event going to be delivered to the learner?

Web _____ Part Web _____

Internet ☐   Intranet ☐   CD ROM ☐   Combination ☐

If combination please describe:

Design

What kind of learning materials are going to be appropriate for the learner?

What should the readability levels of the materials be?

What instructional strategies are going to be used?

How are the materials going to be formatted?

Development

List the templates that will have to be developed:

What are the copyright issues that need to be addressed?

What other materials will be needed to enhance the learning event with respect to learning?

What other materials exist that can be used for this learning event?

Assessment and Evaluation

How will learner achievement be determined?

Evaluation

How will the ongoing appropriateness and overall effectiveness of the learning materials be determined?

How will the effectiveness of the learning environment be determined?

Is a formative evaluation to be carried out? Yes ☐ No ☐
If yes at what step(s) in the development process?

Is a field trial to be carried out? Yes ☐ No ☐
If yes how will it be carried out?

Where will the field trial be conducted?

When will the field trial be scheduled?

Resources

What are the constraints of the project regarding time, money, people and equipment?

Expertise

What people are going to be needed to complete the project?

What will be their role?

Will people be needed from inside the organization?
Yes ☐ No ☐
If yes describe:

Costs

What are the cost implications of the project?

What funding is available?

Will additional funding be needed to complete the project?
Yes ☐ No ☐
If yes describe:

Technical issues

What type of computer will be needed?

What type of Internet connection will be needed?

Software

Which browser will be used?

What plug-ins will be needed?

List the software needed for the learning event:

Chapter 7
Developing learner profiles

INTRODUCTION

A learner profile can be defined as a block diagram that outlines the various topics that have to be learnt in order for that person to complete the learning event successfully. The development of a profile can be completed in a half-day session or it can be extended over a number of days depending on the size of the profile and the group involved in the process. Once validated, the learner profile becomes part of your documentation and forms the basis for the development of the Web-based learning materials. This process is the same no matter whether you are developing Web-based, multimedia or print-based materials.

THE PROFILE

A learner profile is made up of a number of rows, called bands. Each band has a title box (the first box on the left) that describes the competency or skill the learner has to learn. For the purpose of developing Web-based learning materials, consider the title box on the left of the profile as the topic heading and each smaller box, moving from left to right, as a general learning objective (GLO), which describes how that goal is to be reached by the learner. In terms of the development of learning materials, each GLO can represent one topic. The number of bands in a profile and the size of each vary depending on the materials being developed. Some profiles may have as few as two or three bands while others have 20 or more.

The small sample shown in Figure 7.1 is taken from a Web learning event titled 'Brewing for non-brewers'. The audience for this particular event consists of recently hired sales and marketing staff who require an orientation to the brewing process. The profile for this event has eight bands.

Figure 7.1 *A typical profile band*

The development of a learner profile is divided into a number of steps, as detailed in the following sections.

Planning the profile session

Who should attend the session

The first step in the development of a profile is to determine who will take part in the session. Base your choice of subject-matter experts (SMEs) on their:

- overall expertise in the field;
- position in the organization they represent;
- commitment to the methodology being employed;
- willingness and ability to discuss the issues surrounding the topics under discussion;
- availability to be involved in the session.

Determining the size of the group

To ensure a successful profiling session, you will need a group of four to six people. In some cases you can reduce the size of the group to two or three persons but only if you are sure that the participants you have chosen have the expertise, the willingness and the ability to discuss the various issues surrounding each of the learner topics. Any less than this number is not advisable as you may have validity problems later.

Selecting the session leader

Early in the planning process it will be necessary for you to determine who will lead the profile session. The leader need not be a subject-matter expert and in many cases someone not having expertise in the profile under development can ask the kind of questions that in other circumstances would not be tolerated. The person you choose, however, should be skilled in group dynamics, be well-versed in the process of profile development including the writing of learning objectives, and have some knowledge of how people learn.

Session preparation

It is important that all members of the group are well briefed on what is expected of them during the profile session. Included in your pre-session materials should be:

- a copy of the validated Web-based learning event information document (WID);
- a guide to the WID and how it is used as part of the documentation;

- instructions for the review of the goals and objectives listed in the WID;
- a short description of what will take place during the profiling session;
- an outline of the role people are expected to play during the session.

You should send a package of materials, describing each of the above, to each member of the group at least one week prior to the session being held.

Organizing the room

No matter what organization your participants are from, you should try to hold the profile session on 'neutral' territory as this will help reduce any feelings of favouritism. It will also allow the group to concentrate on the task in hand without interruptions from the office.

You need to check out the room you are going to use carefully, as it is essential that it be large enough to seat the group comfortably. Ideally the chairs and tables should be set up in a 'U' facing a large blank wall on which the index cards can be placed. (Although the index card methodology is the most effective, a profile can also be developed using a computer chart-building program and projecting the image on to a screen. Changes would then be made to the various parts of the chart using the computer.) The 'U' should be set up with enough space for the group leader to move into the open end when needed; however, the sides of the 'U' should be close enough to allow people on each side to interact with ease. If a 'U' set-up is not possible, a boardroom style set-up can be used but only if the group is small enough so that everyone can face the group leader and interact with one another. The room should be equipped with a flip chart and/or a portable whiteboard.

Conducting the session

Getting started

Prior to the session starting, the group leader should explain the purpose of the session, state its expected length and, most importantly, list the expected outcomes. This task is necessary to help all members of the group feel part of the process. Before any profile development can take place it will be necessary for the leader to review each of the goals and objectives listed in the WID and to ensure that they are indeed valid.

It should be noted that if the group asks for major changes to the goals and objectives listed in the WID, there may be a problem with either the group who validated it or the profile group itself. You would be advised at this stage in the development of the profile to allow the profile group to redraft the goals and objectives of the WID and then to develop the profile accordingly. At a later date you can revalidate the WID with a different validation group and hopefully determine where the problem(s) occurred.

Where to start

Beginning a profile session can often be a difficult task as the members of the group are often reluctant to speak and in many cases still do not understand what is expected of them. If the session is to get off to a good start the group leader must first explain how each of the major topic headings or band titles is to be developed and enlist the help of one of the group to quickly jot down each of the ideas as they are suggested. The group leader should then have the group 'brainstorm' a list of topics appropriate for the materials being developed. It is very important for the group to understand that:

● the goals and objectives as developed in the WID must be kept in mind;
● no particular order for the titles is necessary or should be made at this stage;
● there are no 'wrong' answers.

As the various band titles are suggested and quickly jotted down on the index cards, the group leader should stick the cards on to the wall. No attempt should be made to order the cards at this time. The session should continue until the group appears to have exhausted the range of topics. At this point the group leader can ask the participants to review each of the cards and reflect on their appropriateness. Once the group has been given the opportunity to review the cards it needs to determine if any should be removed from the list or if any can be consolidated under one title. The group should review the list again, determine if anything should be added and then attempt to order the list. After ordering the topics it will be necessary for the leader to rearrange the cards into a vertical pattern. The list should be in the order in which the learning materials may eventually be presented, or the order in which learners will need to learn the materials if that is different to the presentation of the materials.

If it is appropriate, the leader may wish to introduce the concept of pre- and co-requisites, and have the group consider each of these as the list is ordered. It might also be necessary for the leader to arbitrate differences of opinion regarding the order of the cards by suggesting appropriate alternatives based on knowledge of the audience for the materials, learning theory and the like and/or pointing out the appropriate sections of the WID.

It should be noted that the order of the cards should not be considered fixed. (As the session continues it may become apparent that the order needs to change and the leader should be open to making these changes.) Once the basic ordering is complete the group should be instructed on the procedures for developing each of the bands.

The next step

Bands can be developed in any order that the group feels appropriate. Once a band has been chosen for development, however, the group should concentrate on that band and not move from one band to another on an *ad hoc* basis. Prior to starting, the group leader should review the process for the development of the bands and review the relevant portions of the WID.

When ready, the leader should have the group consider the band under development and through discussion generate a series of topics appropriate for that band. The same process should be followed as with the development of the band titles. As the various topics are suggested the group leader should write each of them on an index card and stick the card on the wall next to the appropriate band title. Again no attempt should be made to order the cards at this time. Typically the development of the topics takes a significant period of time and should undergo a great deal of discussion. It is important that the leader keep the group on topic.

The session should continue until the group appears to have exhausted the range of topics for that band. It will be necessary for the group leader to ensure that all of the needed sub-topics have been listed. This will require frequent checking with the group to determine if anything else needs to be added to the band and if two or more topics can be consolidated under one sub-topic. Remember that the topics do not have to be in order; that will be completed later. The group, however, will frequently want to place topics in order as this process often helps them determine the next title. This process need not be discouraged. Once the band appears to be finished the group leader should again ask which if any items can be consolidated, added or deleted. It is suggested here that, if the group determines a topic card should be discarded, the card should not be thrown away but placed off to one side ready for use in a different band or replaced in the original band as new considerations are made by the group.

Completing the profile

The process of determining each of the band topics should continue until each is completed. As noted above this process can take a considerable amount of time, and breaks should be provided on a regular basis. Once the bands are completed the group should review each band, considering if anything else needs to be added, whether any discarded cards should be placed back into the profile and whether the sub-topics are in the correct order.

The last lap

Profiles are often considered finished once all the topics have been identified. However, two additional tasks should be completed to help ensure
the topic titles are as correct as possible. The first task is to ask that the
group consider in turn each of the topics in each band and determine the
verb that best describes the action required of learners to complete that
task. This will help you later in the development of both general and
specific learning objectives. The verbs in Table 7.1 are applicable to the
various levels in the cognitive domain. You should note that, depending
on their use, some verbs may apply to more than one level.

Table 7.1   *Verbs appropriate to each of the levels of the cognitive*
domain

Knowledge		Comprehension	
arrange	order	classify	locate
define	recall	describe	recognize
duplicate	recognize	discuss	report
label	relate	explain	restate
list	repeat	express	review
memorize	reproduce	identify	select
name		indicate	translate
Application		**Analysis**	
apply	operate	analyse	differentiate
choose	practise	appraise	discriminate
demonstrate	schedule	calculate	distinguish
dramatize	sketch	categorize	examine
employ	solve	compare	experiment
illustrate	use	contrast	question
interpret		criticize	test
Synthesis		**Evaluation**	
arrange	formulate	appraise	evaluate
assemble	manage	argue	judge
collect	organize	assess	predict
compose	plan	attach	rate
construct	prepare	choose	score
create	propose	compare	select
design	set up	defend	support
	write	estimate	value

The second task is a little more complex. You will find, as you try to
develop the actual course materials, that it will be difficult for you to
know what should be included in the materials. Take the band shown at
the beginning of this chapter; albeit without conditions and standards, it
demonstrates fairly typical learning objectives, but these do not tell you

anything about the learning materials that need to be developed. To help you resolve this problem, you will need to complete a sub-profile (see below).

Once the profile has been completed the cards should be numbered, and then removed from the wall. It is possible that at this stage you may have to make minor changes for the sake of clarity. You should remember, however, that no major changes should be made without consultation with the group as a whole. Once you have completed the profile, it should be prepared ready for validation.

Profile validation

The most simple and direct method for validating a profile is to send it, possibly via e-mail, to members of the profile group to be checked for errors. You may also want to consider setting up the profile team with review and tracking software for the validation and/or the sub-profile development. However, you have to consider the costs involved in monetary terms, set-up time and user training. If this is a one-time event for the group, a simple pencil-and-paper methodology may serve you better in the short term.

This section of the chapter described the procedure that should be followed when developing a learner profile. The key to getting the profile right the first time is to ensure you get the right mix of people in the profile group. Ensure that you review the WID and that its goals and objectives are clear with respect to the profile being developed. Be firm but fair with the group and ensure they stay on track as much as possible.

THE SUB-PROFILE

As with the profile, the sub-profile is also a block diagram. However, it goes one step further than the profile, and details the various topic headings that have to be covered to ensure learners reach their appropriate level of learning.

The sub-profile, like the main profile, is made up of a number of rows called bands whose length and complexity can vary depending upon the materials being developed. The sub-profile can be developed in one of three ways:

1. at the end of the main profile session;
2. individually by each member of the profile group after the main profile session has ended;
3. as part of the validation process by the validation group.

Whichever way it is done, the purpose of the sub-profile is twofold. When you are developing your learning materials it will serve as guide and when you are determining both GLOs and SLOs the sub-profile becomes an important information tool.

Developing the sub-profile

Some developers like to stop after the main profile and complete a series of validation steps to determine both GLOs and SLOs, and validate the materials at the formative evaluation stage. The problem with doing this is that you can get a long way off track before being told that what is being developed is not correct. This upsets both budgets and timelines, not to mention the developers!

As noted previously, the profile outlines the major topics you are to develop for the learning event. The sub-profile provides the details for each topic. In Figure 7.2, the details of the topic 'Brewing raw materials' have been determined, and all the various items that will have to be covered during the learning event have been itemized. The sub-profile can also be used as the basis for the development of SLOs. In the brewing example, the topic header, 'Brewing raw materials', can be considered as a GLO and each of the topics listed under it as SLOs. Sub-topics then become the steps learners have to take to reach that objective, and all the objectives are the steps to reach the goal.

The sub-profile SLOs are the ones you incorporate into the learning materials under such headings as telling learners what they need to learn. This might be done using a presentation, or showing learners how those things are done, or you may want to use a presentation and practice tutorial and have learners practise the skills they need to achieve competence. Here you can also use a sample skill-modelling tutorial that demonstrates a specific exercise.

Completing the sub-profile

Completing the sub-profile during the main profile session

Once the profile has been reviewed the leader will need to determine where the group would like to start to develop the sub-profile. In this case profile cards should not be taken down from the wall, as they are needed to guide the group. A new card should be written out for each topic that needs to be expanded and placed on an appropriate blank portion of the wall. Wherever the group decides to start, the leader should ask the group to list the sub-topics contained under each topic. This should follow a similar pattern to the development of the original profile, with various members of the group making suggestions as needed and the group leader writing the cards, asking questions and making sure the session is productive. The new cards can be set up on one side of the profile ready to be numbered and collected after the session is finished.

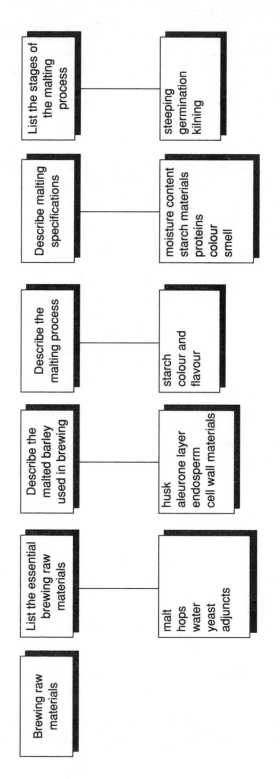

Figure 7.2 *A typical sub-profile band*

As with the profile, once discussion of the sub-topics seems finished the leader should ask the group to review the cards and ask the standard questions regarding removing any cards from the list and consolidating any of them under one title. Further questions will need to be asked regarding any additions to the list and the ordering of the cards. The session should continue until all the sub-topics are determined and the group is satisfied with the result.

Completing the sub-profile by the profile group after the session is over

A second method for determining the sub-profile is to have it completed by the profile group *after* the formal session is over. However, to do this the group leader will have to explain in detail what has to be done and provide the group with an example and a template for them to complete. The group will also need a copy of the profile. Two methods can be used to complete this task. All of the group can be asked to complete all of the profile, or prior to people leaving the profile session, bands can be assigned to various members of the group. The second method is advisable if the profile is a large one. Once the sub-profiles are completed, they and the profile can be put together ready for validation.

As with the development of the profile, getting the sub-profile ready to be a viable part of the course documentation is an important task that needs to be carried out in a systematic manner and added to the documentation ready for use by the developers of the learning materials.

CONCLUSION

A learner profile and sub-profile are essential for the development of learning objectives and the subsequent development of learning materials for use by the learner.

Chapter 8

Developing learning objectives

INTRODUCTION

A useful learning objective is one that allows you to make the largest number of decisions relevant to its achievement and measurement. A meaningful objective is one that communicates intent by excluding the greatest number of possible meanings other than what you intended. This chapter describes the development of objectives and their uses in Web-based learning materials.

Objectives are useful in the design and implementation of Web-based learning materials and the evaluation of the learner. They tell learners where they are going and how they are going to get there. They tell the facilitator of the learning event and the organization how they will know when the learners have arrived. In order to communicate the exact intent, objectives should be written using phrases that are open to as few interpretations as possible. Objectives should consist of as many statements, questions or examples as are necessary to describe the desired behaviour of learners at the time they leave the learning event. Objectives should be prepared in enough detail so that all learners do exactly the same things to reach their learning goals.

WHAT ARE OBJECTIVES?

Objectives describe the kind of performance expected by learners at the end of a learning event. For example, while a highly skilled person may be able to perform a particular task quickly without using job aids as a reminder of the steps, it is unrealistic to expect learners to be able to perform the same task in the same way. It is more realistic to expect learners to be able to perform all of the steps at a basic level, determine if the task has been carried out correctly and correct it if it is not. When this is the case, then the learners have the knowledge and the skills to be able to practise the task to improve their efficiency.

When developing your objectives the key question you must ask yourself is: what kind of things should learners be able to do at the end of the learning event that will most help them become as skilled as possible in the least amount of time? A well-written learning objective represents a clear statement of instructional intent and it can be written in any form as long as it clarifies that intent.

The development of learning objectives often leads to better insights about the purpose, content and delivery methods of the learning materials. Materials that once seemed important may be discovered to be less so, or you may find that important concerns have been left out of your materials or that what was being done during the learning event has little or no relation to the objectives that have been developed. It is important to understand that objectives are not simply written once and for all. As you gain fresh insights into the purpose and methods for the delivery of your learning materials your view of the course goals and the objectives will also change.

As a way of checking if your objectives are appropriate, use the following checklist to make sure your objective statements have the appropriate characteristics:

- An objective says something about learners. It does not describe a Web-based resource or the learning event facilitator or the kinds of learning experience to which learners will be exposed.
- An objective talks about the behaviour or performance of learners. It does not describe the performance of the facilitator, neither does it describe what learners are expected to know or understand. Though you might begin an objective using a general statement such as 'The learner must understand the operation of XYZ machine', you would go on to explain what you mean by 'understand' and describe what the learner will be expected to do to demonstrate the definition of understanding that has been determined for this objective. Whatever is meant by understanding would be defined in the sentences following the general one. However, to make things easier for yourself, do not use the verb 'understand', but rather use a verb such as 'describe' or, in this case, 'demonstrate' ('The learner can demonstrate various operations on XYZ machine').
- An objective is about ends rather than means. It describes a product rather than a process. As such it describes what learners are expected to be able to do at the end of the learning event rather than the means that will be used to get them there. An objective talks about end performance rather than learning materials content.
- An objective describes the conditions under which learners will be performing the end behaviour. In some cases learners will be expected to perform in the absence of any assistance provided by job aids.

- An objective also includes information about the level of performance considered acceptable. If learners are expected to perform a task within a five-minute time frame, for example, that should be stated as part of the objective. If the performance is expected to be error-free or if some error will be tolerated, this should also be indicated.

Useful objectives answer the following questions:

- What should learners be able to do?
- Under what conditions should learners be able to perform that task?
- How well must the performance be carried out?

Well-written objectives are written so that they specify the following:

- performance: what the learner is expected to do;
- conditions: the important conditions under which the performance is to occur;
- standards: the minimum criteria learners must meet in order for the performance to be acceptable.

Performance

Performance refers to any activity engaged in by learners. It can be a visible performance such as writing, sorting or labelling, or it can be invisible such as reviewing or solving. The way to write an objective that includes performance is to write a statement that answers the question: what are learners doing when demonstrating achievement of the objective? For example, an objective written in performance terms might appear as follows: 'Describe the fermentation process.' The main intent of this objective is simply that learners should describe something. It is not clear if it is to be described orally or in writing, but no matter; what is clear is what is expected of the learners when they demonstrate achievement of the objective.

The same is true for the following objective: 'Explain the difference between a malt silo and a malt mill.' Again what is not made clear is how the explanation is to be made, but the expected performance of learners is clear. They have to be able to explain something. Because of the way in which these objectives are written, they are measurable. The quality of the description or explanation can be measured in a number of different ways. Quite often, however, this type of objective is written using the verb 'understand'. Unfortunately, when an objective is written in this fashion, for example 'Understand the fermentation process', it becomes very difficult if not impossible to measure how much if anything the learner has learnt about fermentation.

Conditions

Conditions refer to those things imposed on learners when they are demonstrating their mastery of the objective. The following part-sentences demonstrate conditions:

- Given a problem of the following type...
- Given a list of...
- Given any reference of the learner's choice...
- Given a map of...
- Given a standard set of tools...
- Given a correctly functioning...
- Without the aid of references...
- Without the aid of a calculator...
- Without the aid of tools...

An objective that includes conditions is a statement that identifies the important aspects of the target or end performance to be developed and answers the following questions:

- What will learners be allowed to use?
- What will learners be denied?
- Under what conditions will the behaviour occur?
- Are there any skills that are not to be developed and does the objective exclude those skills?

Consider the following performance objective: 'Without the aid of references, describe in detail each of the five stages of the brewing process.' Once again the intent, or performance, has been made clear: learners have to describe the five stages in detail. The conditions are also very clear. They have to do so without the aid of references.

Consider also the following, more complex, performance objective: 'Given a choice of raw materials, select the correct ingredients, determine the correct amount of each to brew an India Pale Ale and begin the brewing process.' In this objective learners are being asked, first, to select the correct ingredients to brew a particular kind of beer, and then to use those ingredients to start the brewing process. Again the conditions have been clearly stated: learners are to be given the raw materials from which to make a selection.

Standards

Standards refer to how well learners have to perform and is the yardstick by which achievement of the objective is assessed. Standards are set to specify a desired criterion. For example, an acceptable performance could be marginal or must be perfect, depending on the circumstances of the action. The most common way to describe standards is to use time or accuracy, for example: 'Given the correct ingredients and using an appropriate brewing process, the learner will brew a medium-range lager beer that meets or surpasses all of the standards set for colour, strength and taste.'

The following expressions demonstrate standards:

- accurate to the nearest whole number;
- accurate to the nearest gram;
- to three significant figures;
- no more than three incorrect entries for every page in the log.

Consider the following two objectives: 'Given a standard four-cylinder petrol engine exhibiting five malfunctions, and being told one symptom for each malfunction, be able to locate each malfunction in 10 minutes or less' and 'Given a compass, ruler, pencil and paper, be able to construct and bisect any given angle larger than 10 degrees, accurate to the nearest 1 degree.' As you can see, the objectives each contain a performance, a condition and a standard.

In the first objective, the expected performance of learners is to locate a number of engine malfunctions; the conditions under which the performance is to take place involve a standard four-cylinder petrol engine that exhibits a number of malfunctions; and learners are expected to locate each of the malfunctions in 10 minutes or less. In the second objective, learners are expected to be able to construct and bisect a given angle larger than 10 degrees; they are able to use a compass, ruler, pencil and paper to aid in the task; and they are expected to complete the activity to within 1 degree of accuracy. Objectives written in this form make test question development less difficult and help in the development of viable learning materials.

EDITING EXISTING OBJECTIVES

Whenever you develop Web-based learning materials, typically you make two assumptions. First, you assume that the product of the delivery of those materials to learners will result in a change to those learners. And second, you assume that in selecting the means by which to change learners you can do a better job if you state precisely what you will accept as evidence of their competence. As has been discussed previously, you know that a learning objective should describe what learners will be able to do when they have been changed in the desired way. However, not all objectives are written in a way that aids learners in accomplishing what needs to be accomplished as they work through various parts of the learning materials. It is important therefore that you are able to recognize well-stated objectives and edit poorly stated ones.

Consider the following objective: 'Write an essay describing the causes of World War I. The essay must demonstrate an understanding of the more subtle forces leading up to the event and an appreciation of historical relationships.' At first glance it appears to be appropriate. It has a fairly well described intent and appears to have a well-described standard. However, on closer review it becomes evident that it is not well written. For example, it is difficult if not impossible to measure 'demonstrate an understanding' and 'an appreciation of historical relationships'. Here learners would be better served if the objective was edited to read: 'The essay must describe in detail each of the various forces that combined to bring about the war and further describe their historical relationship.' This edited version, albeit not perfect, does help make the objective measurable. From the test question that can be derived from this objective, a comprehensive marking scheme can be developed to aid the person marking the question to grade the quality of the written answer more accurately.

Consider also this next objective: 'Given a functioning but poorly adjusted acquisition amplifier, adjust it within a five-minute time period so that it tracks and locks correctly.' This objective can stand on its own. It describes the learner performance: adjusting the amplifier so it tracks and locks correctly. It has a set of conditions: a functioning but poorly adjusted acquisition amplifier. And it sets out a time-based standard of performance: within five minutes. Again the objective is not perfect but it does clearly specify the intent and is focused on the learner.

For the most part you should be able to list the characteristics of a well-written objective. Even if you are not familiar with the subject matter, you should be able to decide if the objective format is acceptable. However, if you are not competent in the subject matter, you may find it hard to determine the criteria for acceptable performance.

Even when you do have such competence, the criteria may be debatable. If, for example, it is stated that 90 per cent accuracy will be accepted as evidence of proficiency, what does this mean? Presumably it indicates that a high level of performance is expected, but why is 90 per cent the right number? Why not 75 or 80 or even 65 per cent right? Haggling over such details can consume a great deal of time and even be counterproductive. Consider the following when you are trying to determine suitable performance criteria:

- Sometimes 100 per cent is not the only acceptable criterion. However, you would like to think that the surgeon removing your gall-bladder has been trained to 100 per cent, or that the pilot of the plane you are in, which is just about to land at a small landing strip in the middle of the Amazon jungle, has received 100 per cent in landing procedures.
- Often, however, 100 per cent is not a realistic criterion. Those being tested may not have complete control over all the variables that affect

the performance. Perfection may not matter. Competent learners often make 'silly' mistakes under the pressure of a test. Some mistakes are more acceptable than others.

- Some criteria are expandable. Learners may perform all of the steps in an operation successfully but carry them out more slowly than someone with more experience would. If time is not an issue, allow a long time limit or do not use one at all.

- Sometimes the only way to arrive at a criterion is to make it up and see if it fits the case. If it is appropriate in the learning situation, then let it be; if it appears to be too high or too low, adjust it accordingly until it appears right.

All too often what is actually achieved by the instruction and what you hoped to achieve are not the same. Often there are gaps in the instruction, holes that appear because you are the expert in the subject. Sometimes you inadvertently allow assumptions to creep into the development of materials; or you find that the materials 'teach' one thing while the objective calls for something else. One of the most common examples of this is learning materials that have learners discuss or describe something while the objective calls for them to *do* something. Such problems are understandable. Experts speak the language of whatever business they are in and think about their subject. It's easy to forget that learners are not equally familiar with the jargon or comfortable with the way in which it is used and the experienced viewpoint it represents.

When you are in the process of developing objectives as part of your learning materials, you need to be able to review the learning materials and derive from them a good idea of what could be expected from that instruction. If you are in the process of reviewing materials with a view to revising them you need to look at the materials and compare them with current objectives and perhaps develop new and different objectives. One way to proceed in this case is to review the materials and develop the objectives that might reasonably be accomplished by learners who work with that material. This will tell you if the instruction is relevant to the objectives, and it also tells you something about the relevancy of the objectives to that instruction. A final strategy is to review the tests and determine what outcomes are considered important.

Table 8.1 sets out expected learner response for selected action verbs.

Table 8.1   *Developing learning objectives*

Action Verb	Types of Response	Sample Test Task
Identify	Point to, touch, mark, circle, match, pick up.	Put an X next to the triangle.
Name	Supply verbal label.	What is this type of angle called?
Distinguish between	Identify as separate or different by marking, separating into classes or selecting out the common kind.	Which of the following statements are facts (Tick F) and which are opinions (Tick O)?
Define	Supply a verbal description (orally or in writing) that gives the precise meaning or essential qualities.	Define each of the following terms.
Describe	Supply a verbal account (orally or in writing) that gives the essential categories, properties and relationships.	Describe the procedure for measuring relative humidity in the atmosphere.
Classify	Place into groups having common characteristics; assign to a particular category.	Choose from the list the name of the type of pronoun used in each of the following sentences.
Order	List in order, place in sequence, arrange, rearrange.	Arrange the following historical events in chronological order.
Construct	Draw, make, design, assemble, prepare, build.	Draw a bar graph using the following data.
Demonstrate	Perform a set of procedures with or without a verbal explanation.	Set up the laboratory equipment for this experiment.

OBJECTIVES CHECKLIST

The following list is intended as a tool for detecting and correcting any errors in your final list of objectives. Any negative answer indicates an area where improvement is needed.

1. Does each general objective indicate an appropriate outcome for the topic?

2. Does the list of general objectives include all logical outcomes of the topic?

3. Are the general objectives attainable? (Do they take into account the ability of the learners, facilities and time available, for example?)

4. Do the objectives exhibit the principles of learning? (Are the outcomes those that are permanent and transferable?)

5. Does each general objective begin with a verb?

6. Is each general objective stated in terms of learner performance?

7. Is each general objective stated as a learning product (rather than a learning process)?

8. Is each general objective stated in terms of learners' end behaviour (rather than the subject matter to be covered)?

9. Does each general objective include only one learning outcome?

10. Is each general objective stated at the correct level of generality? (Is it clear, concise and definable?)

11. Is each general objective stated so that it is relatively independent (free from overlap with other objectives)?

CONCLUSION

The development of learning objectives is a task whose importance should not be overlooked. A complete objective contains a learner performance, the condition(s) under which the performance takes place and the standards of performance. However, an objective can be stated in performance terms and still be viable for use in learning materials.

Chapter 9
Assessment

INTRODUCTION

Determining your assessment guidelines is a very important step in developing a Web-based learning event. Assessments allow the facilitator to determine if learners have achieved the learning event's objectives, and the information from assessments can be used, in part, to evaluate the overall success of the learning event. In this chapter, three components of assessment are discussed. The first is constructing well-designed test questions. The second is computer-managed learning, an instructional management tool that allows assessments to be delivered and marked online. Finally, assignments are discussed as a means for assessing higher-order objectives. Assignments give learners an opportunity to demonstrate what they have learnt about the topic in a less restrictive testing environment.

Observations are always subjective. They reveal what is in the eye of the beholder, not what really exists. However, information about learners has to be accurate and reflect what is actually happening. Assessments are designed to replace subjective measurement with objective measurement to the greatest degree possible, because without the use of a well-designed and properly used assessment there is no independent basis for assessing learners' behaviour. Assessments allow the facilitator to monitor and evaluate what learners have learnt and diagnose strengths and/or weaknesses as they occur. Assessments often use tests or examinations, which learners complete under direct facilitator observation or examination conditions. Another form of assessment is assignments, sometimes known as projects and reports. Assignments are usually completed by learners or groups of learners, but are not completed under the direct observation of the facilitator. Tests and examinations will be discussed first, followed by computer-managed learning and then assignments.

TESTING

Reasons for tests

There are a number of reasons for using tests as a basis for judgement, some of which are as follows:

- *To give objectivity to observation.* Measuring instruments are needed to help record behaviour from a neutral vantage point.
- *To elicit behaviour under relatively controlled conditions.* How can learner performance be judged when those judgements are limited by the many variables that operate in various situations? The testing situation must occur under conditions that can be reasonably controlled.
- *To sample performances of which the learner is capable.* To determine certain things about a person, you have to create a situation in which you can sample specific capabilities or tendencies.
- *To obtain performances and measure gains relevant to goals or standards.* It is often not enough to know whether a person can do something; the question is how well a person can perform the skill.
- *To apprehend the unseen or unseeable.* The naked eye cannot see a person's attributes, values or developmental levels; instruments are needed to reveal the unseen.
- *To detect the characteristics and components of behaviour.* When given the opportunity to isolate behaviour or explore the performances of which a person is capable, you often need to obtain detailed information that might not be acquired during observation.
- *To predict future behaviour.* Since certain tests have been found to relate to future outcomes or events, it may be possible to predict future performance based on test outcomes.
- *To make data always available for feedback and decision making.* Testing provides data about outcomes such as the quality of learner performance and helps you make better instructional decisions.

Writing test questions

The most important aspect of a test is that the questions truly ask learners to show that they have learnt what was taught them. The criterion for a good question should not be any one of the following:

- 'This one will make them think!'
- 'That sounds good.'
- 'I'll get 'em with this one!'
- 'I think we covered this – anyway, they just *ought* to know it.'

As a general rule, every time you write a test question ask yourself both what the question is *intended* to measure and what it is *really* measuring.

Testing is a controlled and objective procedure by which the performance of learners can be sampled and evaluated against a standard. The testing procedure makes data available for learner feedback to help you detect competence and determine the acquisition and possession of skills and knowledge. The success of any test, however, depends on how well the test is constructed, how well it is used and how it is interpreted. You cannot make valid judgements with a test that is imprecise or inaccurate. The worth of a test is measured in terms of its validity and reliability. Validity means that the test measures what it is supposed to measure. To establish validity you should have some independent way of assessing the property that the test is supposed to measure. Reliability refers to the test's consistency. Does the test measure the same thing each time it is used? Whatever a test measures, it must provide as error-free an estimate of the property to be measured as is possible.

Test questions: essay and short answer/completion questions

A test question either asks learners to provide an answer or it asks them to choose an answer from a list of possibilities. Essay questions and short answer or completion questions are the two forms that ask learners to supply the answer.

Essay questions

Essay questions can be asked in such a way that learners are given complete freedom to express their ideas, for example: 'Discuss changing attitudes toward the use of the Web in learning.' More commonly, however, essay questions are asked in a way that restricts learners' response in some way. You may want to limit the content area or the manner in which learners are to respond, for example: 'In no more than 500 words, describe the changes in attitude of multinational organizations toward the use of online learning as a viable means of imparting knowledge in a corporate environment. To what events do you attribute these changes?'

Advantages
There are a number of advantages to using the essay question:

- It is the best way to assess a learner's writing ability.
- It is the only type of question that can measure verbal self-expression.
- It is the best way to assess a learner's ability to create, organize, synthesize, relate and evaluate ideas.

- The essay question can measure learners' global attack skills on a problem as well as their problem-solving skills.
- It can be used to measure attitudes, values and opinions.
- It can be used effectively when an objective calls for the ability to *recall* rather than *recognize* information.
- Essay questions are *relatively* easy to construct compared to objective questions.
- Learners cannot guess the 'right answer'.
- Essay questions are practical for use with small groups.
- Essay tests can be good learning experiences.

Disadvantages

Unfortunately, the disadvantages of essay questions outweigh the advantages. These disadvantages centre on the basic issues of test design – validity and reliability:

- Because of their length, essay questions can sample only a limited number of course objectives.
- Essay questions are not the best way for you to measure simple comprehension, rote memory of facts or to answer 'who, what, where, when' questions.
- Scoring essay questions is extremely difficult, time-consuming and unreliable.
- Essay tests favour the verbally adept learner.
- Bluffing is common and not always easy to detect.

Design

The following guidelines will help you maximize the effectiveness of the essay-type question.

- Learners have the right to know exactly what is expected of them so the questions must be made as clear and unambiguous as possible.
- Don't give learners a choice of questions, since this makes the scoring very unreliable.
- Use a relatively large number of brief-answer questions in order to sample the objectives adequately.
- Whenever possible, present a novel situation.

Scoring

Two major methods can be used to increase the reliability and fairness of scoring an essay test; these are the analytical and rating methods. The steps of the analytical method are:

1. Before giving the test, construct an ideal answer to each question.

2. Break each question down into its different parts and identify the major points that should be covered by the learners' answers.
3. Read the learners' responses and give points based on a rating scale.

The steps of the rating method are:

1. Before giving the test, construct an ideal answer to each question.
2. Read the learners' answers and classify them into one of three to five categories, such as poor, average, good.
3. Read and classify the responses once or twice and average the ratings.

Regardless of the method of scoring, there are several things you can do to increase the reliability of your scoring:

● Before actually scoring the tests, pick a few answers at random to see how they compare to the ideal answer.
● Grade all learners anonymously.
● Read all the learners' responses to one question at the same time before moving on to the next question.
● Score all answers to one question without interruption so that all learners are exposed to a consistent mood or frame of mind.
● Provide comments and correct the learners' errors so they have a basis for understanding their mistakes.
● Evaluate the mechanics of expression; they should be scored separately from the content.
● Determine a policy for how to score irrelevant responses.

An essay question can be written as a short answer question when it contains only one central idea and can be answered in one or two sentences. Questions that require learners to supply definitions or short explanations of concepts and relationships fall into this category. Answers to extended-answer essay questions can be from 100 to 500 words in length. You can use this type of question to measure a learner's ability to deal with complex relationships, comparisons and evaluations.

You should indicate the desired length of the response in the question. The use of the phrase 'In one or two sentences' or 'Briefly' as restrictive terms do not help learners or you, as they fail to specify your intent. The question should have limits such as time ('This question should take you no more than 10 minutes') or worth ('This question is worth 10 marks'). Limits, such as 'In 500 words or less', should be used to help learners answer the question to the best of their ability.

Short answer/completion questions

The second type of question that asks learners to provide the answer is the short answer or completion question. The completion question can take one of three forms: the question format, the incomplete sentence format and the association format. The best method is the question format, where you present the information as a question and ask for specific, limited information. The incomplete sentence format should be used sparingly because questions written in this format are often obvious or ambiguous. The association form consists of an introductory statement used to establish a frame of reference and a set of related words to which learners are to respond. This type of question is similar to the matching-type question.

Advantages

The advantages to using a short answer/completion question are:

- It is one of the easiest types of question to construct.
- It can be used to measure simple learning, such as recall of information.
- Learners cannot guess the answer or rely on partial knowledge.
- Reliability and validity are increased (as compared to essay questions) because more objectives can be tested.
- The short answer/completion question is the best way to check certain mathematical skills. For example, when you are testing computation skills or the ability to follow a formula, learners can't solve the problem by working backwards from a given solution.

Disadvantages

As with the essay question, the short answer/completion question is characterized more by its disadvantages:

- It is very difficult and tedious to score. You frequently have to make decisions about partial answers or about unexpected but correct (or partially correct) answers that result from a different interpretation of the question.
- The scope of information that this type of question can adequately test is limited to that which can be stated in a single word, symbol or phrase.
- It is almost impossible to design short answer/completion questions that evaluate complex learning, such as the ability to analyse.

Design

Design guidelines for short answer/completion questions include the following:

- The question should be written so that there is only one short, definite, correct answer. Learners, however, will always come up with unexpected but true responses. For example:

Poor: Beethoven was a _____

Better: What was Beethoven's nationality? _____ (German)

Some of the answers you could expect from your learners for the first example could be 'composer, musician, German, great man'.

Poor: A _____ weighs less than a kilogram

Better: What unit of measurement is exactly 1/1000 of a kilogram? _____ (gram)

In some questions the use of the article 'an' indicates that the correct response must start with a vowel, which limits the number of possible answers. When writing your questions, you need to consider the following:

● Specify precisely the terms in which your learners should answer the question.
● Do not remove statements verbatim from your learning materials.
● Avoid giving clues (specific determiners) that give the answer away or make it easier to guess.
● Each question should be independent of all the others.
● Omit only significant words, but be careful not to mutilate the statement. For example:

Poor: Bach created _____ in every _____ form except _____

Better: Bach created masterpieces in every baroque form except _____ (opera)

● Whenever possible, put the blank at the end of the statement.

Scoring
Guidelines for scoring include:

● List all the possible acceptable answers on the answer key before grading the tests and give equal credit for each. Let your learners know if spelling counts.
● Give one point per blank, not per question.
● Put all the blanks for the answers in a column along the edge of the page. This will make scoring faster and easier.

Test questions: true/false, matching and multiple-choice questions

The alternative family of test questions to essay and short

answer/completion questions consists of true/false, matching and multiple-choice questions. This family of questions is otherwise known as objective questions. These questions present learners with a list of possible answers. Learners choose the answers they think are correct. There are several important advantages to objective questions:

- You can use them to test learning at any level, simple as well as complex.
- They are easy to score.
- Objective tests are efficient. Compared to essay or short answer tests, it takes less time to answer more questions. This factor increases the test's reliability and validity, because the test can cover more content at greater depth. The result is a more complete picture of what has been learnt.
- Learners cannot bluff their way through an objective test.

There are some disadvantages to objective testing, not all of which are insurmountable:

- Objective questions are more difficult and time-consuming to design than essay or short answer tests.
- They can encourage rote learning.
- It is difficult to design questions that test complex learning.
- Learners often resort to guessing.

Whichever form of objective question you decide to write, there are some general guidelines to follow that apply to all objective questions:

- Learners must be given a fair chance to show what they have learnt. Help them out by asking clear, uncomplicated questions. This can be done by using precise words and by avoiding complex or awkward word arrangements. Keep the reading level low in relation to the learners you are testing.
  - Avoid using a particular response pattern, such as TFTTFT or babcbd.
  - Avoid making the correct answers consistently longer (or shorter) than the incorrect answers.
  - Avoid using grammar that can provide clues to the answer. For example:

Poor: A newt is an example of a(n)
  1. fish
  2. amphibian
  3. reptile
  4. bird

Better: To which group of vertebrates does the newt belong?
1. Fishes
2. Amphibians
3. Reptiles
4. Birds

–   Be sure each question is independent of all the others. A common error is to include a question that provides a clue to another question later in the test. For example:

An acid spill should be cleaned up using:
1. a caustic neutralizer
2. an acid neutralizer
3. water
4. ptyalin

A neutralizer should be used to clean up:
1. a caustic spill
2. a flammable spill
3. any type of spill in the lab
4. an acid spill

The second question helps provide the answer to the first question. This occurs most often when questions are written at different times and placed in different parts of the test.

●   If a question is written based on an authority's views that are likely to be controversial or debatable, cite the authority.

Poor: There is a direct link between smoking and impotence in men.
True   False

Better: According to the American Society of Addiction Medicine there is a direct link between smoking and impotence in men.
True   False

●   When designing the whole test, group each type of question together so learners won't have to waste time adjusting to different thinking patterns. Write clear, explicit directions.

True/false questions

The true/false test consists of a statement with some way for learners to register agreement or disagreement.

Advantages

The advantages of true/false questions include the following:

- The test can be scored by someone unqualified in the subject area.
- The scoring is completely objective.
- The structure of the question is less complex than with other selection-type questions.
- The statement need not include instructions on how to respond.
- It is less difficult to write and refine true/false questions.

Disadvantages
The disadvantages of true/false questions include the following:

- There is a possibility of a learner getting half of the questions correct by chance.
- The test is of little value in determining gaps in learners' knowledge.
- Questions often do not discriminate well between those receiving the highest test scores and those receiving the lowest scores.
- The true/false test is less reliable than other forms of objective tests of equal length.
- It is often difficult to develop questions that can be judged to be absolutely true or false.
- The true/false question is not appropriate for measuring complex understanding.

Design
When designing a true/false test, consider the limitations of the test format and select only those questions from objectives that lend themselves to measurement with questions of this type. Objectives that do not lend themselves to measurement using a true/false question should be measured using other question types. By following this simple rule you will end up with a more valid test.

Usually the instructions for registering agreement or disagreement for the true/false test are part of the test directions appearing in a separate paragraph. However, instructions specific to a cluster of true/false questions may also appear in the test as an introductory statement for the question cluster. For example:

The following sentences may or may not contain grammatical errors. If the sentence is grammatically correct, mark out the T. If the sentence is not grammatically correct, mark out the F.

T	F	I heard you was at the Marina.
T	F	He didn't plan to study education at the university.
T	F	Are you calling us?
T	F	The back tyres had wore out.
T	F	This mobile phone works good.

You can also write a true/false question in such a way that learners are not only asked for a true or false answer, but also asked to identify the incorrect elements in the sentence and correct it. The disadvantage to this is that the question can often be changed to a true statement in a number of different ways and you must take care to ensure that the question is not ambiguous. In addition, when the learner is asked to answer a question of this type the speed of responding is reduced and fewer questions can be answered during the exam time limit. It also takes you longer to mark this kind of question, as it cannot be done using a scoring machine.

Matching questions

Another member of the objective test question family is the matching exercise, which is in fact a specialized form of multiple-choice. Two parallel columns of information are presented and learners are asked to match each word, number or symbol in one column with a word, sentence or phrase in the other column. The questions the learners are trying to match are called premises (the left-hand column). The questions the learners choose from are called the alternates. The directions usually state the basis on which matches are to be made.

There are some common variations in the design of matching exercises. For example, the question may have an unequal number or premises and alternates, which makes answering more difficult. Another variation is to provide the option of using responses once, more than once or not at all.

Advantages
Advantages of matching questions include:

- They are relatively easy to construct and score.
- They are compact and efficient, and a large amount of related material can be tested in a short period of time and space.
- It is not as easy for learners to guess as it is with true/false questions.
- Matching exercises are best used with homogeneous subject matter to test learners' ability to match terms, definitions, dates, events, cause and effects, and other matters involving simple relationships.

Disadvantages
There are some disadvantages to using matching exercises in your tests:

- They encourage rote memorization by learners.
- Their use is limited to testing homogeneous material.
- It is difficult to design exercises that test complex thinking and learning.

Design

The following guidelines should be followed when you are designing matching-type questions:

- Use only logically related material in a single exercise. Each response should be a plausible answer for each premise.
- Avoid using an equal number of responses and premises. This way learners' answers are not the result of a process of elimination.
- The directions should tell learners the basis on which they are to make a match. The directions should also state whether a response can be used once, more than once or not at all.
- Arrange the exercise so the learner can answer the question efficiently.
  - Arrange the responses in a logical order, such as alphabetical or numerical.
  - Place the entire question on one screen so the learner doesn't waste time scrolling down the screen.
  - Limit the number of premises to no more than 10.
  - Create more alternates than premises.

Multiple-choice questions

The most versatile type of objective question is the multiple-choice question. In its standard format, it consists of a stem, which presents the problem, and a list of possible answers called distracters, whose function is to distract those learners who are unsure of the correct answer. Learners select the one correct or best answer from this list.

There are many variations of the standard multiple-choice question. Some of the most common include the following:

- *Reverse multiple-choice.* All but one of the suggested answers are correct.
- *Combined response.* In addition to the stem, a list of options is presented. The suggested answers are different combinations of these options. For example:

Indicate which of the following statement(s) are **correct**.
In a chemical storage facility:

1. All chemicals can be stored in any cabinet or shelf.

2. Chemicals should be stored higher than 4 feet off the ground.

3. Chemicals should be stored according to their compatibility with other chemicals.

4. Chemicals should be stored according to the size of the container.

    a. 1, 2; b. 3, 4; c. 2, 3; d. 1, 4

- *Analogy.* Three parts of an analogy are given and learners choose the fourth part from the suggested solutions.

    The anopheles mosquito is to malaria as the aedes mosquito is to:
    1. Ebola
    2. Nile River blindness
    3. Dengue fever
    4. Sleeping sickness

Advantages
There are many advantages to using the multiple-choice question, which are given as follows:

- It is possible to design high-quality questions that test complex learning.
- Multiple-choice questions can be used to test material that is neither homogeneous nor clear cut.
- The multiple-choice question is usually less ambiguous or confusing then either true/false or matching questions.
- Multiple-choice questions can provide valuable diagnostic information. By examining learners' incorrect answers, you can find clues about the nature of their misunderstandings.
- Multiple-choice questions avoid the problem of response sets. That is, learners don't have a tendency to prefer a particular response when they don't know the correct answer.
- The effects of guessing are small when compared to that of true/false questions.

Disadvantages
Even though multiple-choice questions are the most highly recommended type of test question, there are some drawbacks to using them, as follows:

- Of all the types of test questions, they are the most difficult and time-consuming questions to design well, partly because of the difficulty of writing effective distracters.
- Multiple-choice questions take more time to answer than the other objective questions, so less material can be tested.
- Learners with low reading ability or limited experience taking tests have more difficulty answering multiple-choice questions.

Design
Consider the following guidelines when designing multiple-choice questions:

- Use clear, unambiguous, precise language. The easiest way to write a clear question is to ask a direct question rather than present an incomplete statement as the stem.
- If an incomplete statement is used, include as much information in the stem as possible. Make sure the solutions come at the end of the statement, not at the beginning or in the middle. This will save reading time as well as printing space. For example:

Poor: What did Margaret Thatcher do after she stepped down as head of the British Conservative Party?

    A. Wrote her memoirs.

    B. Formed a consulting company.

    C. Became a TV talk show host.

Better: Margaret Thatcher, after she stepped down as head of the British Conservative Party:

    <u>A</u>. wrote her memoirs.

    B. formed a consulting company.

    C. became a TV talk show host.

- Try not to make the correct answer consistently different from the distracters, for example by making the answer longer, more detailed or following a systematic pattern (a, b, d, a, b, d).
- Try to eliminate verbal associations between the stem and alternatives. For example:

Poor: The price the buyer pays for goods is called the:

    1. cost

    2. selling price

    3. gross profit

    4. net profit

Better: The amount the buyer pays for goods is called the:

    1. cost

    <u>2</u>. selling price

    3. gross profit

    4. net profit

- Avoid overlapping distracters. For example:

Which of the following play a role in digestion?

1. Tonsils
2. Pancreas
3. Appendix
4. Large intestine

A. 1, 2, 4
B. 2 only
C. 2, 3, 4
D. 2, 4

Since 2 is included in each of the options, learners will always select it. You have not learnt whether they know that the pancreas is involved in the digestive process. The following is another example of overlapping distracters:

In the story of 'Georgie Grows Up', Georgie was a young:

1. boy
2. lad
3. son
4. girl

If the answer to this question is not girl, learners will be right no matter which of the other three options they choose.

● State questions and options positively. The only time you should use a negatively stated question is when it is critical to know what *not* to do. Put 'not' in bold so the learners see it. For example:

In an unwitnessed cardiac arrest with no breathing or pulse, the rescuer should **not**:

A. give the precordial thump
B. maintain a 15:2 ratio
C. open up the airway
D. give four initial quick breaths.

● Use 'none of the above' and 'all of the above' sparingly. Use 'none of the above' as an option only when it is necessary for the learner to know that all the distracters are wrong. For example:

The first president of Singapore was:

A. George Yeo

B. Lee Kuan Yew

C. Ong Teng Chong

<u>D</u>. None of the above

Note that since 'D' is the correct answer, you still have not tested whether learners know who the first president was. Using 'all of the above' encourages guessing. The combined-response question, discussed earlier, avoids the problems of 'all of the above'.

The interpretative exercise

The interpretative exercise is a unique test question that often combines many types of objective questions. An interpretative exercise presents some introductory material to learners, such as charts, graphs or a short reading. The test consists of a series of questions that ask learners to interpret the material. The questions may be of the true/false, matching or multiple-choice variety, or some variation.

Advantages

The advantages of interpretative exercises include the following:

● They can measure more complex learning than most of the other questions. Some examples of the types of learning they can test include measuring learners' ability to:
  – apply principles;
  – identify cause-effect relationships;
  – identify unstated assumptions;
  – assess the relevance of an argument or adequacy of a procedure.
● They are an effective way of simulating a natural situation.
● They are challenging and many learners enjoy them.

Disadvantages

The disadvantages of interpretative exercises include the following:

● They are very difficult questions to design.
● They often place a heavy demand on learners' reading skills.

Design

Guidelines for the design of an interpretative exercise include the following:

● Choose the introductory material carefully. It should be brief, novel, creative and on a non-demanding reading level.

- The questions should be related only to the introductory material.
- Keep the number of questions proportional to the length of the introductory material.

An example of an interpretative exercise graph is shown below.

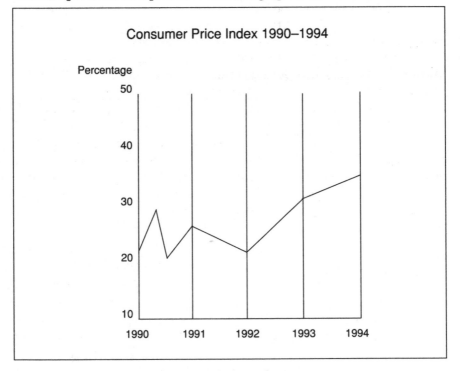

Figure 9.1   *Interpretative exercise graph*

Answer the questions based only on the information given in the graph. Check your answer sheet by marking space if the:

- a. question is definitely true
- b. question is probably true
- c. information given is not sufficient to indicate any degree of truth or falsity in the question
- d. question is probably false
- e. question is definitely false

Test questions summary

Writing test questions is a difficult task at best. However, knowing some of the basic rules and understanding where and how various types of test questions can and should be used will enable you to construct better tests for your learners. It is important to remember that the form of a test gives no certain indication of the ability tested. When you develop your test you must seek to make sure your measurements are as objective as possible and an outline or learner profile of topics learners are expected to achieve should always be the basis for your test questions. Table 9.1 shows a summary of the different types of test questions and when it is appropriate to use them.

Table 9.1 *Summary of test questions*

Question Type	Best Used to Assess	Not Best Choice for Assessing
Essay questions	Creative thinking Global, integrative thinking Problem solving Writing ability Self-expression Organizational skills	Simple recall (who, what, when, where)
Short answer/ completion questions	Simple recall only Knowledge of terminology, formulas, symbols and/or calculations	Any complex thinking Recall of information that cannot be stated in words, symbols or formulas
Objective (questions)	Any simple and complex learning depending on type	Creative, original thinking Writing ability and self-expression
Multiple-choice questions	Simple and complex learning	
True/false questions	Knowledge of cause and effect Attitudes, superstitions and misconceptions Information with definitely correct answers	Complex learning and thinking
Matching questions	Associations and relationships within homogenous material Definitions	Complex learning
Interpretative questions	Applying knowledge to new situations Evaluative thinking skills	Simple knowledge

COMPUTER-MANAGED LEARNING

In an online learning environment, learner assessment is often conducted using some form of electronic assessment program, where the learners can answer questions online and obtain immediate feedback on their answers. This assessment component is called computer-managed learning (CML) and is essentially a management tool for monitoring learners' progress and is available as a dedicated Web assessment program. The main function of a computer-managed learning program is to assist large groups of learners in determining their progress, and assist facilitators and administration staff cope with the inherent problems of tracking learners through a Web-based learning event.

CML is based on three themes. These are:

1. *Individualization.* The most effective type of learning occurs when learners can proceed at their own rate.
2. *Performance objectives.* What learners are expected to achieve is written in performance and measurable terms.
3. *Educational technology.* The use of technology to help improve learning.

A CML system is a management tool that helps facilitators to identify a 'path' for their learners to follow through a series of learning events and, based on that path, track their progress and assess their achievement.

Facilitators and learners typically access CML via the Web. When learners complete the various online activities, they are presented with a series of assessment questions, which they answer and which are marked online. This way learners can receive immediate feedback on their results and in some cases various kinds of feedback can also be provided. The facilitator can monitor the learners' progress by accessing their results and determining which objectives they have or have not achieved. Using this information the facilitator can then determine if the learner is making adequate progress or if some form of remediation or direct facilitator assistance is needed.

Learner interaction with CML

Learners can have a number of different interactions with a CML system. For example, learners first study the learning materials and complete the associated activities. These activities can include reading text, viewing multimedia files, assessing links, e-mailing other learners and contributing to discussion forums. Following these activities, the next step might be for learners to access the CML system and request a computer-generated assessment based on the learning materials (see Figure 9.2). The system then generates the test and learners complete it

---

Attempt 2 on item
'Assessment Generation'

Select all the correct answers. You can choose more than one.

1. (1) Any exam can be made up of a combination of

☐   A)   QUESTIONS WHICH TEST SPECIFIC MODULE(S).

☐   B)   QUESTIONS WHICH TEST SPECIFIC OBJECTIVE(S).

Figure 9.2 *Sample online assessment question,*
http://www.wineducation.com/TLM.htm

(Reproduced with permission of The Learning Manager™, a registered trademark of The Learning Manager Corporation)

as determined by the course map. The course map is developed by the learning event designer and includes details of what test questions are to be included in each assessment as well as other parameters.

Once the learners complete the assessment the computer then marks each question and records the score, the questions used from the question pool or test bank, the questions answered correctly and those answered incorrectly. The computer then displays an assessment report (see Figure 9.3).

The assessment report indicates learner achievement, including questions answered both correctly and incorrectly, and gives the correct answers and learner feedback. If learners achieve the predefined pass mark set by the designer, they are allowed to proceed to the next assessment.

If the predetermined standard is not achieved, learners are expected to review the learning materials based on the objectives they have failed to achieve. The learning event designer can set the number of times learners can attempt each assessment. Typically this is three, based on the premise that if they fail to master the objective three times then they need assistance from the facilitator. Figure 9.4 shows a typical learner results report.

When learners repeat an assessment, each test displays different test questions based on the size of the question pool and the ability of the system to randomly generate the question. When learners feel ready for

Course: TLM001 Year: 2000 Section: SC User: ESO1			
Summary for Attempt 2 on item 'Assessment Generation'			
Qu. #	**Module Objective**	**Your Score**	**Your Answer**
1	Assessment Generation/5	0/1	B
2	Assessment Generation/6	1/1	B
3	Assessment Generation/4	0/1	C
4	Assessment Generation/2	0/1	C
5	Assessment Generation/1	1/1	T
6	Assessment Generation/3	0/1	T
		2/6	**Final Score: 33 %**

Note: Right Click to Print this

Done

Figure 9.3   *A typical online assessment report,*
http://www.wineducation.com/TLM.htm

(Reproduced with permission of The Learning Manager™, a registered trademark of The Learning Manager Corporation)

the next assessment, they simply request one from the system. This cycle is repeated until the unit of study is completed.

For learners the benefits of a CML system can include:

- A consistent user interface where learners can access assessments.
- Completion of assessments at any time when they feel ready.
- Immediate feedback on the results of their assessments to help create more confident learners. They can attempt an assessment again after restudying the relevant learning material.
- A greater opportunity for the facilitator to personalize the learning experience through individual feedback.
- The recognition of prior knowledge using pre-tests. The pre-test determines which objectives learners have achieved before they study the actual learning material. When learners reach the required level of mastery in the pre-test, they are considered to have achieved the required objectives and can move on to the next learning event. If

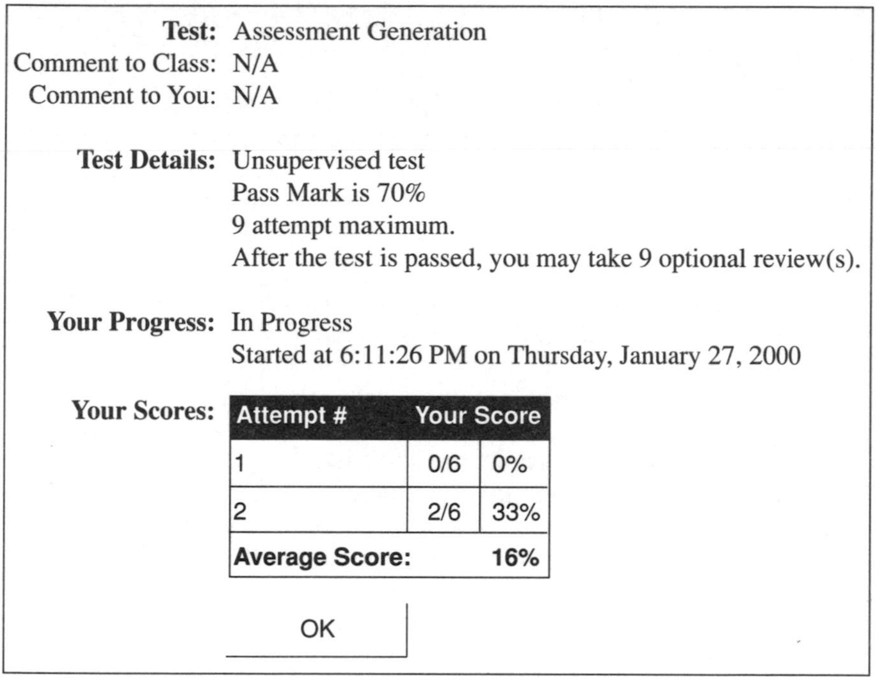

```
┌─────────────────────────────────────────────────────────────────┐
│                   Test:  Assessment Generation                    │
│   Comment to Class:  N/A                                          │
│    Comment to You:  N/A                                           │
│                                                                   │
│       Test Details:  Unsupervised test                           │
│                      Pass Mark is 70%                             │
│                      9 attempt maximum.                           │
│                      After the test is passed, you may take 9     │
│                      optional review(s).                          │
│                                                                   │
│     Your Progress:  In Progress                                  │
│                     Started at 6:11:26 PM on Thursday, January    │
│                     27, 2000                                      │
│                                                                   │
│       Your Scores:                                               │
└─────────────────────────────────────────────────────────────────┘
```

Attempt #	Your Score	
1	0/6	0%
2	2/6	33%
Average Score:		**16%**

OK

Figure 9.4 *Learner results report,*
http://www.wineducation.com/TLM.htm

(Reproduced with permission of The Learning Manager™, a registered trademark of The Learning Manager Corporation)

 they achieve only some of the objectives then they study only the materials associated with the objectives they have not achieved.
- The adaptation of the system to learners' learning speed, learning style and knowledge level.
- The linking to other Web sites as part of the questions or feedback.
- A non-judgemental system with respect to the learners' responses.
- When learners are studying a learning event where all the materials are delivered via the Web, they can assess their progress by completing the CML assessments. CML can also be used in conjunction with a face-to-face learning event, as it provides a means for learners to assess their progress and allows the facilitator to monitor learners' progress. Facilitators can then use this information to determine if the learning event needs to be adapted to better meet learners' needs.
- Decreasing the feeling of isolation because of the immediate personalized feedback they receive on their assessments. This is particularly the case if learners are studying a fully Webbed learning event that has no face-to-face component.

Facilitator and administrator interaction with a typical CML system

Facilitator interaction with a CML system can be classified as one of three functions: clerical, report generation and system management. The clerical function includes such things as the facilitator registering learners on the system, allowing them access to other parts of the system, finding passwords, changing marks and performing other basic tasks.

Report generation has the facilitator performing tasks such as checking report card grades and learner histories, and reviewing the analysis of both the questions and the learning objectives. The system can also be used to identify learners according to specific criteria, for example learners experiencing difficulty mastering a specific objective.

System management functions include such things as making changes to predefined learning sequences and other decisions. However, at this level, facilitator access to the system might be restricted to ensure the testing strategy and course map remain consistent. In many organizations the learning event designer is given the authority to make changes to the event based on participant and facilitator feedback.

For a facilitator, the typical benefits of CML include:

- the opportunity to engage in a more productive interaction with learners through awareness of learner achievement;
- links to other resources that can be included in questions or feedback;
- the random generation of assessments so each one is unique, provided of course that the question pool has enough test questions for each objective;
- the integration of communication tools such as discussion forums and e-mail;
- the ability to incorporate multimedia;
- the ability to launch other programs from within the system.

For administrators, the typical benefits of CML include:

- the provision of a valid and reliable testing procedure, since all learners are completing assessments based on the same objectives even though the actual test questions may not be the same – the analysis component of CML allows facilitators to determine, from the test question report, the ability of the test question to discriminate between learners;
- the use of an automatic, detailed record-keeping system;
- the early identification of learner difficulties, since progress can be monitored on a regular basis;
- the issuing and marking of objective assessments;

- the reduction of learner failure through the early identification of learner problems;
- the consistent monitoring of learners' progress.

A CML system offers facilitators and administrators a viable methodology for tracking learners through a series of diverse Web-based learning activities, each taking place at different times and locations. CML can be a very efficient management tool for learning events delivered over the Web, as it allows learners to 'practise' what they have learnt and receive immediate feedback.

A CML course

A CML course usually consists of a test bank or series of test banks that contain various test questions and a course map detailing the assessments to be presented to learners. The learning event designer designs the CML strategy that makes up the event, while facilitators are given limited rights to access the event and monitor learner results. This method of giving limited access rights ensures that the CML course is not changed without the knowledge of the learning event designer.

Types of test questions used in CML

Any type of test question can be used in a CML system. However, the most suitable are objective-type questions, such as:

- multiple-choice;
- true/false;
- matching;
- short (one- or two-word) answer;
- mathematical random number generation – these are questions that have their values generated by the CML system using a simple algorithm. For example, if the question requires learners to add two numbers together, the algorithm may specify that the first number be between one and nine and the second number between 10 and 100. The CML system then generates the question with the values in the required range.

Subjective-type questions can also be included such as essay and 'short answer' questions. These questions, however, have to be marked by the facilitator and entered in the CML system's individual learner history report. CML test questions can include text, mathematical equations, special symbols, graphics, audio, animation and video. Many CML programs also allow learners to launch other applications such as word processing, which can be used to answer an essay question. Other programs such as spreadsheets can also be launched to assist learners complete various computations. Links can be included as a source of information to assist learners answer various questions or as a source of remediation when feedback is given. Most CML programs allow the event designer to provide some form of feedback for each question. For example, if learners select a correct option they will receive a reinforcing comment. Conversely, if they choose an incorrect option corrective feedback can be provided.

It is of critical importance that test questions be well written to ensure both reliability and validity, and some CML programs provide question analysis options. The writing of test questions for use in a CML environment is no different to writing test questions for the regular classroom assessment.

Assessment strategy/event map

If electronic assessments are included in the Web-based learning event then an assessment strategy or event map must be developed. Before the assessment strategy is developed the operational parameters of the CML system must also be known. Some of the decisions that the Web-based learning event designer has to make regarding assessment strategy are:

- How often do learners have to complete an assessment?
- How much material is covered in each assessment?
- How many different types of assessments are used (for example, tutorials and in-course, pre- and post-assessments)?
- How will each assessment be designed (for example, the mastery level, the number of times learners are able to attempt it, the number of questions to be included in the assessments and which objectives are to be assessed)?

Typical assessment learning strategy

Given a learning event with 10 tutorials, with each tutorial covering three objectives, there is a total of 30 objectives in the learning event. The assessment strategy, in this case, is based on one assessment per tutorial. The designer also wants learners to be able to attempt any tutorial assessment without any prerequisites. This means that learners can attempt the assessment for tutorial 4, for example, before attempting the assessments for tutorials 1 to 3. After the tutorial 5 assessment, the designer wants an in-course assessment covering all the preceding tutorials. After tutorial 10, there will be a second in-course assessment covering tutorials 6 to 10, and at the end of the learning event there is to be an assessment covering all the objectives.

The designer also wants to determine how much learners have gained from the learning event, so a pre- and post-test strategy will be incorporated. The pre-test assesses all the objectives of the learning event, and determines which objectives the learners have or have not achieved. The post-test assesses all the objectives of the learning event and determines which objectives the learners have achieved as a result of the event. The difference between the pre- and post-test is the so-called learning gain. The learning event designer wants to ensure learners have mastered all the objectives covered in the tutorial assessments before attempting the post-test.

Therefore, the assessment design discussed above can be summarized as follows:

- ten tutorials with three objectives each, for a total of 30 objectives;
- an assessment for each tutorial, for a total of 10 tutorial assessments;
- tutorial assessments that do not have any prerequisites;
- the first in-course assessment (IC1) will cover the objectives in tutorials 1 to 5 and the second in-course assessment (IC2) will cover the objectives in tutorials 6 to 10;
- before learners can complete the in-course assessments, they must complete the tutorial assessments;
- before learners attempt the post-test they must have completed and mastered the in-course assessments;
- learners must complete both a pre- and post-test.

Given the above, the assessment strategy would be as shown in the following Figure 9.5.

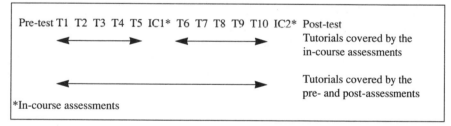

Figure 9.5 *Assessment strategy*

Test question pools for each of the assessments would now be developed as follows:

- ten tutorial assessments – three test questions for each of the three objectives totalling nine test questions for each tutorial or 90 test questions for all 30 objectives;
- two in-course assessments – two test questions for each of the 15 objectives, totalling 30 test questions for each of the in-course assessments;

- pre-/post-course assessments – one test question for each of the 30 objectives, totalling 30 test questions.

Assessment strategy parameters

Typically CML programs have a number of parameters that can be controlled, such as:

- *Pass mark.* Using this feature the designer can set the pass mark for each assessment. The pass mark or the level of mastery is determined by the event designer, with decisions based on the type of learner and past experience with the learning event. Generally the level of mastery is set between 70 and 80 per cent. Each type of assessment can have different levels of mastery. For example, the tutorial assessment may have a lower level of mastery than the in-course and post-test assessments.
- *Minimum number of attempts.* The minimum number of attempts learners are given on each assessment is typically set at one.
- *Maximum number of attempts.* Learners can be given more than one attempt on each assessment depending on its type. It is usual to give learners one attempt on the pre-test because the designer is trying to determine the knowledge of learners before beginning the learning event. In tutorial assessment, it is usual to give learners up to three attempts because if they fail the first attempt they can identify which objectives they have not mastered, restudy the learning materials and reattempt the assessment. For the post-test the designer may want the learners to attempt it in a computer laboratory under examination conditions. In this case it is usual to allow learners just one attempt.
- *Auto pass.* The auto pass function allows learners to proceed to the next assessment without having achieved the prerequisite assessment. For example, if learners have attempted the tutorial 3 assessment three times and failed to reach the required level of mastery, then the system can be preset to allow them to proceed automatically to the next assessment. This is usually done so as not to delay learners. If the auto pass feature is not set, the learners have to contact their facilitator to 'release' another assessment. Although this might be desirable in that the facilitator can assist learners with the objectives they have not achieved, it may not be convenient to contact the facilitator. However, a more effective and efficient strategy is not to allow learners to auto-pass the in-course assessments. Learners will then only have to contact the facilitator a minimum number of times during the event, if they fail to obtain mastery by the third attempt.
- *Time limit.* Generally, no time limits are set for electronic assessment, as most are diagnostic in nature. However, if the learning event designer wants the post-test as part of the final assessment, then a time limit may be imposed.

- *Number of questions.* The number of questions per assessment will depend on the type of assessment the learners are undertaking. Tutorial-type assessment may contain between five and 20 questions, in-course assessments may contain 10 to 30 questions and a post-test may contain 20 to 40 questions. The designer must determine how many questions to include in each assessment.
- *Reviews.* A review allows the learners to access an already-mastered assessment as part of their revision strategy. Learners will usually want to do this just before they attempt the in-course revision strategy or post-test assessment.

The following are typical parameters of a CML program.

Table 9.2   *Parameters of CML programs*

Parameter	Tutorials	In-course Assessment	Pre-/Post-Tests	Choice
Pass Mark	80	80	80	To master the assessment the learners must achieve 80% before they can proceed.
Minimum Number of Attempts	1	1	1	The minimum number of attempts the learners can make to pass the test.
Auto Pass	yes	no	no	Allows the learner to proceed to the next assessment
Time Limit	none	none	none	There is no time liimt for this assessment.
Number of Questions	9	30	30	There are nine questions in each of the tutorial assessments, 30 in each of the in-course assessments and 30 in each of the pre- and post-tests.
Review	review	review	none	The learners can complete reviews even when they have passed the relevant assessment.

The Learning Manager

The Learning Manager (TLM), from The Learning Manager Corporation, was originally developed as a computer-managed learning program, but has now expanded into an instructional management system that incorporates the assessment characteristics of computer-managed learning.

TLM has the following benefits:

- Templates that guide course development. These include test question and learning material templates, where data are entered using a common word processing package.
- Learning materials conform to a customized standard in terms of content and visual presentation. This is done by using the learning material template that specifies the type of information that can be entered.
- Template formats are for both print and online delivery.
- System learning requirements are minimized as a standard word processing package that is used to enter both the test questions and the learning materials.
- Learners can access learning events from any PC connected to an intranet or Internet.
- Learners have greater access, and control over their learning.

A typical methodology for the use of TLM in a Web-based learning environment is outlined in the following sales training learning scenario.

Assumptions

ABC.com has had its sales training materials put up online. The materials are held in a secure server off-site and are managed by a local service provider. Because of the overall structure of the sales training course, all facets of the programme, with the exception of the orientation session, have been put into the Web-based environment in their entirety. In the case of the orientation session, part has been put on the Web and part has been retained in a face-to-face environment, although the session is available in an interactive video format for use where face-to-face sessions are not possible.

The application

The sales training materials are delivered to learners using TLM. This application comprises three components: those of testing, record keeping and study generation. As part of its last iteration a fourth component, the delivery of instruction, was added to the TLM software. These four components allow ABC.com employees participating in the sales training programme a complete range of resources to help engage them in the learning process, while at the same time providing for the monitoring and tracking of activities by ABC.com to ensure the learners are performing to the appropriate level of mastery.

The scenario

ABC.com employees sign on to the TLM system at any one of the many computers in their office or via a terminal in the new learning resource

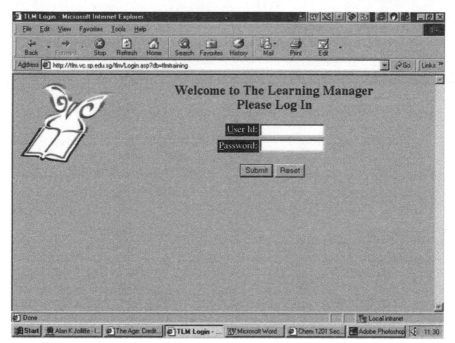

Figure 9.6 *The Learning Manager log-in screen,*
http://www.wineducation.com/TLM.htm

(Reproduced with permission of The Learning Manager™, a registered trademark
of The Learning Manager Corporation)

centre (LRC). At the log-in screen (see Figure 9.6), learners new to the
system are required to provide both their name and the password
supplied by the ABC.com local co-ordinator. Immediately on log-in,
learners are given the opportunity to change their password to something more suited to their personal tastes.

Once the new password is entered and approved, learners are shown
the user interface screen (see Figure 9.7).

The user interface screen shows a number of different options.
However, because the learners are new to the system only one option is
actually available. After clicking on that option learners are taken to a
personalized training map (developed by ABC.com human resources
from various skills profiles) of all the courses they as ABC.com
employees will be expected to complete as part of their probation and
subsequent first year with the organization. The first module in the sales
training course deals with understanding the learning system as a whole.
The first screen seen by learners shows a course map to aid in orientation. The course map screen also includes a number of course menu ques-

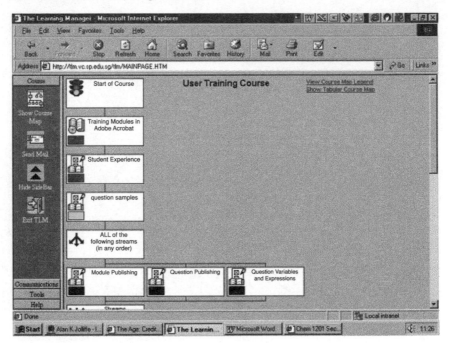

Figure 9.7   *The Learning Manager course map,*
http://www.wineducation.com/TLM.htm

(Reproduced with permission of The Learning Manager™, a registered trademark
of The Learning Manager Corporation)

tions positioned on the left side of the screen. This fully customizable
menu allows learners, among other things, to select the other modules in
the sales training programme as they become available, allows access to a
personal notepad to record course notes and provides access to a discussion room for both synchronous and asynchronous communication with
the programme facilitator, local and regional co-ordinators, subject-
matter experts and management staff as well as fellow learners. The
course menu also provides access to both the ABC.com home page and
the ABC.com world-wide resource library.

The learners can select to view the instructional component and
complete the activities, which include:

- reading text;
- viewing graphics and photographs;
- listening to audio files;
- viewing video and animation files;
- accessing other computer programs;
- accessing the Web using links;

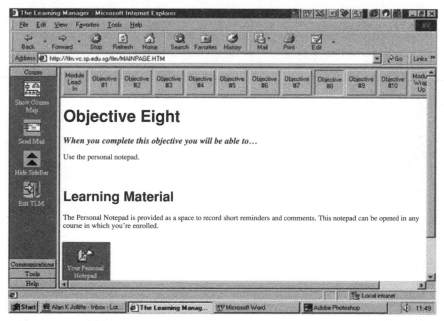

Figure 9.8   *Instructional activities,*
http://www.wineducation.com/TLM.htm

(Reproduced with permission of The Learning Manager™, a registered trademark of The Learning Manager Corporation)

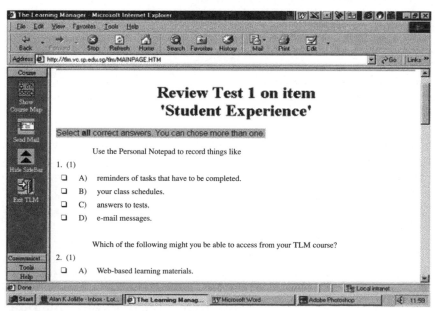

Figure 9.9   *A sample CML assessment,*
http://www.wineducation.com/TLM.htm

(Reproduced with permission of The Learning Manager™, a registered trademark of The Learning Manager Corporation)

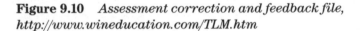

Figure 9.10　*Assessment correction and feedback file,*
http://www.wineducation.com/TLM.htm

(Reproduced with permission of The Learning Manager™, a registered trademark
of The Learning Manager Corporation)

- e-mailing other learners;
- contributing to discussion forums;
- making their own course notes.

Once into module 1, learners work through the materials and assessments at their own pace (within a given time frame, however) until
completed. Figure 9.8 shows a typical instructional activities screen.

At completion, learners are asked to answer a test designed first to
determine what has been learnt and second to highlight learner strengths
and weaknesses. Figure 9.9 shows a test screen.

Learners complete the assessment and submit it for marking.

Once marked, the learner can access his or her assessment report (see
Figure 9.10). These data are captured and used by ABC.com ready for use
in month-end reports. If learners meet or surpass the criteria set they can
move on to another module. If they do not meet the criteria they can,
depending on the parameters set for the test, attempt the test up to two
more times. If at the third attempt the criterion is still not met, a 'flag' is
set and the learners are 'locked out' of the system until it is reset by the

local co-ordinator. In this way, learners having difficulties are identified immediately for intervention by ABC.com coaches. In such cases the system will suggest a remedial path for the learners, who would then be 'sidelined' from the mainstream on a temporary basis to complete the remedial learning materials.

In this scenario, as already noted, the first module was determined to be compulsory while all subsequent modules use a recognition of prior learning (RPL) protocol and have a pre-test attached. On successful completion of the pre-test learners are assumed to 'know' the materials contained in the module and are allowed to pass through to the next module.

Moving on

Once learners have completed and passed module 1 they may make the choice to move directly to module 2. As part of the requirements for module 2, learners are expected to use various resources as part of an assignment. They access the resources via the TLM Desktop (these resources are standard HTML pages residing in the local service provider's TLM server and are printable, based on the parameters set by ABC.com). While working through other portions of the module learning materials, learners now require access to a series of other resources including the sales training QuickTIPS, which are also accessed directly from the TLM Desktop (again standard HTML pages, and printable as determined by ABC.com).

However, yet more resources are needed to explain the concept in greater detail. One such resource is a video that is accessed via the TLM library option in the course menu. This video is delivered to learners' screens in a 2.5 by 2.5 inch format via a CD ROM juke-box attached to the local service provider's server. Other resources needed to complete the module are print-based and are available from the ABC.com world-wide library in an HTML format. Learners are able to access these resources, like the video resource, via the course menu on the TLM Desktop.

Putting it all together

After learners have completed and passed module 2, data are again collected and stored for future reference. The learners then proceed to work through the remaining modules in the sales training programme. As learners progress through the programme, the general manager fulfils the role of ensuring that the system is functioning as needed by the organization. The general manager also reviews the monthly reports that are issued via the TLM system to the local service provider and forwarded to regional co-ordinators for dissemination (see Figure 9.11). The reports are used as interview guidelines when setting up employee/management performance appraisal (EPA/MPA) interviews.

The Learning Manager - Microsoft Internet Explorer

File Edit View Favorites Tools Help

Back Forward Stop Refresh Home Search Favorites History Mail Print Edit

Address http://tlm.vc.sp.edu.sg/tlm/MainPage.htm

Student History for TRAINING ONE 1998 – User Training Course – class 1

No. of students in class: 20

it16–1, it16–1 (IT16–1)

Item	Start/End Date	Status	Attempts	Reviews	Scores
Training Modules in Adobe Acrobat	11/16/99 11:06 11/16/99 11:10	SP	0	0	
Student Experience	11/16/99 11:11 11/16/99 11:20	AP	1	0	70
question samples	11/16/99 11:22 11/16/99 11:30	AP	1	1	37
Module Publishing	11/16/99 13:53	AC	0	0	
Question Publishing	11/16/99 11:33	AC	0	0	

it16–10, (IT16–10)

Item	Start/End Date	Status	Attempts	Reviews	Scores
Training Modules in Adobe Acrobat	11/16/99 11:22 11/16/99 11:22	SP			
Student Experience	11/16/99 11:20 11/16/99 11:24	AP	1	0	60

Done   Local intranet

Start Re: Philippin The Lea... Microsoft W Adobe Phot... IntranetWare M... Hassall and   03:03

Figure 9.11   *Learner history report,*
http://www.wineducation.com/TLM.htm

(Reproduced with permission of The Learning Manager™, a registered trademark
of The Learning Manager Corporation)

Local co-ordinators also work in the background to ensure the TLM
system meets the needs of both the ABC.com organization and the
learners. They play the role of systems administrators, helping learners
with sign-on and password problems and providing other general 'help'
services. In their role as local co-ordinators they also serve as conduits
through which SMEs pass materials for system updating to regional co-
ordinators. Local co-ordinators have limited access to the TLM system as
required by their job function.

Regional co-ordinators take on the responsibility of liaison with the
TLM service provider, who adds materials to the various courses on the
TLM server, updates the system and generates all required month-end
reports, including an up-to-date multi-level learning log. Also included in
the reports are the general manager and SME performance checklists for
business cases. These checklists are accessible online for completion as
required. Regional co-ordinators, like general managers and SMEs, have
no access to the TLM system.

Table 9.3 *Assessment strategy*

Guideline	Indicator(s) of Success
Set up a typical CML system to track learner progress and achievement	The course map has been developed to follow the correct sequence of learning topics.
	The course map provides, at a minimum, one mid-module and one end-of-module test.
	The test questions are correctly linked to an appropriate learning objective.
	Any appropriate end-of-event examination is in evidence.
	The test question pool(s) contains a minimum of 10 test questions per objective.
Test Questions – Multiple-Choice Questions Develop an assessment using multiple-choice questions consistent with the formalized learning strategy specifically developed for the learning event.	Question answers are evenly spread across all question distracters throughout the test.
	The number of distracters per question is consistent throughout the test.
	A set number of plausible distracters have been used for each question in the test.
	The stem of each question in the test is concise and to the point.
	The use of negative has been avoided in the stem, the distracters and the question answer.
	All of the above and/or none of the above have been used sparingly if at all.
	Response choices have been arranged in a logical order.
	The distracters are presented vertically, to increase readability.
	Grammatically consistent construction of each question is used to avoid revealing the answer.
	Each test question has one logical, correct answer.
	The use of absolutes is avoided in answer choices.

Test Questions – Matching Questions Provide a test using matching questions consistent with the formalized learning strategy specifically developed for the learning event.	Precise instructions have been provided to help the learner answer the question. The basis for matching the premise and the response has been specified. An unequal number of responses in relation to premises has been provided. Questions have been developed to determine either recall or application of knowledge. The choice statements are listed in chronological or numeric order.
Test Questions – True/False Questions Provide a test using true/false questions consistent with the formalized learning strategy specifically developed for the learning event.	The question is constructed in one of three forms, simple, complex or compound. The statement is concise without more elaboration than is necessary to give clear meaning. Negative statements have been avoided. A regular or predictable response pattern has been avoided. Words such as all, every, always, none, never, nothing, something, usually, often, may, seldom, frequently, could, many and some have been avoided.
Test Questions – Short Answer Questions Provide a test using short answer questions consistent with the formalized learning strategy specifically developed for the learning event	Precise instructions have been provided to help the learner answer the question. The blanks for answer completion are all the same length. A key word list has been provided. Excessive numbers of blanks in any one question have been avoided. Blanks have been placed at the end of the stem sentence rather than the beginning. There is only one correct answer for each question. The answer word or words have parameters set to allow for a range of correct responses.

Assessment design guidelines

Table 9.3 lists design guidelines and basic indicators of success that should be applied to the design and development of a viable learner assessment.

WEB-BASED ASSIGNMENTS

Computer-managed learning can be used as part of the assessment strategy as it is effective in assessing lower-order objectives such as arranging, labelling, describing, solving and calculating. However, CML is somewhat less effective in assessing higher-order objectives, such as applying, analysing, evaluating, comparing and interpreting. This kind of objective is more difficult to assess as it is more time-consuming to produce effective test questions. Written or facilitator-marked assignments can assess learners' performance for the entire learning event and assess cognitive (knowledge) skills and affective (attitudes) performances. Subjective assignments can be included in the assessment strategy, but they need to be marked by the facilitator. Assessments in a Web-based learning event can include both CML and facilitator-marked assignments.

Assignments inform facilitators how learners are progressing and who needs or does not need their assistance. Assignments give the facilitator the opportunity to assist learners by providing corrective feedback. Assignments are also used to prepare learners for final examinations and with deadlines to help them structure their study. Since the assignment is usually used as part of the assessment requirements for the learning event it requires careful consideration and planning to ensure it assesses the learning event objectives.

Assignment elements

When setting assignments for a Web-based learning event the designer must decide which elements of an assignment to use. The elements of a typical assignment include:

- the question itself;
- model answers;
- marking criteria;
- feedback.

The question itself can be open-ended or a series of structured short answer questions. Model answers can be provided so learners can see exactly what is required of them. The format of the assignment could be a report or essay discussion. When the question has been set and the type of assignment format determined, the learning event designer must then determine the assignment's suitability for the learner. Determining if the assignment is suitable depends on a number of factors, including the educational background and level of ability of the learners. Assessment guidelines need to be developed so that learners know exactly what is expected of them.

It can be difficult to obtain consistency in the marking of assignments, so marking criteria are essential. The last element is feedback from the facilitator, which provides learners with information on their progress and the future direction they should take with their study.

Determining the purpose of the assignment

Typically, the specific learning objectives identify the key knowledge concepts and principles that must be assessed. Once these have been identified the designer has to determine what learners are expected to do with this knowledge. Following are some examples of what the learning event designer might want learners to achieve as part of an assignment:

- acquaint learners with an issue, concept or principle;
- question learners' attitudes;
- attempt to develop learners' ability to gather, collate and express ideas;
- develop learners' skills;
- make learners responsible for their own decisions;
- develop creativity;
- develop problem-solving skills;
- foster collaborative learning and teamwork;
- develop written and oral skills;
- develop practical knowledge of the subject;
- develop Internet research skills;
- develop negotiation skills.

Selecting the appropriate aims helps the learning event designer determine on the form of the assignment, and whether the objectives should be assessed individually or collectively.

Testing the objectives in the assignment

The learning event designer needs to decide what form the assignment will take or what exactly learners are being asked to do. Here are some examples of what learners could be asked to do in an assignment:

- analyse information that describes ideas and their assumptions, relationship and importance to one another;
- argue for or against a particular proposal;
- compare a proposal or idea for similarities and differences;
- contrast a proposal or idea by focusing upon the differences;
- criticize a proposal, giving a judgement and supporting it with evidence and discussion;
- present a balanced argument showing the positive and negative points;
- define the meaning of a phrase or theory;
- describe a theory, process or idea giving examples and non-examples;
- evaluate a proposal or idea giving its strengths and weaknesses, discussing its merits and forming a conclusion;
- examine a proposal or idea in depth and investigate its implications;
- explain information or concepts and interpret them in detail;
- illustrate information and concepts in detail using diagrams or figures;
- justify a proposal or idea, showing there are clear grounds for the decision and conclusion;
- outline the main principles of a proposal or idea and leave out the details, but show the structure and relationship;
- prove the truth behind an idea or proposal by presenting logical evidence as an argument;
- relate how things are connected to one another and how they are alike, and explain the relationships between them;
- trace the development or history of a proposal, idea or subject from the beginning.

What the designer asks learners to do will depend very much on the objectives of the learning event. Once these are determined, the designer must then decide on the form or type of questions to be included in the assignment. The types of questions you can choose include:

- essay – discussing a proposal or idea, or examining an argument by giving the pros and cons and making a conclusion (a critical discussion should include a conclusion);
- summary/review – summarizing the main points of a topic;
- practical work – conducting an experiment or investigation;
- completion of diagrams – designing a series of diagrams to represent a process or concept;
- short answers;
- practice examination questions – completing questions from previous examination papers.

Suitability

Now that purpose and the method of assessing objectives have been identified, it is necessary to ensure the assignment is appropriate to the learner's background and ability level. Here the designer's experience with other learning events will be of assistance. A good option is to pilot the assignment with a group of learners to determine how effective the assignment is at measuring the attainment of the learning objectives.

Assessment guidelines

For the learners' benefit, the learning event designer should develop assessment guidelines to give learners guidance regarding the materials they need to present in order to fulfil the requirements of the assignment. The assessment guidelines should include:

- the format or organization and presentation required – how are learners to complete the assignment?
- the parameters and scope of the assignment, including the time to complete, the number of words, the areas to incorporate, the resources to be accessed and the areas for individual and collaborative work;
- the structure of the assignment – what are the topics and sub-topics?
- a breakdown of marks for individual components – this will give learners an idea of the importance of each component and an indication of how much time they must spend on each;
- how learners are to submit their assignment.

Determining the effectiveness of assignments

After the assignment questions have been developed, the designer can use the following checklist to help ensure all the appropriate elements are included in the question:

- Is the question clear and unambiguous?
- Does the question relate to the performance objectives?
- Are the tasks in the assignment similar to the ones learners would be expected to carry out in the real world?
- Must learners acquire knowledge, and construct and apply new forms of knowledge?
- Are the tasks complex enough to allow for the assessment of a variety of performance areas?
- Are the requirements of the assignment clear without revealing the solutions?
- Has a marking scheme been included?

- Has a list of the Web resources learners are expected to use been included?
- Have learners been told what topics have to be covered?
- Does the assignment include details on presentation and format?
- Have learners been adequately prepared for the question?
- Have learners been told how to submit their assignment?
- Have learners been told if they can include multiple-media files and links?

One of the best ways to determine the effectiveness of an assignment is to have it reviewed by others and make suggestions for improvement.

Sample assignment

A cave diving learning event is being conducted for deep sea divers. The learners all live in isolated areas, but can come together for one weekend when they will undergo practical training. The event designer decides to deliver the theory component of the learning event via the Web using CML to monitor progress. As part of the assessment plan the designer wants to assess one of the main objectives of the learning event, which is to plan and conduct a cave dive. While this will be carried out during the learners' practical training, the designer feels it is important that the learners develop a dive plan prior to the practical session.

The learning outcome the designer wants to assess is: 'Given a group of at least six divers, develop a dive plan for a level two cave. Include the following information in your plan: potential problems, pre-dive plan, special equipment required, procedures to follow during the dive and post-dive procedures.'

The designer also wants to assess the learners' practical knowledge by developing the dive plan in practical terms and so decides that some form of pro forma document using a series of dive-related categories for the learners to complete would be most suitable. For example:

You are the most experienced diver in a group of six, three of whom are newly qualified cave divers. The group intends to dive the (specified) cave. Outline your dive plan under the following headings:

A. Potential problems – list at least five.
B. Pre-dive plan – include how to obtain permission to dive, and the dive brief.
C. Special equipment – list everything apart from basic scuba equipment.
D. Procedures during the dive – list the descend, bottom and ascend procedures.
E. Post-dive procedures – include what should **not** be done after the dive.

Marking schemes

To aid in marking consistency, an assessment marking scheme should be developed. This involves breaking the question down into its various parts and producing the best possible answer.

An assessment marking scheme for the sample assignment might be as follows:

A. Potential problems
Loss of surface; reduction of light; reduction of buoyancy; problems of depth (ie narcosis and decompression sickness); air consumption; entry and exit points; silting. *Allow one mark for each point.*

B. Pre-dive plan
Gain permission to dive – arrange up to two weeks beforehand; carry and show qualification. Dive plan – nominate leader; decide purpose; decide duration; calculate air consumption rate; assign groups according to experience, water conditions and previous dives; describe emergency procedures; equipment and signal checks. *Allow one mark for each point.*

C. Special equipment required
All sinkhole diver equipment; decompression line/shot-line; reel and tethers; spare tank and regulator on the shot-line; ladder; extra rope for lowering gear. *Allow one mark for each point.*

D. Procedures during the dive
Check everything is OK with your buddy; set your watch; descend following the shot-line down; clear ears constantly on descent; go to the bottom slowly; trim for neutral buoyancy; check that your buddy is OK; constantly monitor your pressure gauge, depth and bottom time; tie off reel on the bottom; both divers attach to the guideline; when the bottom time is up, signal your buddy to ascend; untie the reel and ascend; complete a safety stop. *Allow one mark for each point.*

E. Post-dive procedures
Ensure that your buddy has surfaced; check he/she is OK; rest on the surface for several minutes; check your remaining air; provide feedback on the dive; retrieve all gear and clean up the area; report to the land owner. Do not exercise immediately after surfacing; avoid repetitive dives. *Allow one mark for each point.*

CONCLUSION

The most important step in developing a Web-based learning event is developing the assessments. Assessment is used not only to monitor the learners' achievement and progress but also to assist the learning event designer(s) determine the success of the learning event. Computer-managed learning can alleviate much of the workload of marking from facilitator(s), and allow learners constantly to monitor their own progress. However, the effectiveness of computer-managed learning depends on a well-thought-out assessment strategy and, above all, effective and well-constructed test questions. Assignments are also an important component of the assessment, and are useful for assessing higher-order objectives. They allow learners to demonstrate what they have learnt without the stress of examinations.

Chapter 10

Developing instructional strategies

INTRODUCTION

In this chapter a systematic approach to developing instructional strategies is outlined. Instructional strategies can be considered at both the micro- and macro-level. The micro-level is concerned with developing instructional strategies for an individual topic, and the macro-level with developing an overall instructional strategy for the entire learning event. At the micro-level, a five-step approach should be used: pre-instructional activities, information presentation, activation of learning, follow-up and remediation. At the macro-level, there are a number of different types of learning events including: structured, unstructured, presentation, choice of explanation, adaptive, how-to, supervised, knowledge-driven, troubleshooting, simulation or laboratory, and reference guide.

The instructional strategy is concerned with how learners are going to learn from your Web-based learning event and describes how learners are going to achieve the learning objectives. The instructional strategy is more than just sequencing the content. It is concerned with how learners will interact with and learn from your Web-based learning event.

When developing your instructional strategy you need to consider the:

- characteristics of the learners;
- type of knowledge you are delivering;
- learning outcomes and the objectives of the learning event;
- prerequisite knowledge.

Depending on the objectives, there are different types of approaches that can be used in designing and developing learning events to ensure learners do in fact learn.

LEARNING STRATEGIES

There has been much research conducted, regarding the development of learning strategies. Gagné (1977) developed the nine events of instruction, as follows:

1. gaining the learner's attention;
2. informing the learner of the objective;
3. stimulating recall of prerequisite learning;
4. presenting the stimulus material;
5. providing learning guidance;
6. eliciting the performance;
7. providing feedback about performance correctness;
8. assessing the performance;
9. enhancing retention and transfer.

Dick and Carey (1990) summarized the sequence of instructional strategies as follows:

1. pre-instructional activities
   - motivation
   - objectives
   - entry behaviours;
2. information presentation
   - instructional sequence
   - size of the instructional unit
   - information
   - examples;
3. learner participation
   - practice
   - feedback;
4. testing
   - pre-test
   - embedded tests
   - post-test;
5. follow-through
   - remediation
   - enrichment.

For a Web-based learning event a five-step instructional strategies approach is appropriate.

Pre-instructional activities

Pre-instructional activities consist of gaining learners' attention to help motivate them to learn. It also includes informing learners of the objective and assisting them to recall prerequisite knowledge.

The most important step in any learning event is to focus learners' attention on the task at hand and try to ensure that this attention is enough to sustain their interest throughout the learning event. Attention can be gained through the use of an unusual or different graphic interface, or some eye-catching sequence. Colour, graphics and photographs can also be used to attract learners to events. Movement is always eye-catching, so using animations and video may be appropriate to attract and motivate learners. Text in the form of a story or case study can also be used.

Learners need to be informed of what is going to happen during the learning event so they can focus on that event and determine what is relevant to them and what is not. A learning plan can also be developed that includes the event objectives. At this level, the objectives can be written in less formal terms to aid learners to better understand what is required of them during the event.

To enable learners to put the new information into a context based on what they already know, it is important that the learning event should contain something that causes them to recall a prior event, evaluate it and use it as the foundation on which the present event will build. One way of doing this is to link the current event to relevant sections of the previous event. Learners more easily understand information if they know the similarities and differences between their existing knowledge and the new knowledge to be learnt.

Information presentation

When the new materials are presented it is important that learners are told of the generalities of the operation, linked to a context or background, along with the facts, knowledge and skill associated with what is to be learnt. It is also important that attention is focused on the relevant parts of the instruction. Content sequencing is very important when presenting information to learners. There are a number of different ways in which content can be sequenced:

- *Chronological.* Using the chronological approach your topics are arranged according to when various events occurred. A typical example here is a history lesson.
- *Order of performance.* Here topics are arranged in the order they are performed. A typical example here is the taking apart of a machine or similar device where it is important for learners to know the correct sequence of events. In some circumstances, backward chaining can also be used with great success.
- *Known to unknown.* This approach asks you to consider what learners already know and build on it. An example of this approach is the learning of a new computer software program, with prior knowledge of a relational database used to introduce the topic and relevant links inserted.

- *Taxonomic.* This approach is common in science and engineering, and has been used to classify learning objectives. A typical example is the structure of organisms in biology.
- *Simple to complex.* Here the topic is arranged to begin with the most simple concept or task and to add to it in a logical fashion until the topic has been covered. An example of this is the very young child learning about the members of the immediate family and the relationship of each to the others, and then moving upward and outward into the wider community. The simple-to-complex approach also has some of the elements of the known-to-unknown approach.
- *Problem-centred.* A learning event may be centred around a problem or exploration of an issue. The learners are presented with a problem and have to develop solutions or interpretations. The Web-based learning materials need to provide learners with a context to learn the essential knowledge and skills involved in the problem. For example, a learning event on Web page layout may be based on the problem, 'Which Web development tool do I use to develop my Web pages?'

One of the most important things Web-based learning materials can do for learners is to provide them with a means of encoding, or understanding, the information. The materials might show the steps involved in carrying out a task or they might suggest how learners can complete a task. A list of annotated links might be provided that gives learners some guidance on which links are relevant for them. Accessing many links can be time-consuming and inefficient in terms of learning, but providing information about the links helps learners know which sites will be most beneficial.

When designing informational materials for the Web environment, it is important to keep one major characteristic of learners in mind: they prefer to scan from screen to screen to find information that is relevant to them. Learners rarely read entire screens and seldom read in a linear manner. For this reason it is important to have the information 'chunked'. A chunk of information is the smallest piece of information that makes sense by itself. It may be a paragraph or a multimedia file, but it must be independent enough to make sense to learners without further explanation.

When information is chunked it must be arranged so that learners can move easily between chunks within the Web page. The chunks should be arranged so that learners can quickly browse the information by scrolling (although this should be kept to a minimum) and linking, but should also be arranged in such a way that they do not become lost in cyberspace. This means that directories, table of contents and a list of links are included in the information presentation component.

Activation of learning

In the activation of learning component, activities are included that allow learners to apply the knowledge they have learnt, and feedback should be given on their performance.

At this stage, learners are expected to respond to all that has gone on before and demonstrate their learning. It is important that this stage is not confused with evaluation. Learners at this stage are still learning; they are not being assessed. There are a number of learning strategies that can be used, requiring learners to compare, classify, induce, deduce, analyse errors, construct support and make abstractions of information given to them. There are many different types of activities that can be used, ranging from open-ended questions, note taking, summaries and researching to the more controlled quizzes, computer-managed learning strategies and facilitator-marked assignments.

As well as providing an opportunity to practise what they have learnt, feedback should be given so that learners can determine if they have performed correctly. If true learning is to take place, learners have to be able to judge how well they have performed compared to some set criteria. This feedback may be in the form of an electronic quiz and the use of more formal feedback available from a CML program. Feedback can also come directly from the facilitator and other learners, for example, when learners submit assignments, the facilitator can comment and return them. For learner comments, the assignments can be placed into a discussion forum.

Assessment of learning

Assessment of learning is concerned with learners demonstrating their total understanding of the topic. This is the evaluation portion of the learning event in which the event designer must devise a methodology to determine if the Web-based learning event has been successful and learning has taken place.

Electronic assessment strategies play a role through the use of CML programs or other assessment packages. However, assessment methods such as tutor-marked assignments and peer assessment are also essential to determine whether learners have achieved the objectives.

Follow-up and remediation

In this component learners are given an opportunity to transfer what they have learnt to other situations and use it in different ways. To help ensure that this happens in an appropriate manner it is important that the facilitator provides sufficient learning practice and feedback to learners about their performance so adjustments can take place. If learners cannot apply what they have learnt to new situations then remediation activities should be provided.

Collaborative learning is a good method of ensuring learners can apply what they have learnt to new situations. Here learners can work on a group project with each having a different role and communicating via a computer forum or e-mail. For remediation, a series of links each with a description can be given and learners can access the ones they need. A more systematic method is to recommend the links that learners should access, based on the results of their CML assessment. Many CML programs can embed the links in the program and learners access them through the feedback section of their results.

Web-based instructional strategies

Table 10.1 overleaf outlines some of the instructional strategies that can be used in a Web-based learning event.

INSTRUCTIONAL STRATEGIES AT THE MACRO-LEVEL

At the micro-level the instructional strategies should follow a five step approach. However, at a macro-level there are a number of different instructional strategies that can be followed for different types of learning events. Following are a series of guidelines for the development and structure of Web-based learning materials. As you consider the design structure of the learning event you need to understand that these structures can be mixed into an infinite variety of combinations. For example, a learning event might consist of a number of modules, each having a series of topics. All of the modules with the exception of module 1 can be set up in an unstructured environment where learners can make choices regarding which module to study first, which second and so on. Module 1, however, is compulsory and would be set up in a structured environment. Within the module itself a variety of structures can be used. The topics can be structured or unstructured, or set up in a presentation mode; part of the module may be adaptive and part may be a troubleshooting guide. The combinations are endless, restricted only by the imagination of the designer.

Structured learning event

A structured learning event simply presents the materials as a hierarchy of topics, one following the other, as in a textbook.

Uses

The structured learning event has a step-by-step format where learners

Table 10.1   *Instructional strategies in a Web-based learning event*

Components of Instruction	Instructional Strategies
Pre-instructional activities	Use text or audio overviews. Pre-test learners to give them some idea of what to expect in the learning event. Issue a challenge to learners: they must solve a problem. Use a case study approach to create interest. Use humour to introduce the topic. Use appropriate multimedia materials to introduce the topic. Use links to stimulate learners' prior knowledge.
Information presentation	Ensure the information proceeds from known to unknown, concrete, to abstract, observation to reasoning and whole to detail. Ensure the information is broken down into manageable chunks. Ensure the information is logically sequenced. Use scenarios to analyse and solve problems. Include examples and non-examples. Include tables of contents and lists of links. Include a frequently asked questions section.
Activation of learning	Use open-ended questions, quizzes and computer-managed learning assessments. Use collaborative work. Use a discussion forum. Make use of e-mail communication. Use the Web for research.
Assessment of learning	Use quizzes and computer-managed learning assessments. Use facilitator-marked assignments. Include collaborative projects and assignments.
Follow-up and remediation	Provide feedback from computer-managed and instructor-marked assignments. Use hyperlinks to enrichment materials. Challenge learners to complete learning activities.

have to move from one piece of information to the next in an organized manner. It is best used in conjunction with other types of learning events.

Pros

It is straightforward to construct. However, other elements such as animation and sound could be added.

Cons

It is not ideal as a total instructional method, as it is designed in a linear fashion and it can contribute to information overload.

Table 10.2   *Structured learning event*

Guideline	Indicators of success
Provide a structured learning event with a list of appropriate topics and sub-topics.	A standard start page that includes a navigation bar that learners can use to move from one level of topic page to another, backward and forward, is provided. A navigation link that brings the user from page to page is provided. Asks learners if they would like their pages in a different language. A structure of topics into which the learning event is divided is provided. A consistent set of links is in evidence. A recap page is included. An assignment and/or additional resources page is in evidence.

Table 10.2 shows the indicators of success for a structured learning event.

Unstructured learning event

An unstructured learning event is one that allows learners to follow links to relevant keywords, words or concepts that catch their attention. An unstructured learning event is like the Web itself, where learners can look up a topic and that topic can provide a list of new links. The unstructured learning event should begin with a start page leading to a main page that introduces the topic or provides a summary of the topic. In the topic's description, words can act as links to other pages in the learning event that explain the topic and provide yet more links. This type of learning event allows learners to explore the topic quickly and easily and to see how the pieces of information relate to one another.

Uses

The unstructured learning event allows learners to explore all the relevant information in the learning event in a manner suitable for them. It can be used with the structured learning event if all the topics in the learning event are unstructured while the topics themselves are structured.

Pros

It allows learners to see how the materials they are engaged in learning are structured.

Cons

It can contribute to information overload. Learners can be lost in 'hyper-space' or become disorientated, and they can be distracted with nice-to-know information.

Table 10.3 shows the indicators of success for an unstructured learning event.

Table 10.3   *Unstructured learning event*

Guideline	Indicators of success
Provide an unstructured learning event with a list of appropriate topics and sub-topics.	A standard start page that includes a navigation bar that enables learners to return to the start of the learning event at any time is used.
	A navigation link is provided that brings the user from page to page.
	A structure of topics into which the learning event is divided is provided.
	A consistent set of links is provided.
	A recap or overview page is provided.
	An assignment and/or additional resources page is in evidence.
	Asks learners if they would like their pages in a different language.
	Learners are able to use the learning event to explore all the topics.
	Learners are able to construct their own knowledge maps of the system, showing how the elements relate, thus teaching them to categorize and create a hierarchy of information.

Presentation learning event

A presentation learning event is designed simply to provide information and is typically delivered in a linear fashion. Presentations can be in the form of a slide show or a guided tour of a topic. It should be made clear to learners that the linked pages are intended as a presentation. Tell them that they are free to move from screen to screen going backward and forward, taking their time to read and understand the information.

Uses

This learning event is used to give the learner an overview or guided tour of the topic, and is ideal where the structure is complex or where a simple step-by-step procedure is called for as part of the topic. It can be used with either a structured or an unstructured learning event.

Pros

It is an ideal way to introduce a topic and/or provide a guided tour.

Cons

It is not ideal as an instructional method by itself, as it is designed in a linear fashion.

Table 10.4 shows the indicators of success for a presentation learning event.

Table 10.4   *Presentation learning event*

Guideline	Indicators of success
Provide a presentation learning event with a list of appropriate topics and sub-topics	A standard start page that includes a navigation bar that enables learners to return to the start of the learning event at any time is provided.
	A navigation link that brings the user from page to page is in evidence.
	A structure of topics into which the learning event is divided is provided.
	Asks learners if they would like their pages in a different language.
	An overview of recap page has been included.

Choice of explanation learning event

In a choice of explanation learning event, learners are offered a choice of topic. They may be offered an outline, a detailed explanation or an explanation written with their particular needs or experience in mind. The structure of a choice-driven learning event consists of a start page with a link to a page that contains a list of explanation choices. Learners can view any of these explanations and carry on to the next topic or they can return to the choice page and view another explanation.

Uses

This learning event is best used where there are different levels of learners within the same job family. Here learners can make choices about what they want to see. The choice of explanation learning event can be combined with a structured learning event.

Pros

It can be developed or individualized for a particular type of learner.

Cons

It can contribute to information overload. Learners can be lost in 'hyperspace' or become disorientated.

Table 10.5 shows the indicators of success for a choice of explanation learning event.

Table 10.5   *Choice of explanation learning event*

Guideline	Indicators of success
Provide a choice of explanation learning event with a list of appropriate topics and sub-topics.	A standard start page that includes a navigation bar that enables learners to return to the start of the learning event at any time is provided.
	A navigation link that brings the user from page to page is in evidence.
	A structure of topics into which the learning event is divided is provided.
	The various choices are displayed to learners allowing them to choose one.
	Learners can return and view an alternative explanation if the initial explanation was not satisfactory.
	Asks learners if they would like their pages in a different language.

Adaptive learning event

An adaptive learning event picks the material to be displayed based on information about the particular learner. This structure is similar to the choice of explanation learning event with the difference being that learners have no idea that there are other explanations available. There are a number of possibilities for collecting information about the type of learning event learners will get. Learners can be given a quiz and the level of the learning event set accordingly, or they can be given a choice of explanation learning event.

Uses

This learning event is best used where there are different levels of learners within the same job family. However, learners do not make a choice, as the materials used are based on the learners' profile. The adaptive learning event can be combined with a structured learning event.

Pros

It can be individualized for a particular type or group of learners. The learners' profile can be changed at any time. For example, if learners are having difficulty with a part of the materials it may be that the initial selection was too ambitious. The learners could then be rerouted to a lower level to receive a simpler explanation.

Cons

It can be difficult to implement. Learners can become disorientated.

Table 10.6 shows the indicators of success for an adaptive learning event.

Table 10.6   *Adaptive learning event*

Guideline	Indicators of success
Provide an adaptive learning event with a list of appropriate topics and sub-topics.	A standard start page that includes a navigation bar that enables learners to return to the start of the learning event at any time is provided.
	A structure of topics into which the learning event is divided is provided.
	The various choices are displayed to learners allowing them to choose one.
	Asks learners if they would like their pages in a different language.
	The action page automatically directs learners to different forms of an explanation.
	The links to point the learners back to the preceding page are available.

How-to learning event

A how-to learning event guides learners though the process of performing a specific task so the structure is usually linear, but some diversions to other learning events such as a troubleshooting event can be built in. In this type of learning event, learners are told to follow step by step. A feedback link is provided so that learners can indicate if there is a problem with any of the explanations. If learners are being shown how to use a program, parts of the screen can be used to show illustrations.

Uses

The how-to learning event is used when a guide or procedure is needed for a specific task. It can be used in conjunction with both the presentation and the structured learning event.

Pros

It can be used in a variety of different ways, and can be combined with a number of animation and video utilities.

Cons

It can be difficult to develop.

Table 10.7 shows the indicators of success for a how-to learning event.

Table 10.7   *How-to learning event*

Guideline	Indicators of success
Provide a how-to learning event with a list of appropriate topics and sub-topics.	A standard start page that includes a navigation bar that enables learners to return to the start of the learning event at any time is in evidence.
	A navigation link is provided that brings the user from page to page.
	A structure of topics into which the learning event is divided is provided.
	The basic structure is linear but has diversions to other learning events such as a troubleshooting guide.
	It is combined with a choice of explanation tutorial to take account of situations in which learners are starting from different points.
	It is combined with a reference structure to help learners look up terms they are unsure of.
	Asks learners if they would like their pages in a different language.

Supervised learning event

In a supervised learning event, learners undertake various tasks with the help of a tutor or mentor. In this kind of event a tutor can send learners to a certain page in the material, and can monitor learners' actions there. Similarly, learners can monitor the actions of a tutor, thereby learning by example. Learners can also start a communication session with a tutor to discuss various relevant topics, and the tutor can assign a list of pages for learners to read. The structure of a supervised learning event will vary depending on the system of supervision being used. Two possible structures that can be used in this type of learning event are the directed and the observed.

Uses

The supervised learning event is used when learners need guidance through a complex learning task.

Pros

It can be used in a variety of different ways. It allows practice and direct intervention in the learning process.

Cons

It can make learners overly reliant on tutorial help. It can be difficult to set up.

Table 10.8 shows the indicators of success for a supervised learning event.

Table 10.8   *Supervised learning event*

Guideline	Indicators of success
Provide a supervised learning event with a list of appropriate topics and sub-topics.	A standard start page that includes a navigation bar that enables learners to return to the start of the learning event at any time is in evidence.
	A navigation link is provided that brings the user from page to page.
	A structure of topics into which the learning event is divided is provided.
	The tutor is able to send learners to a particular page.
	The tutor is able to observe the learner's page and intervene to point out relevant parts of the page, give advice or make suggestions.
	Asks learners if they would like their pages in a different language.

Knowledge-driven learning event

A knowledge-driven learning event is one that operates by asking learners a question at the end of the topic. Selecting the correct answer will bring learners to the next page of the learning event. The structure of a knowledge-based system is related to the questions asked. The learner proceeds from a topic page to an answer page; an incorrect answer page can provide a link back to the topic page, but a link can also be provided back to the prerequisites given in the start page so that learners have a chance to do some basic revision before trying again.

Uses

The knowledge-driven learning event is best used in conjunction with either a how-to or a structured event, as learners are asked a question at the completion of one topic and selection of the correct answer will bring them to the next topic.

Pros

It is easy to develop. It allows learners to work through the materials by revisiting previous materials before proceeding. It can be useful in getting learners to read the materials more carefully.

Cons

Development of poor questions can hamper learners' progress.

Table 10.9 shows the indicators of success for a knowledge-driven learning event.

Table 10.9   *Knowledge-driven learning event*

Guideline	Indicators of success
Provide a knowledge-driven learning event with a list of appropriate topics and sub-topics.	A standard start page that includes a navigation bar that enables learners to return to the start of the learning event at any time is provided.
	A navigation link is provided that brings the user from page to page.
	A structure of topics into which the learning event is divided is provided.
	A random question methodology that discourages learners from pressing the answer links until they get the correct answer is provided.
	Flags are set to prevent learners from proceeding until the question has been answered correctly.
	Asks learners if they would like their pages in a different language.

Troubleshooting guide

A troubleshooting guide usually consists of a set of questions representing common problems and actions to perform in response to those questions. It is ideal for hypertext implementation because links can be provided to relevant pages to match the answers to the questions learners ask. A troubleshooting guide may need to provide links to other topics or modules. For example, if learners find themselves in a situation where they need to follow a step-by-step guide, a reference can be placed to a link to instruct the browser to open a new browser window and load the new link. This is done to prevent learners from getting lost after completing a step-by-step guide or another learning event. Each subsequent page after the start page should consist of a question designed to narrow the area of the problem. Learners answer the question by clicking on an appropriate link and follow the pages until they reach a successful solution or there is nothing else to try. Learners reach a resolution page if they obtain a successful solution or a 'failure' page if a resolution to the problem cannot be found. The 'failure' page should contain contact information for someone who is able to solve the problem.

Uses

A troubleshooting event is best used to step learners through a transfer-of-learning scenario. A decision matrix is provided for the learners to determine the most appropriate answer. A troubleshooting guide can also be used as part of a how-to learning event.

Pros

It is ideal for hypertext implementation as links can be provided to relevant pages to match learner questions.

Cons

Learners can get lost in 'hyperspace'.

Table 10.10 shows the indicators of success for a troubleshooting guide.

Table 10.10   *Troubleshooting guide*

Guideline	Indicators of success
Provide a troubleshooting guide with a list of appropriate topics and sub-topics.	A start page that includes a navigation bar that enables learners to return to the start of the learning event at any time is provided.
	A navigation link is provided that brings the user from page to page.
	A structure of topics into which the guide is divided is provided.
	The start page is made up of a series of conditions. Once learners have established that the guide is suitable for them, they can move on to the next page.
	Person contact information is given.
	Person contact information is accurate and the information is included on the final or 'failure' page not the start page.
	Asks learners if they would like their pages in a different language.

Simulation or laboratory learning event

In a simulation or a laboratory tutorial, learners are given the chance to interact with something. It could be a very simple interaction, such as selecting a link representing an action, which will cause the link to load a picture or a video of an experiment after the corresponding action has been performed.

Uses

The simulation or laboratory learning event is used when it is necessary for learners to interact with something. It can be used in conjunction with all types of learning events.

Pros

It allows learners to enter into discussions by getting them to record and discuss predictions. It turns learners into active observers of the simulation's outcome. It helps them build a mental model of the process.

Cons

It can be difficult to design.

Table 10.11 shows the indicators of success for a simulation or laboratory learning event.

Table 10.11 *Simulation or laboratory learning event*

Guideline	Indicators of success
Provide a simulation or laboratory learning event with a list of appropriate topics and sub-topics.	A start page that includes a navigation bar that enables learners to return to the start of the learning event at any time is provided.
	A navigation link is provided that brings the user from page to page.
	A structure of topics into which the learning event is divided is provided.
	The simulation is relevant to the topic.
	The simulations, limitations and assumptions are described to learners.
	Asks learners if they would like their pages in a different language.

Reference guide

A reference guide is a simple list of terms learners may find useful. It can be made up of a menu of terms that provide links to a more complete description of terms, either on the same page or on a different page. It is customary to put the referenced elements all on the same page unless it makes the page too large. A reference guide usually consists of a single page with a main menu and a menu of terms.

Uses

A reference guide is used when a simple list of terms is needed by learners, and has many links to other materials.

Pros

The reference guide is simple to design and develop.

Cons

Learners can get lost in 'hyperspace'.

Table 10.12 shows the indicators of success for a reference guide.

Table 10.12   *Reference guide*

Guideline	Indicators of success
Provide a reference guide with a list of appropriate topics and sub-topics.	A start page that includes a navigation bar that enables learners to return to the start of the learning event at any time is provided.
	A navigation link is provided that brings the user from page to page.
	A structure of topics into which the guide is divided is provided.
	Asks learners if they would like their pages in a different language.

CONCLUSION

It is important to systematically plan the instructional strategy for your learning event to ensure your learners achieve the objectives. On a micro-level, you should use the five-step approach made up of pre-instructional activities, information presentation, activation of learning, assessment of learning and follow-up and remediation. At a macro-level, you should identify the type of learning event you are designing and follow the design guidelines outlined in this chapter.

Chapter 11
Selecting and reviewing learning resources

INTRODUCTION

This chapter outlines the selection of learning resources and Web sites on a systematic basis, so that they assist learners in achieving the learning objectives. The advantages and disadvantages of each learning resource are discussed and a systematic method for selecting the resources outlined. A method is also shown for the selection of relevant Web sites using a checklist.

One of the advantages of a Web-based learning event is that you can use many different sources of information, including multimedia resources. The use of such resources is one of the great attractions of a Web-based learning event. However, if they are used inappropriately it can lead to the gratuitous use of resources and distract learners rather than assist them in attaining the learning objectives. The appropriate use of media can clarify issues and show examples and concepts that would take a great deal of text to explain to learners. To develop media resources takes a great deal of time and effort and may be technically quite difficult, so you must ensure that they are essential to your learning event.

Since it is time-consuming to produce media resources it seems logical to use the existing resources you have available. These may be text files, graphics, photographs, animation, videos and other computer-based programs. These can all be adapted for Web-based delivery, and will complement your learning event and save you time, money and effort. Among the resources you can make use of are other Web sites, since there is so much existing material already available on the Web. But once again you need a systematic method for ensuring the resources are suitable for your Web-based learning event and assist learners in achieving the objectives.

TYPES OF RESOURCES

There are many different types of resources that can be used on the Web, including individual computer files, segments of video-tape and Web sites. In addition, the facilitator is also a resource with whom learners can communicate using computer-mediated means. The types of resources you can include in your Web-based learning event are:

- text;
- graphics;
- photographs;
- presentation programs;
- audio;
- video;
- animations;
- Web sites;
- other computer-based learning materials;
- e-mail;
- discussion forums;
- telephone tutorials;
- tutorials.

Multimedia files including text, graphics, photographs, audio, videos and animations are the traditional instructional resources and form an important part of the information presentation in a Web-based learning event. Electronic presentations are becoming increasingly important resources and are easy to convert to a Web-based environment. Other computer-based learning materials are also a good source of information. However, before they can be used on the Web they may need to be redesigned.

Web sites are very important sources of information and it seems that there is a Web site on any topic your care to mention. One of the major advantages of a Web-based learning event is that you can link to other sites to enhance your learning event. This can save you time and effort in developing instructional materials.

Another advantage of a Web-based learning event is that you can communicate with learners through both synchronous and asynchronous means. While the synchronous methods of communication can be problematic at present they will become increasingly important. Asynchronous methods of communication such as e-mail and discussion forums are useful resources as they allow learners to communicate with one another and the facilitator and this information can be stored for later retrieval.

The traditional forms of synchronous communication, such as the telephone and face-to-face tutorials are still relevant in a Web-based learning environment. The telephone allows synchronous communication in the form of learners asking questions of the facilitator. Face-to-face tutorials allow synchronous discussion between the facilitator and learners and between learners.

Text

Text is used widely and is a common source of information. The advantages of text are that it:

- can be developed or individualized for a particular type of learner;
- is relatively simple to convert to HTML;
- can supplement other types of media;
- is easy to update;
- can be easily structured using headings, summaries and reviews;
- will download relatively quickly.

The disadvantages are that a great deal of text is often needed to explain visual types of information, and can create visually boring screens.

Graphics

Graphics form a significant part of the instructional message. The advantages are that they:

- enable better communication, especially when used in conjunction with text;
- can be used to present facts and figures in a different way;
- can emphasize certain points;
- can show relationships and ideas;
- act as a form of visual shorthand;
- help learners remember;
- are an effective way to show concepts;
- are an ideal way to vary the presentation.

The disadvantages are:

- They can only use GIF and JPEG file formats on the Web.
- Depending on the size of the graphics, they can take a long time to download.
- They can take a long time to produce.
- The number of colours may be limited depending on screen set-up.

Photographs

Photographs can form a significant part of the instructional message, and the use of digital cameras makes photographs relatively easy to produce and incorporate into the learning event. The advantages are that they:

- can show an actual object or process;
- are relatively easy to incorporate in the learning event;
- are an ideal way to vary the presentation.

The disadvantages are that they:

- can only use JPEG format on the Web;
- can contain superfluous and distracting detail;
- date quickly, especially when people are involved;
- make it difficult to see the internal working of objects;
- can take a long time to download;
- can be quite large from a file-size perspective, if not compressed correctly.

Presentation programs

Electronic presentation programs are easy to convert to HTML and they can be used in a variety of ways. Quite often they come with their own Web navigation features. The advantages are that they:

- can incorporate multimedia;
- can include embedded links;
- can be easily updated;
- allow learners to control the pace;
- can be presented in a fixed sequence.

The disadvantage is that they may not be consistent with the format of the learning event.

Audio

Audio can be used to enhance and personalize an instructional message to learners. Audio is simple to record but can be slow to download because of the relatively large file size. The advantages are that it:

- is relatively simple to record and edit;
- can be used to highlight or emphasize the instructional message;
- can be controlled by the learner;
- permits learner review;

- adds a human touch to the presentation;
- can be updated relatively easily;
- helps the facilitator to motivate and encourage learners by varying intonation, pace and sound effects;
- is ideal for learners who have reading difficulties.

The disadvantages are that it:

- can be large from a file-size perspective, if not correctly compressed;
- can take some time to download;
- requires digital editing;
- requires learners to have speakers attached to their computers;
- lacks the speaker's visual cues;
- has a fixed rate of information flow.

Video

Video is used to show movement as part of the instructional message. Because of file size limitations, only short segments should be used in a Web-based learning event. The advantages are that it:

- can be recorded quickly using digital cameras;
- can show movement;
- can be used in conjunction with audio;
- can be controlled by learners;
- permits learner review.

The disadvantages are:

- file size can be large if not compressed correctly;
- it can take a long time to download;
- quality may be poor and may break up depending on the bandwidth;
- the window size may make it difficult to see fine details in the video.

Animation

Animation is effective in showing the internal working of a variety of things such as a machine. The advantages are that:

- it can be used in conjunction with audio;
- learners can control the animation;
- it is an ideal way to vary the presentation.

The disadvantages are that they can be time-consuming and expensive to produce and large files may be slow to download.

Web sites

There is a vast array of information and resources existing on the Web. This gives both event designers and facilitators access to materials that can be linked to the learning event to assist learners in achieving the learning outcomes. The inclusion of links to other Web sites can save a great deal of time and expense in the development of Web-based learning materials. The advantages are that:

- they are an ideal way to include multimedia resources;
- sites are easily accessible;
- they are easy to incorporate into the learning event;
- other Internet-based resources such as Usenet are available, as are FTP sites;
- they can be used for remediation and/or enrichment;
- learners can interact with sites and people outside the realm of the learning event;
- they are a good way to add interest and motivate learners;
- they allow access to libraries and government sites;
- they are a good way to vary the presentation.

The disadvantages are that the:

- site may be so interesting that learners become sidetracked;
- site may contain technically incorrect information, or misinformation;
- site may not be at the appropriate level for the learners.

Computer-based training programs

With the availability of plug-ins, the use of relatively small file size computer-based training programs over the Web now becomes possible. However, the design of the material must be relatively simple to play over the Web or else it will be very slow to run. The advantages are that they:

- can be interactive;
- can be learner controlled;
- can give immediate feedback;
- can provide some tracking of learner progress;
- can incorporate multimedia;
- are a good way to vary the presentation.

The disadvantages are that they:

- should be relatively simply in design;

- may be slow to download depending on the bandwidth learners are using;
- may require the download of a plug-in.

E-mail

Today e-mail is used extensively and can be an essential component of a Web-based learning event, as it allows the facilitator and learners to communicate with one another. Stored e-mails can be another information resource. The advantages are that:

- they are an easy, rapid and readily available method of communication;
- they can be used with groups;
- listserves can be used;
- they can be relatively inexpensive;
- address books make it easy to send e-mails;
- they are a good way to supplement Web-based learning materials;
- they can be used to focus on learners' specific learning problems;
- they can be used to overcome learners' feelings of isolation;
- the facilitator can provide rapid feedback on assignments;
- they can create a feeling of a learning community;
- learners can communicate with others not directly involved in the learning event;
- they can be sent at any time that learners have a question;
- they are a good way of sending reminders;
- they can be stored for future reference.

The disadvantages are that:

- the facilitator can become overloaded;
- attachments may overload learners' e-mail accounts;
- learners can have an unrealistic expectation of turn-round time for mail from the facilitator;
- learners may ask questions that require long, detailed answers;
- many learners ask the same questions.

Discussion forums

Discussion forums allow interaction between facilitator and learners, and between learners, and help overcome some of the learners' feelings of isolation. The information stored in the discussion forum can also be useful as a resource for learners. The advantages are that they:

- can allow learners to ask questions and have them answered;

- can help overcome learners' isolation;
- can allow for interaction;
- can allow the facilitator to track learners' performance;
- can help keep discussions on track;
- allow learners time to formulate questions and answers;
- are a good way to vary the information presentation.

The disadvantages are that learners:

- may have unrealistic expectations of the facilitator;
- may get off track if the discussion is not moderated correctly;
- may not participate;
- may exhibit inappropriate behaviour.

Telephone

The telephone has long been used as a synchronous method of supporting distance learners, and it is still relevant and useful for a Web-based learning event. The telephone allows learners to access a very useful resource, the facilitator. The advantages are that:

- it is a synchronous method of communication;
- it can personalize discussion and instruction;
- learners are familiar with the medium;
- learners can discuss specific learning problems;
- learners can discuss non-instructional problems;
- the facilitator can keep in regular contact with learners and monitor their progress;
- the costs of local phone calls are relatively cheap.

The disadvantages are that:

- learners can telephone the facilitator at inappropriate times;
- learners' problems or questions may be repetitive;
- some learners may not want phone calls from the facilitator at the office or at home.

Tutorials

In some cases it may be necessary to have traditional tutorials in a Web-based learning event. This is particularly true when skill-based training is involved. In a face-to-face tutorial, learners not only gain access to physical resources but can use the facilitator and other learners as sources of information. The advantages are that:

- learners can interact with one another, which helps overcome the feeling of isolation;
- learners can interact with the facilitator;
- learners are more likely to interact with other learners and the facilitator if they have met them;
- learners are more relaxed about asking questions;
- many different activities can be undertaken in the tutorial;
- the tutorial can have a motivational effect on learners.

The disadvantages are that it may be difficult to organize a common time and date, and learners also need to progress to the same point in the learning event for the tutorial to be useful.

SELECTING RESOURCES

There may be a range of useful resources existing in your organization or commercially available. If so, it may be both cost- and time-effective to include this material in your Web-based learning event. However, since the resource has not been designed specifically for your learning event, you must be careful in selecting which materials should be included.

Two things should be kept in mind in selecting resources for your learning event. The first is the cost of purchase or development. The resource may be ideal for your learning event, but if it is very expensive to produce or purchase then it is probable that you cannot use it. The second point is the bandwidth with which learners access your learning event. If they access the event via a narrow bandwidth then it may not be possible to download large video files because of long download times. However, if learners access the event via a wide bandwidth then it may be possible to use video files.

Other Web sites and pages will be a resource that you can include in your learning event as hyperlinks. The number of Web sites on any particular topic is vast but, since they can be produced by anyone and cost very little to place on the Web, you must apply selection criteria to determine what is and what is not suitable. The number of Web sites is so extensive that a separate checklist has been developed for evaluating Web sites.

When reviewing existing resources, use the following information from your WID to ensure the resource is appropriate.

- The characteristics of the learners, including their preferred learning styles.
- The bandwidth learners will be using to access the learning event.
- The learning outcomes and objectives of the learning event.
- The content to be covered in your learning event.
- The learning activities that will be used in conjunction with the resource.

All resources should be reviewed in the light of the learning outcomes and objectives for your learning event. While the resource may be instructionally sound, it is of little use if its objectives don't match your learning event's objectives. Alternatively, it may be of little use if the resource's objectives do match your learning event's objectives and if it is not aimed at the learners' learning level.

Resource characteristics can be classified as:

- learning outcomes;
- information presentation;
- instructional strategy;
- audience;
- authenticity;
- format;
- cost;
- copyright.

Information should be presented in a structured way to ensure learners obtain maximum learning effectiveness. For effective learning materials, you should include good advanced organizers, summaries and glossaries. The technical quality of your resources depends on information being up to date and, above all, correct. It should be free of spelling and grammatical errors, as well as advertising, gender and racial bias.

The most useful kind of resource is designed to be self-instructional. If items such as interactive exercises, self-help and review questions are included, it makes the material more valuable as a learning resource. The resource should hold learners' interest and motivate them to learn more by including exercises, and the information should be relevant and written in an interesting way.

The usefulness of a resource for your learners will depend on the audience for whom it was originally designed. Also important is whether learners other than those for whom it was designed can use the material or whether it is too specific.

The resource you are reviewing should be authenticated, that is you should know who the authors are, their qualifications and positions, and who the producers and publishers are. Information such as intended audience and other users of the resource will also help you establish its authenticity.

The format of the resource has an important bearing on whether it is useful for your learners. If the resource is a video file, for example, can it be used in sections and converted to a file type that can be downloaded or streamed in a reasonable amount of time? If the video is viewed at a reduced size, will it still be distinguishable and useful? If the resource is a large graphic file, can it be converted to a GIF or JPEG file and downloaded in a reasonable amount of time? Alternatively, can a thumbnail be used in most cases with learners rarely needing to expand it? Does the resource require a specific plug-in for viewing? If it does it may be a disadvantage, as the installation of a plug-in could present learners with difficulties. The quality of the resource is also important. For example, if you are using a high-quality video file that has been converted to a streaming format and streamed at a low bandwidth, will it still be of an acceptable quality? The amount of effort required to convert the resource into a useful format will be important. For example, you may have a very useful computer-based training program, but for viewing on the Web it may need to be completely redesigned. In addition, a plug-in will have to be used, so the effort in converting the program may not be worth it compared with developing another resource.

Cost is always a factor in using an existing resource. If it is free, it may be appropriate to use the resource. Alternatively, if it is expensive or requires a run-time licence per user, it may not be feasible. Another factor is the cost of conversion for use on the Web. If the resource is copyrighted, copyright release will have to be obtained. Not only is that time-consuming but copyright fees can also be costly. If it is both costly and difficult to obtain copyright, then it may not be appropriate to use that resource.

Checklist for evaluating existing learning resources

The following checklist will help you evaluate resources to determine if they are suitable for your learning event.

Learning outcomes

1. Does the resource cover your learning outcomes and objectives?
2. What percentage of the objectives does the resource cover?
3. What objectives are not covered?
4. What proportion of the resource is not relevant?
5. Does the resource cover the main body of instruction?

Information presentation

1. Are the learning outcomes and objectives explicitly stated?
2. Is the resource well structured and organized?
3. Does the resource teach or act as an information source?
4. Are there adequate examples?
5. Does the resource contain advanced organizers, summaries and glossaries?
6. Does the organizational content of the resource match those of your learning event?
7. Is the resource designed for the specialist or for general use?

8. Is the resource up to date?
9. When was the resource last updated?
10. Is the resource likely to be updated in the future?
11. What percentage of the total resource is usable?
12. Is the resource factually correct?
13. Is the resource free from race, gender, religious and other bias?
14. Is the resource free from undesirable advertising and other bias?

Instructional strategy

1. Is the resource designed for independent learning?
2. Are there interactive exercises including self-help and review questions?
3. What role do learners have to play with the resource?
4. Does the resource provide meaningful learner participation?
5. Does the resource arouse interest, hold attention and provide motivation?
6. Is the pacing of the resource appropriate for your learners?

Audience

1. Is the resource at the appropriate reading or viewing level for your learners?
2. For whom was the resource originally designed?
3. Can the resource be used with your group of learners?

Authenticity

1. Is the producer of the resource reputable and an authority on the topic?
2. Is there any evidence that the resource was effective for its original purpose?
3. Who else uses the resource?

Format

1. What is the physical format of the materials?
2. If the resource is a computer file, is it suitable for your learning event platform?
3. Does the file format need to be converted to suit your learning event?
4. Is the file size suitable for the bandwidth your learners are accessing from?
5. Does the material require a special plug-in for viewing over the Web?
6. If the resource has to be reduced in size for viewing on the Web, will it still be suitable?

7. What is the technical quality of the resource, and is it suitable for your purpose?

Cost

1. How much does it cost to use?
2. Is there a run-time cost per learner?
3. How much will it cost to convert the resource to a format suitable for your learning event?

Copyright

1. Is the resource copyright-free?
2. If you need copyright release, will it be difficult to obtain?
3. Are there any copyright release fees?

Overall

1. What is your overall opinion on using this resource in your learning event?

Web site evaluation

One of the greatest advantages of Web-based learning is that you can make use of the considerable amount of information already available on the Web. However, unlike other forms of published information anybody can put anything on the Web. In many cases there is no form of editorial review as there is with a book or video production. If you are going to include links to other Web sites you must have some way of evaluating the Web site. Otherwise you may provide your learners with erroneous information that will hinder rather than help them achieve the learning event objectives.

Evaluating Web sites can be considered under the following headings:

- access information;
- technical aspects;
- learning outcomes;
- information presentation;
- multimedia;
- design;
- authenticity;
- navigation;
- links.

Access information includes information about the browser used to access the Web site. This is important as different browsers behave differently. The speed of access to the Web is also of critical importance. A site with a great deal of multimedia, no matter how good the content, will be of little use if access is via a 23.8KB modem. The access speed will be so slow that it will annoy your learners rather than provide them with useful information. You must also have a means of identifying a Web site, usually the URL and a name.

The technical aspect includes points such as the stability of the site. A site that is stable one day and not the next is of little use in your learning event. One of the basic things you must consider is whether the Web pages download in a reasonable amount of time, taking into account the speed your learners will access the Web. Another consideration is the speed at which multimedia files download. While a text page may download at an acceptable speed it may be extremely slow at downloading the associated multimedia files. If a special browser is required, it may not be the one that your learners are using, in which case they will have to purchase or download it, which can be troublesome.

You are interested in the Web site under evaluation in the light of its ability to help learners achieve the learning objectives of your learning event. Therefore it is important to determine which objectives the Web site has the potential to allow learners to achieve. It is unlikely that a Web site will allow learners to achieve all the objectives of your learning event. However, it is important to give an estimate of the percentage of the learning outcomes the Web site has the potential to allow your learners to achieve. You should also determine if the information contained in the Web site covers the main body of your instruction or simply the 'nice-to-know' materials. At the same time you should determine how much non-relevant material the site contains. If your learners need to sieve through page after page of irrelevant material simply to get to the right page, the site may not be worth including.

The way the information is designed and presented on the Web page also has an important bearing on how useful the Web page is to learners. It is of benefit if the objectives are explicitly stated, as this is helpful to learners in letting them know why they are viewing a particular page. The information must also be structured in both content and design. The contents should make use of a heading and subheading structure with the appropriate use of advanced organizers, summaries, glossaries, and self-help questions and tests. The information must also be broken down to manageable chunks so it can be understood and absorbed. Presenting technical or academic articles to a group of learners not familiar with the topic will be of little use even if the article is relevant to the topic under discussion.

An important aspect is the audience for which the site has been designed. If you are reviewing a site designed for medical doctors then it will probably be of little use for other learners. The information on the pages must be correct, otherwise it will only confuse learners. The site should be free of any bias such as race, gender and religion, and free of undesirable advertising. The site should also be free of spelling and grammatical error, and should use either American or British spelling as appropriate.

Another consideration is the design of the Web pages themselves. They should be designed to be functional and attractive, so as to encourage learners to use them. If a background colour is used that makes the text difficult to read, then learners will be less likely to read them. Using too small a font or one that is difficult to read also inhibits the site effectiveness.

As Web sites are established and maintained by a wide variety of individuals and organizations, you must try to authenticate the site as far as possible. You should look for full contact information, as well as information indicating the type of organization, its location and perhaps e-mail addresses and telephone numbers of selected personnel. The domain name gives an indication of the type of site:

- .edu – reserved for educational institutions;
- .com – generally indicates a commercial or for-profit organization;
- .gov – reserved for governmental sites (mostly in the USA);
- .org – once reserved for non-profit organizations, but now used by a wide variety of organizations.

Sites with the above domain addresses have more credibility than others because they are from large organizations, which will have some sort of editorial control over them. The date of production and last update also affects the site's credibility. A site that was produced many years ago and not updated since may very well be out of date and not of much use to your learners.

Recently, a number of new domain names have been considered, including .biz for business sites, along with names to indicate sites for children and young people. These names are scheduled to become available in 2001.

The navigation structure of the site must be clear and easy to use. You must be able to tell from the first page how the site is structured and organized so that learners can find the information they want. There must be adequate links between the pages, and learners must be able to move backward and forward between them. If any icons are used for navigation, it must be clear what their function is.

The hyperlinks used must be easy to identify and logically grouped together, and they should be consistent between each page. Each page should also contain a link back to the site's main or start page. The links must be reliable; there is nothing more frustrating than a 'dead' link or a link that leads to a 'page not found' error.

Web site evaluation worksheet

The following checklist will help you evaluate a Web site.

Access information

1. At what speed are you accessing the Web site?
2. What Web browser are you using?
3. What is the URL of the Web site you are evaluating?
4. What is the name of the Web site?

Technical aspects

1. Is the site stable?
2. In general, are page loading times acceptable?
3. Do you have to download software to view the pages or multimedia elements?
4. Do pages with multimedia items take an acceptable time to download?
5. Can you view the pages with all common browsers?

Learning outcomes

1. Does the site cover the learning outcomes and objectives?
2. What percentage of the objectives does the site cover?
3. What objectives are not covered?
4. What proportion of the site is relevant?
5. Does the site cover the main body of instruction?

Information presentation

1. Are the objectives of the pages explicitly stated?
2. Is the site well structured and organized?
3. Does the organization of the content match that of your learning event?
4. Is the information broken down into manageable 'chunks'?
5. Is the material logically sequenced?
6. Have the same kinds of items been placed together?
7. Are advanced organizer, summaries, glossaries and self-help tests included?
8. Are there adequate examples?
9. Is the Web page designed for specialist or for general use?
10. Is the information accurate?
11. Does the page use correct spelling and grammar?
12. Is the Web page free from race, gender, religious and other bias?
13. Is the Web page free from undesirable advertising and other bias?

Multimedia

1. Do the sounds, graphics or video files enhance the site's message?
2. Are the multimedia files clearly labelled?
3. Is it easy to view the multimedia files?

Design

1. Is it your overall impression that the screen designs are effective?
2. Do the pages have a cluttered look?
3. Are appropriate colours used to enhance the readability and visual appeal of the Web page?
4. Is the overall design both functional and attractive?
5. Is the font readable at the given size?

Authenticity

1. Have the authors been clearly identified?
2. Are the authors of the site authorities in their fields?
3. Has the author's e-mail been included?
4. Can you tell from the domain name where the page originates (ie .edu, .com, .gov, .org)?
5. Has the site been produced by an organization?
6. Has this organization been clearly identified?
7. When was the page first written?
8. When was the page first placed on the Web?
9. When was the page last updated?

Navigation

1. Can you tell from the first page how the site is organized and what options are available?
2. Do the icons clearly represent their function?
3. In general do you have to scroll to obtain all the information?
4. Are there adequate links between pages?
5. Are the links both forward and backward?

Links

1. Are the links easy to identify?
2. Are the links logically grouped?
3. Is the layout consistent from page to page?
4. Is there a link back to the home page on each supporting page?
5. Are the links relevant to the subject matter?
6. Are the links reliable?

Overall

1. What is your overall opinion on using this resource with your learning event?

CONCLUSION

Using existing learning resources and Web sites can save the designer a great deal of time and effort in developing a learning event. However, learning resources used must be selected on a rational basis or they may distract learners more than assist them. Web resources must also be selected on a systematic basis, as not all the material on the Web is technically correct. Finally, Web sites must be selected on the basis that they assist learners achieve the objectives of the learning event.

Chapter 12
Designing the GUI and screen templates

INTRODUCTION

In any type of learning event it is important for learners to be able to see a recognizable structure. A typical learning event can use a combination of templates and tutorial types. For example, one part might use a step-by-step tutorial while the next part uses a troubleshooting tutorial.

In order to fully understand the learning event, learners need to be able to form their own ideas about the materials and understand the event in their own way. Learning events should encourage learners to develop their own knowledge map(s) and help them better understand what they are learning. A good Web-based learning event should contain some or all of the elements outlined in the following guidelines.

Learning event advanced organizer page

Guideline

Provide a learning event advanced organizer page that contains the appropriate elements.

Indicators of success

- A 'why this topic is important' to learners area is included in the introduction.
- A general guide as to how to approach the material is included.
- Details are included of what is expected of learners and how the learning event is intended to be used.
- A list of the prerequisites required (and links to those prerequisites) is included.
- A guide to completing the learning event and a tentative schedule are included.

- A list of learner goals and objectives is provided.
- A list of the resources learners will need is included.
- Learners are asked if they would like their pages in a different language.

Learning event main page

Guideline

Provide a learning event main page (or pages) that contains the appropriate summary elements.

Indicators of success

- A graphic or icon-based summary is in evidence that places the materials in the context of information learners have already learnt and provides links to that information.
- Learners are asked if they would like their pages in a different language.

Learning event page – general

Guideline

Provide a typical learning event page that contains the appropriate elements.

Indicators of success

- There are links to pages that include answers to questions learners may want answered.
- There is an introduction and a brief summary of the topic.
- There is a review element to consolidate learners' knowledge.
- There is a 'lesson' area, where instruction takes place and examples are presented.
- There is the opportunity to practise.
- There is a feedback element to help identify learners experiencing difficulty with the materials.

Learning event assessment page – general

Guideline

Provide a typical learning event assignment page that contains all the appropriate elements.

Indicators of success

- The opportunity is provided for learners to put the knowledge learnt into their own words and/or understanding.

- There is a practice area, where learners can test their knowledge by answering quizzes or problems.
- The opportunity is provided for learners to perform 'experiments' and try simulations using what they have learnt.

Learning event laboratory page – general

Guideline

Provide a typical learning event laboratory page that contains all the appropriate elements.

Indicator of success

- The opportunity is provided for learners to perform 'experiments' and try simulations using what they have learnt.

MATERIALS DEVELOPMENT AND DESIGN

The design and development of good visual materials for any learning event is fundamental to learning. For any learning event to be successful a number of elements must be taken into consideration. This includes analysis of the information you have gathered to date and the determination of the various templates including the text, illustrations and graphics to be used. It should also include consideration of the way the learners' visual perception is applied to the screen design.

It is difficult, however, to state categorically how much material should be presented to learners, as this is based on the topic being presented and the stated objective(s). For the most part, if the guidelines and indicators of success are followed and the learning materials have been broken into manageable 'chunks' for learners to digest, then the mix of text, audio and graphics can be considered appropriate.

There are two standard methods of communication used in the design and development of learning events: graphics, such as illustrations, maps and graphs; and text. Learners are generally very good at recognizing and identifying visual patterns. Graphics are useful where the information to be presented requires that complex relationships between items are both shown and made clear. Text deals with abstract notions and expresses logical deductions.

Item association

Guideline

Provide a screen design for learners appropriate to the requirements of the materials and the needs of learners.

Indicators of success

● The same kinds of item are placed together.
● Those items functionally related to one another, such as text and graphics, are placed together.
● The order of the various elements is logical and systematic.
● Item importance is apparent and a hierarchy has been established.

Learning materials

Guideline

Provide standard methods of communication within the body of the learning materials.

Indicators of success

● The design includes illustrations, maps, graphs and text as appropriate.
● Graphics show overall patterns, trends and shapes.
● Graphics show complex notions such as single, multiple or sequential diagrams.
● Graphics depict spatial relationships.
● Graphics depict objects and create an impression of immediacy.
● Graphics attract and engage learners.
● Graphics remain meaningful when scaled down.
● Error messages that are placed below the response area are provided.
● All required display components fit into the available space.
● Prompts that tell learners what to do are in evidence.
● Prompts that are only displayed when active are in evidence.

Other kinds of information

Guideline

Provide for other kinds of information, in particular the active components, and visually emphasize the most important parts of the materials to direct learners' attention.

Indicators of success

● Titles are emphasized using a larger type size and put at the top of the screen.
● Particular components of a diagram are distinguished using colour.
● Parts of the screen are emphasized using movement.
● Colour is carefully used as a means of grouping and emphasizing.
● No more than two or three colours at a time are used except where it helps clarify the logical structure of the information.

- Extra colours are not used just for their own sake.
- Colour complements the layout.
- Colours are not used in ways that contradict their conventional meanings (for example, red is not used for an 'all clear' sign).

Amount of materials

Guideline

Provide visual relief (space) for learners.

Indicators of success

- Information is not crammed on to a single screen.
- The screen is not artificially filled out.
- Large amounts of space are used around a group of related components rather than having each item spaced out.

Screen templates

Guidelines

Provide screen templates that have several standard menu items presented on every screen.

Indicators of success

- The title of the materials, individual topics, frame numbers and the like are for the most part placed at the top of the screen.
- Routeing information such as back, next, search and quit are for the most part placed at the bottom of the screen.
- Templates are used as a way of ensuring consistency between screens.
- Templates are consistent in their layout to help learners quickly identify items.
- Template items appear in the same place on each screen.

Font type and size

Guideline

Provide a font and text size appropriate to learners' needs and consistent with the requirements of the materials.

Indicators of success

- Text size is approximately three to four millimetres tall.
- A serif typeface is used and kerned for maximum legibility.

- For maximum font legibility the use of the following fonts has been considered: New Century Schoolbook; Bookman; Palatino.
- The following fonts have been avoided for use in text-based materials on learners' screens: Times; Times New Roman; Arial; Helvetica.
- Arial and Helvetica fonts have been considered for use in banners and/or headlines.
- Approximately one and a half line spacing is used.

Displaying text

Guideline

Provide text-based materials reduced to its essential minimum without appearing to talk down to learners.

Indicators of success

- The text is written in 'good' English, in a conversational style, with the normal rules of grammar and punctuation applied.
- The required text fits into the space available.
- The difficulties for learners in scrolling back and forward through a sequence of screens is avoided by presenting the text in sections, each on a single page.
- The print-on-paper convention of filling the entire screen with text is avoided.
- The amount of text that can be displayed on a single screen based on font size, line spacing and the space taken up by permanent screen features has been correctly determined.
- The text is divided into screen-size sections, by using short words and short sentences including the use of point form.
- The number of words per screen varies so that only complete sections of the text appear on one screen.

Arranging text

Guidelines

- Provide text arranged on the screen to suit the reading needs of learners and consistent with the requirements of the materials.
- Provide text arranged on the screen to suit the reading task(s) of learners and consistent with the requirements of the materials.
- Provide text colour appropriate to the reading needs of learners and consistent with the requirements of the materials.

Indicators of success

- Left-justified text is used to format the text.

- Right-justified text or centred text is avoided, since it produces a ragged left margin that disrupts reading.
- Titles and headings are centred, and the location of the heading (centred or left-justified) is used to signal different levels of heading.
- Line endings coincide with the grammatical boundaries rather than splitting words at the end of a line.
- Paragraphs are indicated by an additional blank line rather than by indenting the first line.
- Space is used to separate text items – the greater the distance, the greater the distinction.
- Indenting is used to indicate subsidiary information.
- Subheadings separate items and also summarize their content.
- Colour is carefully used to distinguish and highlight text components.
- The reading tasks of learners are considered, and the presentation of the material is compatible with the style required.
- If learners have to pick out one item from a set of items, the items are displayed as a vertical list.
- Different font sizes are used to distinguish and emphasize headings – the larger the size, the greater the degree of importance to be conveyed.
- Underlining of text is not used except to highlight a link.
- Capitals are used for headings but not for continuous text.
- Bold-face and italics are used occasionally for highlighting words or phrases, bearing in mind that italics can be difficult to read depending on the font used.
- Flashing text is used sparingly, if at all, and only to draw attention to critical warnings or important messages.
- No more than three text colours are used in a display, as learners find it difficult to keep track of different colour codes.
- Colour coding, like other techniques, is consistent across screens.
- A text and background colour combination is chosen that maintains a high contrast between the text and the background.
- The following colour combinations are used on screens throughout the learning event:

Text	Background
White	Magenta, red, green, blue
Yellow	Blue
Cyan	Blue
Green	Yellow, white
Magenta	Blue, white
Red	White, yellow, cyan, green
Blue	White
Black	White, yellow

- When using dark text on a bright background, contrast is good but the brightness of the display does not make reading unpleasant.
- The brightest colours are used for the most important information.
- On black backgrounds the hierarchy of importance – white, yellow, cyan, green – is followed. White or yellow is used for headings or other emphasized items, and cyan or green is used for the main body of information.
- Distinctions between items that are not intended to imply an order of importance are made by choosing colours close together in the hierarchy, for example white and yellow.

Text and graphic linkage

Guideline

Provide linkage between text and graphics appropriate to the needs of learners and consistent with the requirements of the materials.

Indicators of success

- When text and associated graphics are presented on the same screen the graphic is placed as close as possible to the text.
- When text and associated graphics are presented on separate screens a simple and clear method of flipping from one screen to the other and back again is provided and the learner is told how this is done.
- Perceptual grouping is used to indicate the relationship between the graphics and text. For example, if data are shown in a graph in green, then the same data should also be displayed in green text.
- Thumbnails are used whenever possible to reduce physical graphic size.
- Captions are included in the graphic whenever possible.
- Graphic labels are adjacent to the graphic elements to which they refer rather than in a 'key' system.
- Graphics are not interspersed irregularly throughout the text, but rather they are placed in a consistent position from screen to screen.

Text lists

Guideline

Provide text lists appropriate to the needs of learners and consistent with the requirements of the materials.

Indicators of success

- When items in the text form a list this is shown visually by placing the items in a column.

- Lists are differentiated from the surrounding text by spatial positioning such as indentation.
- When lines in a list have more than one item they are not separated by using extra space unless they need to be compared. For example, in a list of family names a separate column is not required for forenames.
- Different colours are not used for things that are the same.

Tables

Guideline

Provide tables appropriate to the needs of learners and consistent with the requirements of the materials.

Indicators of success

- The table is designed in the same way in which it is to be read.
- Horizontal reading of the table is not impaired. Data within each column are related, but items in rows have a functional relationship, that is they all belong to an item in the first column.
- Where information in the table is to be compared in two directions, the tables have both row and column headings.
- A brighter colour is used to distinguish headings from the body of the table.
- Headings are repeated on each screen in the same positions when the table extends across more than one screen.
- Generous spacing is used between table rows but with just enough space between columns to separate them.
- Columns are not spread out just to fill the screen.
- Large gaps between columns are avoided when items vary greatly in length. This is also improved by reversing the order of the columns.
- Single, hairline or dotted lines are used to outline each cell in the table.
- Double vertical lines are not used between columns or different coloured columns, as this draws the eye down the page.

Graphics

Guideline

Provide graphics appropriate to the needs of learners and consistent with the requirements of the materials.

Indicators of success

- The type of graphic used (photographs, drawings, cartoons, illustrations and icons) is determined by reviewing its role or function.
- When the function of the graphic is to motivate, attract attention,

excite, amuse or persuade, photographs, illustrations or cartoons are used.

- Photographs are used to convey a mood (photographs are very accurate, and they show everything, whether relevant or irrelevant).
- Illustrations are used selectively so as to portray only what matters.
- A sequence of graphics is used for showing a series of events or a process.
- Consideration for the target audience is carefully considered before selecting the graphic.
- The graphic does not distract learners from the material to be learnt.
- The image is effective because it fulfils the precise role for which it is intended.
- All graphics have captions or titles.
- Images with too much detail are not used at a small scale as this detail is lost on the screen.

Icons

Guideline

Provide icons appropriate to the needs of learners and consistent with the requirements of the materials.

Indicators of success

- Colours are harmonious and kept to a maximum of two.
- Icons are regular in shape, and positioned on the screen so the active areas do not overlap.
- Borders and/or outlines are used to separate icons when they are in close proximity.
- Icons are grouped into their respective categories of navigation (back, next, forward, etc) and service (print, glossary, resources, etc).
- The number of icons is limited to the essential.
- The icon does not obscure other valuable information on the screen.
- The icon is understandable.
- The icon is unambiguous.
- The icon is informative.
- The icon is distinct and memorable.
- The icon is familiar.
- The icon is legible.

Diagrams

Guideline

Provide diagrams appropriate to the needs of learners and consistent with the requirements of the materials.

Indicators of success

- Diagrams exploit the two-dimensional space and portray information that is already spatial, such as a map.
- Diagrams depict processes such as the changing of a wheel on a car or more conceptual things such as the flow of money within the economy.
- Diagrams explain structures or relationships, such as chemical diagrams that show the structure of compounds, Venn diagrams that show logical relationships and family trees that show genealogical relationships.
- Diagrams rely on simplification for their effectiveness, as highly realistic images are likely to confuse learners.

Charts and graphs

Guideline

Provide charts and graphs appropriate to the needs of learners and consistent with the requirements of the materials.

Indicators of success

- The charts and graphs are graphic representations of numbers.
- Different forms of charts or graphs are used for different purposes.
- The graphical formats enable quantitative relationships to be grasped quickly and provide visual relief.
- Charts and graphs are used as the complexity of the data increases.
- Charts and graphs are used as the accuracy of the data decreases.
- Charts and graphs are used when learners are expected to see two or more distinct visual relationships or studies in the data.
- Pie charts are used for showing the proportion of parts to a whole.
- Bar charts are used for comparing amounts independently of the total.
- Bar charts are combined to show more complex relationships.
- Pictorial charts are used for less numerate learners and for special visual impact.
- Line graphs are used for showing trends involving a variable scale, such as time or temperature, and for showing relations between mathematical variables.
- All the components of the chart are labelled, including the title of the chart or graph, the axes and what they represent, the increments and the amounts that each sector, bar or symbol stands for.
- A visual hierarchy and coding system are established for the chart or graph.
- All colours, increments and labels are consistent throughout the learning event, so that comparisons can be easily made.

- The size of the symbols remains constant throughout the materials.
- Relationships are not exaggerated.
- The overall shape of a graph is largely unaffected by changes in size, given reasonable screen resolution, and the text attached to the graph remains readable.
- Numbers and words are used where accuracy is required to aid in the understanding of the chart.
- The visual organization of the display matches the structure of the content.

3-D graphics

Guideline

Provide 3-D graphics appropriate to the needs of learners and consistent with the requirements of the materials.

Indicators of success

- The graphic is used to encourage three-dimensional thinking.
- The graphic is used in the depiction of objects whose spatial construction is of particular importance.

Interaction

Guideline

Provide learner control over the materials and the examples used.

Indicators of success

- Alternative routes through the materials are developed.
- Learners are given control over the rate at which information is displayed.
- When displaying text that does not fit on a single screen, paging is used rather than scrolling.
- A simple mechanism is provided to enable learners to control forward and backward movement.
- The display of graphics is paced for best visual effect and maximum information transfer.
- Interlacing graphics are used, that is learners are able to watch an image form rather than see a blank screen that suddenly switches to a full display.
- Graphics are displayed before text on a screen.
- Speed and order of presentation are used to draw attention to parts of complex images in order to focus on parts of the images that have changed from one screen to another.
- Auto-scrolling is not used.

Movement through the learning materials

Guideline

Provide movement through the materials appropriate to the needs of learners.

Indicators of success

- A routine is incorporated that times the interval between learner paging of successive screens so that if the response rate is abnormally slow the program can take alternative action or provide additional prompts.
- A method is provided for rerunning part of the program without having to start again at the beginning.
- A method is provided for the program to recognize learners via the use of passwords. This enables learners to come back to the materials and be able to start where they left off.
- Orientation information is displayed continuously, letting users know where they are within the program.
- A consistent means for moving from one screen or module to the next is provided.
- A facility is provided for getting back to the main options the program offers, such as using a pull-down menu or offering learners the option of taking an alternative route through the program.
- The learner route through the program is shown without cluttering up the screen.
- Learners have access to a course map, which shows the paths that can be taken through the materials.

Menus

Guideline

Provide a menu or menus appropriate to the needs of learners, the topic and the program.

Indicators of success

- A short form or abbreviated menu of single words is used and arranged down the left- or right-hand side or along the bottom of the screen.
- A menu is avoided when a free response in some dialogue form would be more suitable.
- Full-screen menus are used at the start of a topic or when the main activity is complete and it is a question of what to go on to do next.
- A random order is not used when the items have a natural sequence.

- When items fall into groups, the grouping is shown visually. Otherwise alphabetical order is used.
- When a selection is made from a displayed menu, the item about to be picked is highlighted.
- When the result of the selection cannot easily be reversed, then the selection is confirmed by some secondary action.
- Menu items not currently selectable are indicated by the use of grey on a black and white display.
- The selected item is clearly indicated.

Controlling the cursor

Guideline

Provide cursor control appropriate to the needs of learners and consistent with the requirements of the materials.

Indicators of success

- The cursor is used for various kinds of interaction as well as for menu selection.
- Cursor movements are sufficiently accurate for the purpose intended.
- The selected object is clearly indicated.

Audio

Guideline

Provide audio appropriate to the design of the materials and consistent with the requirements of learners.

Indicators of success

- Files are less than five minutes in length.
- The narration is active and interesting and uses a personal style.
- There is good tonal variation and the voice is clear.
- The sound volume is consistent from screen to screen.
- The user can pause and play back the file an unlimited number of times.

Video

Guideline

Provide video appropriate to the design of the materials and consistent with the requirements of learners.

Indicators of success

- The video is essential for learning the topic.
- Users can pause and play back the file an unlimited number of times.

CONCLUSION

Learning events should be designed so as to allow learners to perceive the structure of the event because this will help learners to develop a better understanding of what they are learning. The guidelines set out in this chapter support this approach to design.

Chapter 13

Developing flowcharts and storyboards

INTRODUCTION

Some people will argue that both flowcharting and storyboarding for Web-based course development are obsolete given the nature and variety of course development 'tools' available in the market-place. However, without a route map, a direction and a list of places to visit, as a developer of Web-based learning materials, your journey may be a waste. You may miss sights along the way, and worse still you may never know when and if you have reached your final destination.

FLOWCHARTS

Simply put, a flowchart is a map of the place where the journey begins, the various detours that can be made along the way, where the journey will end and when it will be reached. Like any good map it should show alternative routes between the various places that can be visited on the journey, and how quickly a person can travel from one place to another using the alternative 'routes'. Typically a flowchart is developed to help the designer link all the information that together makes up the Web-based learning event. It also helps the designer get back on track after yet another distraction.

A typical flowchart can and will change, depending on the nature of the project, the materials under development and the people doing the development work. There are no established rules or protocols for flowcharts. Some will use different box shapes to identify different screen types and others will simply use information boxes linked together in a particular way. A flowchart will also evolve as the information in the WID is refined.

Following is a description of two kinds of flowcharts. The first is a very comprehensive chart, which for the sake of simplicity will be referred to as a Type 1 chart. It is made up of information boxes that show how each screen is linked to the others. It is based on the learner profile and is typically used by three of the people in the materials development team:

1. The materials designer, who uses the chart to ensure all topics are covered, all screens are linked to one another and each screen has a unique identification number.
2. The programmer, who uses the chart to ensure that all screens are put into the learning event and that they are linked together correctly.
3. The evaluator, who uses the chart to verify the navigation in the learning event and to ensure that no screens have been omitted.

As is detailed in Chapter 7, a learner profile is an outline of what learners need to learn in order to become competent in a particular skill area. A typical profile is made up of a number of rows called 'bands', and each band contains a number of title boxes that describe the competency or skill that has to be learnt. Typically these competencies or skills are written in the form of learning objectives, which describe how that competency or skill is to be attained. When you are planning a Type 1 flowcharting task, consider the profile band title as a general learning objective (GLO) and look on each of the topics in the band as specific learning objectives (SLOs) (see Figure 13.1).

When developing this kind of flowchart, the band title or GLO typically becomes your topic overview screen, preceded by the topic menu page. At the topic overview screen, you outline the topic and provide an advanced organizer for learners to help them construct knowledge from their experience (see Chapter 2 for a discussion of the concepts of constructivism). Each topic in the profile band then becomes the screen or screens where the actual learning is presented. These are your SLOs.

The learning materials content is derived from the sub-profile (see Chapter 7). For example, under the GLO, 'List the essential brewing raw materials', malt, hops, water, yeast and adjuncts are listed. It is from this list that you will develop the learning materials such as text, animation, video and the like that will appear on the learners' screen. The information contained in the sub-profile is the basis for your instructional learning objectives (ILOs) (see Figure 13.2).

Regardless of the kind of flowchart, it should provide those who use it with an overview of the topics that have to be covered during the learning event and directions on how to get from one place to another.

The Type 1 flowchart contains very specific information for its users. Figure 13.3 shows a typical Type 1 flowchart box.

Figure 13.1 *Typical profile band showing general and specific learning objectives*

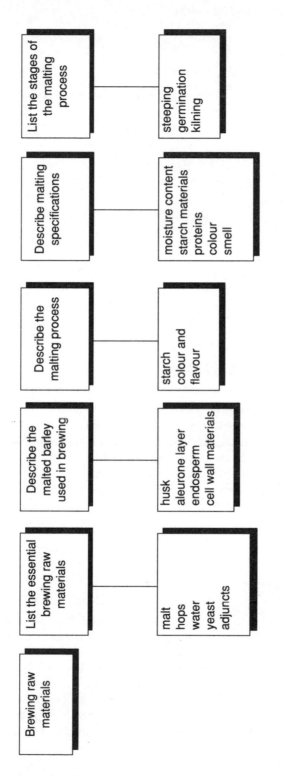

Figure 13.2 *Typical sub-profile showing instructional learning objectives*

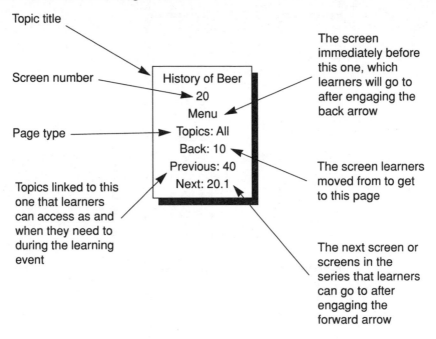

Figure 13.3   *Typical Type 1 flowchart box*

Figure 13.4 shows all the various topics in a particular learning event.

The second kind of flowchart, the Type 2 chart, is also based on the learner profile but presents the information in a very different way. This type of chart uses different box shapes to show the various kinds of screens used in the learning event (see Figure 13.5).

In the Type 2 flowchart the information contained in each box is much less than in the previous chart. Here the event designer simply uses topic titles and screen numbers, and lets the arrows depict previous, back and next screens.

STORYBOARDS

Storyboards like flowcharts have no established rules or protocols. As with the flowchart, a typical Web-based learning materials storyboard evolves from a basic plan to fit the needs of a particular learning event development project. For the most part, storyboards developed for a Web-based learning event are not typical visual outlines used to track visual information. They are usually descriptive, and outline in plain text notes for the programmer, screen text and possibly a basic outline drawing of what the intended graphic, illustration or chart is to look like. They might also list video and/or animation files.

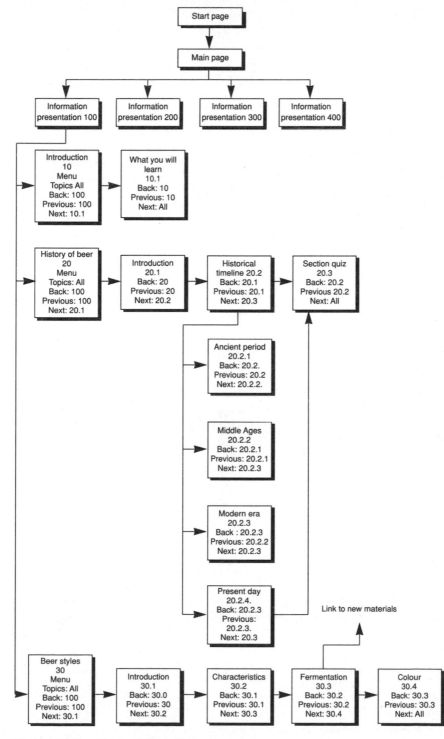

Figure 13.4 *Typical Type 1 flowchart*

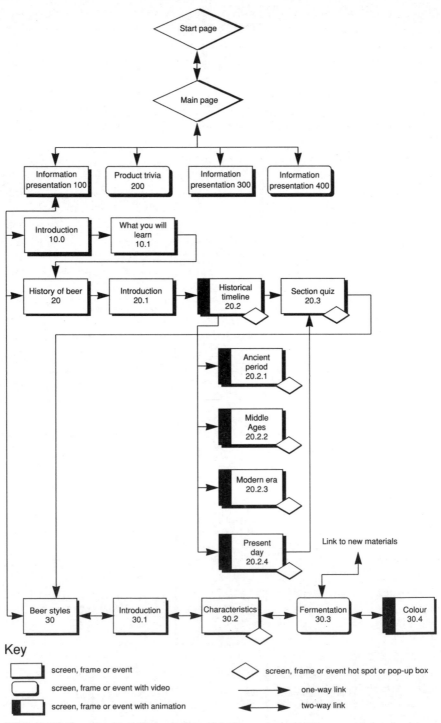

Figure 13.5   *Typical Type 2 flowchart*

Unlike a film script, a Web-based learning event's storyboard does not require a sequential storyline. When you develop the flowchart it is done in a sequential format, that is, one topic physically follows the previous one. The same is true for the storyboard; one topic will follow the previous one. This is done, however, just for the convenience of writing the storyboard and putting it together. The random access nature of a Web-based presentation means that as a designer you have to focus on the potential connections to other pages, resources, modules, topics and Web locations as you develop the storyboard.

Based on your flowchart you will need to link various parts of your storyboard together. These links can be bi-directional, connecting two topics that depend on each other for support and clarification, and unidirectional links, which have a one-way dependency. For example, if you have a series of cross-references between a particular procedure and a number of text screens that describe that procedure, these are bi-directional links. Learners in this case may first read the procedure from the text screens or just follow the procedure until they need help, when they refer to the screens.

Learning materials with the most dependencies are those where the topics being described are concrete and hierarchically organized. For the most part, given the current restrictions with the technology for Web-based learning, much of the materials you will be designing will be developed in a hierarchical manner. However, as you develop the materials, you will have to map out the dependencies based on how you think learners will access the information, not on how the information itself is organized.

Following the brewing example, if learners need information on yeast dosing, for example, they want rapid access to the part of the learning event that shows how it is done. But yeast dosing happens to be in the middle of a learning event topic that begins with the brewing process. So when learners look up the screens that describe yeast dosing, it's important that they are able to get to the information very quickly, but it's equally important for them to be able to get back to the beginning of the topic. This mirrors the way learners using a textbook as part of a traditional learning event reference the material. They look up the topic in the book's index, turn to the page that discusses it and then flip backward until they get to the beginning of what they need to know. Technical documents, instructional materials and reference materials are constantly being consulted in the middle of procedures, because that's where learners run into problems and need additional information. It is very important therefore that learners should be able to page both forward and backward in the procedure and get to the beginning of the procedure with a single button.

Storyboards for different kinds of learning events have different dependencies between the various elements. For example, the actual procedure for yeast dosing has far fewer unidirectional links between each of the operations. Within the procedure itself the flow is pretty much set. The primary bi-directional links in this kind of learning material are those where there is a common technique that is explained in a common section and used in a number of other topics. This way, learners who already know how to carry out yeast dosing can simply follow it on the screen. Learners who don't know can review the materials and then return to the methodology. The screens for yeast dosing, on the other hand, are predominantly simple and merely follow each step in the process.

A reference guide, however, is very different. Here the materials presentation section is strongly dependent on the implied procedures involved in whatever is being taught, if for no other reason than because the materials take learners through each of the steps of learning. It is critical for learners to begin at the right place and to understand what is to be learnt over the course of the learning event, as each part of the event builds on the previous one.

More important from your point of view as the developer is the sense of building learners' knowledge in a structured, ordered way and understanding how the materials should be organized to support this. The storyboard provides a useful way for you to control and track the learning event by letting you see its overall layout and how it flows from one part to the next while permitting you to examine the contents. This way the storyboard can begin defining the screens in terms of the information that has to be covered along with providing a view of the overall structure of the learning materials and how the connections are necessarily more complex in a Web-based learning environment than in a traditional face-to-face learning environment.

As your learning event evolves, your storyboard will grow, serving as a reference for what's already been done and where it fits with the other parts of the learning event.

Developing the storyboard

When developing a storyboard, a simple rule of thumb suggests that a short series of four or five screens can be used to describe one competency or skill shown in the learner profile. Generally speaking you can assume this one competency or skill to be a module. A module is typically described as a basic unit of learning materials, a block of information that can take the form of text, an audio component, a video component or a graphic of some description, which stands alone in its informational integrity while at the same time serving as part of the materials you are developing. The key to a module's definition is that it should be a complete body of information based on its position and function in the storyboard.

As you review your flowchart you have to consider how learners are going to deal with each page or screen that you are describing. For example, many of the current concepts for structuring information comes from the organization of print-based materials. In terms of actual style, Web-based learning materials are no different from print-based media. What is different, of course, is the environment and the way linking allows learners to access the page with little or no preamble. What this means is that the designer has to give careful thought to how Web learning materials are developed and linked together. Should the learning event be developed as a presentation? Should it be in an unstructured environment where learners can enter at any point and make further choices once into the topic? Or should the event be structured so that learners are linked from one concept to the next in a building-block approach? Or can the event be designed using a mix-and-match approach that combines a variety of structures?

Whatever choice you make, you must constantly keep in mind that the Web page, or at least the first page in the 'set' of four or five pages that make up a module, needs to be more independent than similar pages in print-based learning materials. Headers and footers need to be more informative and possibly more elaborate in that you may want to repeat certain information on each page to help make the page or presentation free-standing. This, of course, presents you with the problem of creating materials that are both easy to use yet full of complex content.

One strategy is to apply one of the fundamental rules of writing, that is telling the reader who, what, when and where. A Web page always needs to tell learners who created it so that they are confident it is part of the learning event they are dealing with. All learning materials need clear titles to capture learners' attention. Bear in mind that the header may be the only thing learners see for valuable seconds as text and graphics download, depending on the speed of the page in loading on to their computer screens. A misleading or ambiguous header will not help them recall prerequisite learning or enhance its retention and transfer. The page should be dated in some way, as it is important for learners to evaluate the worth of the learning materials under consideration, and learning materials have to be current. In an age where information is considered to have a 'worth', timeliness is an important element in helping learners know that the materials are worth interacting with. In terms of where the page originated, make sure the materials are identified as belonging to a particular learning event or presentation in a learning event. This is particularly useful when learners have to 'drill down' into unstructured resource materials as part of an assignment.

One of the keys to developing a good storyboard is to remember that in a Web-based event you have no way of knowing what learners have read, seen or heard before getting to the topic you are developing. In the traditional learning environment you can assume that learners have finished

Part 1 before starting Part 2, and you can introduce technical terms in Part 1, knowing they will be needed in Part 2. Another assumption is that learners have taken the responsibility to learn these terms. However, in a Web-based event no such assumptions can be made as you have little or no control over what materials learners have encountered before. You need therefore to develop your storyboard assuming learners have seen nothing else before getting to your materials.

Having determined the topics, the next thing to consider is the links. Links are the way you direct learners from one part of a module to another. You roughed out the links in the flowchart, but now you have to consider how each one will work. A cross-reference, for example, is one kind of link. In a book, when one paragraph ends at the bottom of the page, you can assume that the next paragraph begins at the top of the next page. You can also assume that when learners finish one paragraph, they will automatically start reading the one below it. In a Web-based learning event neither of these assumptions will necessarily hold true.

Once you open up the prospect of linking from one part of the story-board to another, the assumptions about sequence and flow no longer apply. If there is no screen, there can be no next screen to go to. It becomes necessary therefore for you to define the flow from topic to topic and to define the connections within those modules. Getting around in this network of links between topics is the most basic kind of navigation required of any Web-based learning event, and at each point you need to determine exactly what will come next.

More difficult for you to track, however, is navigation within the modules. You need to consider the following:

● What part of each topic needs such a link and where will the link take learners?
● How do you let learners know that such a link exists?
● Why link to another topic when you could include the information where it is needed?

As you continue to refine the storyboard you have to build in sets of very clear navigational aids. Linking learners from one point of the learning event to another or to resources either in the event itself or on the Web often leaves learners lacking a sense of where they are within the local organization of information. This means that you have to consider your graphic identity schemes (See Chapter 12) and through the use of text-based overviews and summary screens give learners the confidence that they are where they have to be or want to be, and have found what they are looking for.

Navigation is, however, more than simply moving from one screen to the next. The source of the link is the piece of data that takes learners out of where they are; the destination link is the point where they are to continue after they have clicked on the information. Learners should always be able to return easily to the start or menu page or to some other major navigational point in the learning event, and these basic links need to be present on every page in your storyboard. You will also need to create a graphic identity that signals to learners that they are in a particular part of the learning event, for example the introduction or the advanced organizer or the quiz.

Not all links are so self-contained. Many links are one-way and learners may or may not return to the point they left to pursue the link. Likewise, the destination of a given link might itself contain a number of other links that learners might follow instead of returning to the original source location. Links from text out to graphics, to explanatory text or to some other kind of material should be considered closed, so that learners navigate the link, see, read or hear the information at the other end and have no choice but to return to the source. Links from one screen to another, to video segments or to any other part of the learning event from which there is no such logical closure can be considered open-ended links.

Every learning event page should contain at least one link. Dead-end links have no place in learning materials, as they frustrate learners and are a lost opportunity to move them forward in their learning. If pages, particularly subsection pages, do not contain links back to the start page or some other menu screen, then learners are effectively locked out and unable to access the remainder of the learning materials.

Not all learners enjoy the 'browsing' concept the designer sometimes builds into the storyboard through links. Learners of time-critical documentation systems, for example, are more interested in quick, reliable search and access, not only to related information at the destination end of links but also back to the original source from which they began searching.

As you link the various elements and components of your learning event together, remember the goal is to provide learners with the information they need in the fewest possible steps and in the shortest time. This means that you have to develop an efficient hierarchy of information to minimize the number of steps through the various menu pages. Research has shown that learners prefer menus with a minimum of five to seven links (sound familiar?) and they prefer a few 'dense' screens of choices rather than many layers of simplified menus. You don't need many levels of menus to overwhelm learners with too many choices. For example, if you follow the research and provide just five menu items, and then drill down through two layers of nested menus, the total number of choices would be 25. Not too bad, you say, but if you used three levels of nested menus, the number would increase to 125! If you provided seven choices and three nested menus, choices would add up to more than 340! It becomes very important therefore that you give a lot of consideration to the structure and organization of your materials.

CONCLUSION

For maximum functionality and legibility your learning event design should be built in a consistent pattern of topic units all sharing the same basic layout, themes, writing conventions and hierarchies of information. Your goal is to be consistent and very predictable. Learners should feel comfortable exploring and learning from the materials you have produced. This consistency and predictability starts with the development of materials standards, continues with the development of the graphic user interface and screen templates, and culminates with the development of flowcharts and the writing of storyboards.

Chapter 14
The process of inputting your learning materials

INTRODUCTION

The process by which your learning materials are inputted into your Web-based learning event is similar to the way articles make their way from draft copies to published documents. The materials are initially created, keyed in, edited, proofread, formatted, assembled, tested and eventually published. This is most often done by circulating and recirculating the materials through a systematic series of checks and tests, performed by different individuals with different responsibilities.

This chapter examines the process by which your learning materials are assembled and arranged into a publishable online course, and includes development and design guidelines, which can serve as a useful reference during the process of inputting your materials.

MEMBER ROLES

Most Web-based training courses require the skills and expertise of at least three and (depending on the size and complexity of the materials) sometimes more individuals. In Chapter 6, you were presented with a detailed description of the particular responsibilities required of each team member in building a Web-based learning event. From previous steps, you will have also created and established the instructional elements, assessment guidelines, and GUI and screen templates that will be used in your learning event. Now you are ready to input your materials and complete the final stages of publishing your online course.

For the purposes of describing the process of inputting your learning materials, this chapter focuses attention on the responsibilities of the core team members of most Web-based learning events:

● instructional designer (ID);

- subject-matter expert (SME);
- Web application programmer (WAP);
- graphic artist (GA).

As the materials are crafted into a publishable format, the core members (and possibly others) will participate in one or more of the following steps:

1. keying in all textual materials;
2. proofreading the materials;
3. formatting the materials for delivery to a Web browser;
4. adding graphics and other multimedia elements;
5. programming assessments and required interactivity;
6. quality checks and software testing.

These steps are shown in Figure 14.1.

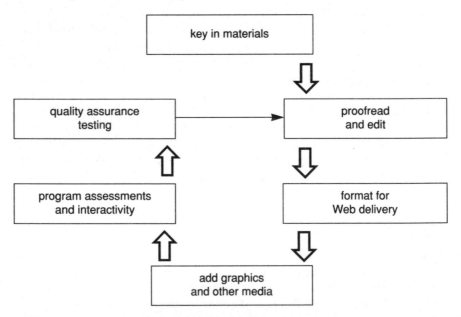

Figure 14.1   *Inputting your materials*

Keying in textual materials

Before any learning materials can be presented in your course, they need to be created or converted into an electronic format. While some of the materials may need to be keyed into a computer from hard copy, most will probably be assembled from a collection of hard and soft copy originals.

If your materials already exist in a soft copy format, the process becomes relatively easy, as they can be edited, proofread and passed directly to the WAP for conversion to HTML (or other page formatting language you may be using). If your materials exist as hard copies only, they will need to be either scanned in and converted via optical character recognition (OCR) software to a usable software format, or typed directly into a word processing program.

If you have several hundred pages of hard copy materials, it's probably wise to establish a method for scanning and conversion, as it will greatly reduce the time and effort needed to turn hard copy text into an electronic format. Diagrams, illustrations and photographs can also be scanned relatively quickly, and passed to the graphic artist for any touch-ups and/or needed modifications. If the learning materials are new, the person generating them will probably be using a word processing program, which may also have the ability to save documents directly to HTML. This can help reduce a step in the overall process.

Once the materials have been converted into an electronic format, they can then be passed to the WAP (who may also participate in this initial stage) for final formatting.

Proofreading the materials

The responsibility for proofreading the learning materials generally lies with the instructional designer and the subject-matter expert. It can also help to have an independent person review the text, who will read it solely for the purposes of catching any errors that may have been missed by those who are more concerned with the actual content itself.

The materials will need to be checked for their accuracy and to ensure they are free of any grammatical, spelling or logical errors. Likewise, drawings, illustrations and other images will need to be reviewed to ensure they are current and accurate.

Formatting the materials for delivery to a Web browser

Once the ID and the SME have edited and proofread the learning materials, they can be passed to the WAP for input and formatting. If a template is being used, this is a relatively straightforward task, as the WAP can cut the text from a word processing document and paste it directly into the HTML page-editing program. The template will also have pre-established tags to define font type, size, positioning etc, which frees the WAP from having to format each and every page individually.

If your learning event uses a page viewing technology such as Adobe Acrobat, the WAP will need to convert the original materials into the appropriate format and test them in the required viewer or plug-in. The formatting stage is also a good time to code and test any required hyperlinks, as well as test the materials for proper display in the targeted Web browser(s).

Adding graphics and other multimedia elements

Once the graphic artist has created, scanned or modified the course's required images, he or she will normally pass them to the WAP to input or embed into the courseware. The images themselves will typically consist of GIF and JPEG files, and it helps if they are named according to a pre-established naming convention. If a template is being used, the WAP can quickly modify the HTML tags to reference the appropriate images. If each page is free-formatted, the WAP and graphic artist will need to work together to decide on the best placement and positioning of the images.

While many graphic artists can also create and modify HTML documents, it is generally best if only one person handles the final HTML code. This will help avoid confusion, stylistic differences or, worse yet, the complete deletion of someone else's work.

Once all images and other media have been added to the courseware, the WAP and graphic artist should review them together. They will need to ensure the images are presented and displayed properly in the target browser(s), and that such issues as placement, resolution, file size and download time are appropriately addressed.

Following a thorough quality check by the WAP and the graphic artist, the draft version of the learning event can then be handed back (or placed on a staging Web server) for review by the instructional designer and subject-matter expert.

Programming assessments and required interactivity

Once the WAP has received the applicable materials, he or she can then begin the process of building the assessments and adding content to the interactive routines in the courseware. The materials themselves may include questions and answers for the assessments, and any text or graphics used in the learning event's interactive routines or exercises.

Normally, any interactivity included in the learning event will have been outlined during the initial design stages and indicated on the course's storyboard or script. The WAP will spend time writing and testing the code (with trial content), and will input the actual content when received.

In cases where a courseware management system is used, the instructional designer or subject-matter expert may use the system to build the assessments. In such a case, he or she then passes the final files directly to the WAP, who integrates them into the appropriate area(s) of the learning event.

Quality checks and software testing

The process of checking and testing the software is the responsibility of all development team members. This may also have to be extended to the Web master or system administrator, who will need to load the courseware on to a Web server, and make any necessary configurations to the Web server itself and any applicable database or courseware management software.

The learning event should be tested from as many different computers, with as many different configurations, as possible. If the event is to be accessed over the public Internet, the team will need to verify acceptable performance when accessed by computers with differing modem speeds and, if applicable, different computer platforms.

It is best to approach this stage systematically, and use a checklist to make sure nothing is missed. The items on your checklist will depend on many factors, including the complexity of the software, targeted browser types, bandwidth issues and other software and hardware requirements.

Quality assurance checklist

A typical quality assurance checklist consists of the following:

- All learning content is accurate and presented without errors or confusion.
- The materials are free of spelling and grammatical errors.
- The general arrangement of the materials correctly follows the pre-established guidelines.
- All navigational links are set correctly.
- All pages have been formatted correctly and display properly in the target or required Web browser(s).
- The page numbering scheme or nomenclature is correct.
- Graphical elements display properly at the targeted screen resolution and colour depth.
- Any included audio, video or animation clips play correctly.
- If applicable, the learning event performs properly in different versions of Web browsers and browser plug-ins.
- Download times are acceptable (given the user access and bandwidth requirements).
- Any required client-side software works properly on the required platform.
- The courseware performs acceptably when accessed by many simultaneous users (load testing).
- Learner log-in names and passwords work properly.
- Assessment pages display their questions properly.
- The results from assessments are correctly submitted to the back-end

database or courseware management system.
- Courseware features such as live chat, e-mail, discussion forums and audio/conferencing work properly.
- Any security requirements are properly adhered to.

Once the quality assurance tests are completed, copies of the checklist should be given to all team members, who can make any necessary corrections or modifications to the materials or the software. The entire process then repeats itself, until all tests pass without fail, and the learning event is ready for publication.

CONCLUSION

Learning materials undergo a process of inputting, arranging and testing, which culminates in the published online course. This chapter discussed the requisite steps in the process.

Chapter 15
Evaluation

INTRODUCTION

The evaluation of a Web-based learning event can be used to help you better understand the environment in which the learning takes place. This environment includes the organization, the learning materials themselves and the use of media, delivery methodologies and various administrative details. It also includes learners' belief as to the overall effectiveness of the learning event or the learning materials being used.

Evaluation is a judgement regarding the worth or value of something. Typically the evaluation process is divided into two parts. The first is a formative procedure related to learning event management while the second is a summative procedure related to the learning event as a whole. The outcome of the first procedure is for the most part learning event modification. The outcome of the second procedure may also be learning event modification. However, its primary function is to help you address issues of learning event continuance.

EVALUATION MODEL

There are many evaluation models that can be used to assess the worth of a learning environment. However, the Kirkpatrick model stands out in terms of its overall simplicity and ease of administration. Furthermore it addresses both the summative and formative procedures needed for Web-based learning materials evaluation.

The Kirkpatrick model outlines four evaluation levels (see Table 15.1). The model suggests that a number of different evaluative tasks have to take place at each level. This would appear to indicate that as the impact of the evaluation becomes apparent the tasks have to change to ensure the validity of the evaluative procedure.

Table 15.1   *Model overview*

	Evaluation Content	Data Collection
Level 1: Reaction	This evaluation is a measurement of learners' feelings and opinions about the course just completed.	The type of information collected here relates to methods of instruction, course content and institution, learning materials and facilities.
Level 2: Learning	This evaluation is a measurement of what has been learnt as a result of the learning event. It examines the facts, skills and attitudes the learners have gained from the event.	The type of information collected here relates to learners' achievement of the learning event objectives.
Level 3: Behavioural Changes	This evaluation is a measurement of the behavioural changes occurring as a result of the learning event just completed.	The type of information collected here examines individual learner behaviour/performance after the learning event. It looks at the changes that can occur and the impact of those changes in a new situation.
Level 4: Results to the Organization	This evaluation is a measurement of the overall impact of an innovation on the institutional environmental.	The type of information collected here relates to costs, improvement of employee morale, turnover rates and productivity on a total organizational/institutional basis.

LEVELS OF EVALUATION

That you should evaluate needs no discussion. The decision that you will need to make has to centre around which level of evaluation you should use to ensure that the learning event or materials retain their high standing. Many organizations do have a commitment to both Levels 1 and 2. A strong argument can be made for the use of Level 3 evaluation to determine the extent of the behavioural change with learners involved in Web-based learning. A case can also be made for the conducting of a Level 4 evaluation to review the viability of a learning innovation. However, in practical terms the inherent difficulties of such an undertaking may result in a less than positive outcome.

Level 1 evaluation overview

Reaction to the learning event or the learning materials

Measuring the reaction to a Web-based learning event or Web-based learning materials at Level 1 involves an evaluation of learners' feelings and opinions about the event and the materials to which they have just been exposed. It is important to emphasize that this reaction is not a measurement of the learning that may or may not have taken place. However, learning theory strongly suggests that if learners are interested and enthusiastic about the topic they are learning, they are more likely to internalize the material.

Evaluation characteristics

Generally a Level 1 evaluation is carried out by an independent evaluator either during a learning event or just after its completion. Level 1 evaluations accomplish two things: first, they provide feedback on the effectiveness of learning events and/or learning materials; and second, they encourage learners to share responsibility for their own learning. Evaluation at Level 1 should be as non-threatening and efficient as possible. If too high an emphasis is placed on the evaluation, it can have an impact on how the learning event itself is perceived by the learners.

Level 1 evaluation can be used to assist you in appraising the overall design of the materials, learners' beliefs as to the effectiveness of the learning event, the use of media, the delivery methodology and various administrative details.

It is important that you understand that the results of a Level 1 evaluation can be subject to a number of variables such as the duration of the event and its content. One of the most important variables, however, is the sense of support learners feel they are receiving from the facilitator and the organization delivering the event. A good Level 1 evaluation instrument should focus on the content of the learning event rather than the amount of perceived support.

In a Web-based environment data can be collected at various points during the event as well as at its conclusion. The compilation of the data is simplified when you use some form of scale. A purely subjective instrument makes it difficult to collect the data, average the results and summarize the comments. But at the same time, if you develop an instrument or methodology that focuses only on answers to direct questions, you may be deprived of possible solutions that could be provided by learners who perceive a deficiency in the learning event.

Conditions necessary for successful evaluation

In a Level 1 evaluation, learners are supplying information regarding their personal reactions to a learning event, and it is important that they feel as protected as possible. In an online environment, learners cannot remain anonymous as they can with a paper-based questionnaire. However, they should have assurances that the data will not be shared with others in any detrimental way.

It is important that your data collection instrument focuses on those other activities that support your learning event and the physical aspects of the Web-based event as perceived by the learners. Failure to do so can result in your evaluation being reduced to a 'happiness index', which simply asks learners how they liked the learning event. One result of a 'happiness' form of evaluation is that it is sometimes difficult to generalize to the population, because the suggestions are often self-cancelling. It is important therefore that you design something that is more than a happiness index. You must decide what you wish to evaluate and then design the questions that will assist learners to supply you with this information. Keep in mind that compiling a large number of responses to short answer questions is a time-consuming process and you really should consider using some form of scale or rating system to quantify reaction.

Since the data are self-reported, you will need to provide a structure to assist learners to focus their comments. Your questions should be clear and capable of being answered briefly, or marked on some form of scale such as a Likert scale, or answered by ticking a simple yes or no. Likert scales are a popular method of choice and usually employ four or five choices that express different degrees of agreement or disagreement and yield ordinal measurements. Using this method your statements are never neutral but favourable or unfavourable to a certain degree. The scores are computed by weighting the responses from five to one for a favourable statement, beginning with strong agreement. This is reversed for unfavourable statements. For example:

The objectives of the learning event were clearly explained in the opening screen	SA A N D SD
My participation in the discussion forum was not a valuable experience for me	SA A N D SD

If the respondent agrees with the first statement and crosses out the A, it becomes a statement that is favourable to the learning event so it can be assigned a value of four. However, if the respondent crosses out the A in the second statement it becomes a negative response to the learning event so it is given a reverse score of two.

When designing your questionnaire remember that people have difficulty making decisions and judgements based on scales of more than five choices. You may also want to consider eliminating the 'N' from the scale and therefore the fence-sitters, and making the scale 'forced choice'.

Strengths

A Level 1 evaluation that uses a large sample from the population avoids the possibility that changes will be made to learning events based on the comments and impact of a few vocal individuals who are either extremely satisfied or unsatisfied. This kind of evaluation can assist you in examining the effect of the event on learners and help you to uncover the reasons behind certain kinds of behaviours. Failure to deal with learner concerns can be extremely costly in terms of dissatisfaction towards other learning events. If you administer a Level 1 questionnaire mid-way through a learning event it could help you to make the next part of the event or subsequent events more effective. As noted previously, if learners generally like a learning event, they are more likely to obtain maximum benefit from it.

Finally, a Level 1 evaluation provides learners with an immediate opportunity to become involved in providing input to decisions made during their learning process. This may result in a feeling of increased involvement and has the potential to increase support for your learning event.

Limitations

The major limitation of a Level 1 evaluation is that it does *not* measure any changes in what has been learnt. In addition, the impact of just one part of the event can taint the instrument. For example, if a simulation exercise does not work as well as it should or the technology overwhelms one part of the event, this may result in learners downgrading the scores they give other things. In some cases, because they are easier to identify and associate, the negative aspects of a learning event are described, often to the detriment of observing the positive points.

Methods of administration

Three methodologies can be used to administer a Level 1 evaluation in an educational setting. These are:

1. an online evaluation administered at different times during the event;
2. an online evaluation administered at the conclusion of the event;
3. individual e-mail correspondence with learners conducted after the event has finished.

Evaluation data can be collected either during or at the conclusion of the event. However, because of the time-consuming nature of post-learning-event correspondence, this methodology is not considered appropriate for use in many organizational settings.

A typical reaction evaluation is designed to help gain insight into the dynamic flavour of the learning event by having learners respond to questions regarding the learning environment, the online coach or event facilitator, the learning materials, the use of media, delivery methodologies, administrative details and learners' belief as to the overall effectiveness of the event.

In a Web-based learning scenario, the learning environment plays as important a role as it does in a face-to-face environment. Consider for a moment the various ways learning online can take place. For example, learners can access the learning event from their organization's learning resource centre or library. Access may also be gained from a public library, learners' offices, home or laptop. Materials can be accessed at a local school, college or university. No matter where and how the materials are accessed, the environment has to be conducive to learning.

From an evaluation perspective you will want to determine how well the learning materials performed in a particular environment. Were learners able to change quickly and easily from one activity to another, and did they accept and understand how the event was designed? You will be concerned with whether the event takes place in the way it was designed to take place and whether learners can achieve all that the event demands of them.

The online coach

The role of the online coach is to provide support to learners in a variety of ways. For some learners, just the fact that a coach is available is enough to provide the confidence needed to meet the needs of the event. For others, the coach provides a variety of support roles via synchronous and asynchronous communication. Like the facilitator in a face-to-face environment, the coach has the capacity to interpret the learning event and shape the kind of learning people get.

The evaluation questions you need to consider here revolve around the coach's ability to interact with learners and his or her ability to interpret the materials in a way that is meaningful. Specifically, evaluation questions should ask learners to consider whether the coach was able to explain to them what needed to be explained and answer learners' questions to their satisfaction.

Questions should also be developed to focus on the how the coach used the learning materials and whether the synchronous portion of the event was presented in a way that was stimulating, interesting and helpful. It is very important that other aspects of what happened during the learning event should also be described, such as the ability of the coach to adjust to differences in learning abilities. Consideration should be given to the coach's encouragement, or lack of it, of active participation through the use of examples and illustrations, the explanation of concepts and the enthusiastic answering of questions.

The learning materials

The questions that need to be considered for this portion of the evaluation have to do with how well the learning materials performed in the eyes of learners. Considerations here include how well the materials matched the real world of the learners, whether the content was organized into manageable 'chunks', whether the sequence was from simple to complex and from concrete to abstract, and whether the materials were presented in a way that was both interesting and stimulating. Your evaluation of these materials should include gathering data regarding the relevance of various assignments and the quality of the various assessments. Questions in this regard should take into consideration directions for the assessments, their length and their difficulty.

The use of media

In an online environment, media are used to provide variety to what is essentially a text-based methodology. Such media may include video, although this is limited unless learners have access to a broadband network, graphics, illustrations, simulations, other visual effects and synchronous and asynchronous communication. In this portion of your evaluation you need to develop a series of short questions that relate to the topic of media in general terms. One question might simply ask, for example, whether the use of the various media was appropriate for this learning event.

Delivery methodologies

With respect to delivery of the learning materials, evaluation questions, like those in the previous section, can be general in nature. Here, however, you should focus on the organization of the learning event, the amount of material covered and time allocated during various parts of the event. Depending upon the nature of the learning event, questions might need to be raised regarding the mix of theory and practice to determine what, if any, skills were learnt.

Administrative details

This portion of your evaluation should determine the ease or difficulty with which information about the event was available to learners. You may want to consider such things as access response time and technical difficulties. You should also determine how information regarding the event was first gained by learners.

Learners' belief as to the overall effectiveness of the event

Your focus in this final portion of the evaluation should be on the relevance of the event to learners. Did they learn what they wanted or needed to learn? Do they now understand the various concepts and principles of the field? And finally, can they apply those principles to other situations?

As well as developing questions in each of the preceding areas, there are three other questions that you should consider for use. These are:

1. What did you like best about this learning event?
2. What did you like least about this learning event?
3. What, if anything, would you like to see changed in this learning event?

Answers to questions like these can provide you with a great deal of insight into various aspects of the event itself. However, you should remember that these responses are very difficult to analyse and should only be used as an indicator of where possible problems might lie. Rather than transcribe all of the responses verbatim, you may wish to consider developing a number of categories, under each of the three questions, such as readings, assignments, tutorials, opportunity to work at one's own pace, forums, coach and the like and simply place the total number of respondents who noted that area on the questionnaire next to the appropriate category.

Level 2 evaluation overview

Level 2 evaluation is the determination of what has been learnt as a result of a learning event. This should include learners' attainment of the learning objectives, and assessment of changes in knowledge, skills and attitude. While Level 1 examines how well the learning was received by learners, Level 2 evaluation focuses on what has been learnt. It is important to understand that there is a difference between the skills learnt and skills that can be demonstrated in another setting. Level 2 evaluation only examines those skills learners are able to demonstrate in the learning setting, and this is not a guarantee that they are transferable to other settings.

Characteristics

There are a number of reasons for evaluating at Level 2. These include the need for quantifiable data about a learning event or learning materials, and the need to determine if the learning objectives have been achieved. A Level 2 evaluation also provides information to learners about their progress, and provides information about learners' progress to the organization. A well-designed Level 2 evaluation can give you information to help improve the learning event or learning materials and assess whether or not specific parts of the materials have structural defects that need to be corrected. A Level 2 evaluation is used when there is a need to certify learners on completion of the learning event.

For each of the three areas assessed by Level 2 – changes in knowledge, attitudes and skills – a pre-test/post-test and control group design can be used, so that any changes in learning can be attributed to the learning event. This design should also include using the same measurement before and after the event, measuring those who have taken advantage of the learning event against those who have not and randomly assigning individuals to learning events and control groups.

Strengths

The major strength of a Level 2 evaluation is that it is easier to measure the learning that has taken place than to measure learner performance in a setting different to that in which the learning happened. Quantifiable data can be easily obtained and can provide the organization with data that are statistically defensible. Knowledge gain measurements have more rigour than other instruments because they are not easy to falsify. You also have a high degree of control of the evaluation at Level 2, since it often takes place during the learning event.

Limitations

Although you can infer transfer of learning to another setting, an increase in knowledge or change in attitude does not necessarily ensure an increase in performance on the part of learners. A second limitation is that learners can have a negative response to the evaluation because of an aversion to being tested.

Methods of administration

In a Web-based learning environment, test questions such as multiple-choice, true/false and matching are useful methods for assessing knowledge. Multiple-choice testing is probably one of the better methods for assessing principles and facts; it is among the most objective forms of testing and can measure higher orders of learning, such as understanding, judgement and application of knowledge. The method is often superior to other objective test methods as other methods often encourage guessing, can provide clues and generally speaking test lower levels of learning such as memorization. Short answer and essay questions are not appropriate test methods for use in an online environment because of their subjective nature and the time needed to complete and mark them, and because they often test unrelated skills such as spelling, which can penalize learners who cannot express themselves clearly in writing. Short answer questions can be considered for use in a less rigorous assessment environment such as a reflection exercise under the direction of an online coach where learners respond in either a synchronous or an asynchronous mode to the questions posed. Measuring skills can be carried out using behaviour checklists, while attitudinal change can be measured using questionnaires, attitude surveys and self-rating scales.

The construction of test questions is a difficult and critical task, and a great deal of experience on the part of the event designer is needed to develop questions that measure at the higher levels of the cognitive domain and to ensure that distracters are not obvious. Any Level 2 evaluation should, of course, follow as soon as possible after the learning event, as any delay could result in outside influences affecting the scores.

Level 3 evaluation overview

Evaluation Levels 1 and 2 look at learners' reaction to the learning event and/or learning materials and whether they gained any new knowledge, skills or attitudes. Level 3 evaluation measures the extent to which learners are now able to apply what they have learnt in a different setting. Here you seek to measure changes in behaviour and/or increases in level of performance. Level 3 evaluation is especially important in training, and is concerned with the impact of the training on real-life situations. The issue here is that understanding the concept or applying a skill in a learning setting does not automatically guarantee that learners have the ability to transfer it to a new situation.

Characteristics

Level 3 evaluation is characterized by measures that take place outside the setting of the Web-based learning event. Since the intent is to measure the impact of new behaviour in a different setting, the evaluation must take place in the learners' places of work. Because of this, the evaluation also involves a wider variety of people than do Levels 1 and 2, which typically involve just learners and possibly yourself. Designing a Level 3 evaluation can be time-consuming, and implementation may be complex.

Conditions necessary for successful evaluation

Measuring changes in people's behaviour can be a difficult and frustrating process since a number of significant requirements are needed in order for change to take place. It is extremely important that you consider each of the following conditions before designing your Level 3 evaluation scheme:

1.   The learners must want to improve themselves.
2.   The learners must recognize their own learning deficiencies.
3.   The learners must work in a receptive organizational climate.
4.   The learners will need help from someone else who is interested and skilled in that area of learning.
5.   The learners must have the opportunity to try out the new ideas.

You should consider using a Level 3 evaluation when your major concern is to provide evidence or proof regarding the effectiveness of the learning event. It is possible to evaluate at Level 3 without evaluating at Level 2. However, it may be useful to evaluate at both Levels 2 and 3, as you may discover that knowledge is gained by learners during the learning event, but that the environment of a different setting is not conducive to the changed behaviour. This becomes especially important if the rationale for the learning event is being questioned because of some perceived failure, when the real reason is an environment that does not support learners but discourages or extinguishes new behaviour.

Strengths

Level 3 evaluation will provide more meaningful information about the workplace than a Level 2 evaluation and may bring about an increased commitment to innovation. One of the consequences of a Level 3 evaluation can be the change in the focus of a learning event from facilitator-centred to learner-centred.

Limitations

By measuring individual behaviour you may be measuring how the conditions of statistical measurement are met, such as the match between learner performance and the learning objectives and information for decision making, rather than measuring the quality of the learning event.

Level 3 evaluation is more time-consuming than a Level 1 evaluation and more difficult to implement than a Level 2. Learners may not react as positively to involvement in a Level 3 evaluation because of its observational nature. However, because more people are involved in the evaluation it is important that the organization is carefully prepared for the event. Because evaluation must be done after individuals have had a chance to demonstrate behaviour, longer timelines are an inevitable result. In addition, if the learning event is attempting to teach a skill that is used infrequently there may be a significant time lag before you are able to measure the effectiveness of that learning on the behaviour of learners.

Level 4 evaluation overview

In order to determine if an innovation has been successful, it is necessary to conduct an evaluation at Level 4. At Level 4 the evaluation is concerned with linking any recent changes to the innovation. Although Level 4 is a desirable level of evaluation because it represents a truly indicative measure of the outcome of an innovation to the organization, it is the most difficult and time-consuming to conduct. Change in an organization can be the result of a number of factors, and it is the role of the evaluator to link the change to the innovation but at the same time to try to eliminate all other variables as factors in that change. The task requires the total support and commitment of everyone involved. There is no set formula or process that applies to Level 4. To determine if the innovation did result in the perceived change, it may be necessary to use control groups. The use of control groups in large organizations, however, is not always practical and you may have to use other methods to gather the evidence you need.

Characteristics

Level 4 evaluation concerns the net effect of an innovation on an organization. It helps measure the overall costs of an innovation and improvement in people. In a training setting, it can measure productivity and increased efficiency in an organization and how this might lead to better service. In a learning setting, a Level 4 evaluation may be concerned with the effectiveness and appropriateness of learning and how that affects the ability of a school, college or university to attract high achievers, teachers or learners, grants, sponsorships and academic ranking.

The effective application of a Level 4 evaluation can help to ensure a cost justification for the innovation as well as reinforce the concept of goal achievement and goal clarity. The evaluation of the effect of an innovation on an organization is often cause to assess the mission of that organization.

Conditions necessary for successful evaluation

For a Level 4 evaluation to be successful the organization must be committed to its success.

Level 4 yields qualitative data primarily on behavioural changes brought about by an innovation. These changes may have been those intended by the innovation or they may have been incidental. Depending on the questions asked during the evaluation, information may also be obtained on learner reactions to the learning event, on what they felt they learnt and on the results to the organization of these behavioural changes.

Strengths

Level 4 can be used to assess a variety of learning events, particularly those difficult to measure through objective techniques. It can be used by itself or in concert with other evaluation approaches and, dependent upon the design of the process and the nature of questions asked in follow-up, it can be changed to meet particular information needs and organization circumstances. The time required for the evaluation is related to the conducting of the various interviews and the analysing of the results.

Limitations

The application of a Level 4 evaluation can require significant human resources and an additional commitment of effort. However, because people can become naturally protective of various innovations, there may be a 'fear of cancellation syndrome', which could influence the true response to the evaluation. Further, its high cost might cause the organization to avoid an evaluation of this nature.

The time required for interviewing and analysis is often a serious concern. When online questionnaires are used, time may limit both the quality and the quantity of response. While a Level 4 evaluation can raise concerns for those areas needing improvement, additional data will usually have to be gathered if discontinuing the innovation is to be considered.

Context of the evaluation

The context of the evaluation at Levels 1, 2 and 3 should be seen as one of improvement rather than effectiveness, whereby the information you gather is used to affect ongoing learning events. At Level 4, however, the context should be one of effectiveness based on the impact of the innovation on the organization.

Evaluation questions

The evaluation questions you formulate should be derived from your learning event documentation.

Data collection

Data collection can take place using adapted and/or already developed information collection instruments. The collection techniques you can use include rating scales, observation, interview and questionnaires.

Data analysis

The data analysis should seek to make order out of the collection of diverse facts and data gathered. The analysis should accurately communicate the nature of the reaction that needs to be described, summarize the information and describe how seriously to regard the observations to help determine the degree of relationship among data sets.

Reporting evaluation information

Finally your evaluation report should detail the instruments you used to gather the data as well as the relevance and quality of those instruments. The rate of progress of what is being evaluated should be described along with a prediction for its success based on its observed progress. The features that appear to promote or hinder progress and your recommendations for improvement will form an important part of your report.

A Level 4 evaluation is an important process, which needs to be carried out with a clarity of purpose sufficient to give those concerned with the innovation an understanding of how it might be improved.

THE ONLINE LEARNING ENVIRONMENT

Because online learning is still very new, distinctions between the various types are still forming. For the purpose of this discussion, the primary distinction between the different uses of online learning is based on the level of interactivity and the amount of other media used. In the context of any evaluation, levels of interactivity are a somewhat arbitrary measure based solely on an overall amount of learner activity throughout the total learning event. Learner activity is a relative act based on the design of the event. True interactivity is based on a series of factors including motivation or the 'want to learn' element, useful feedback and reflection.

The key to any learning is that the event must be relevant and it must keep learners wanting more. In a technology-based learning event this is often accomplished through the use of appropriate graphics, illustrations, colour and sound. What appears to matter is how well it all works and whether the elements included in the event mesh with the way learners want to learn.

It is important to remember, when considering the evaluation of online learning materials and the learning environment, that holding learners' attention and engaging their minds are necessary for learning to occur. Interactivity makes the difference between an event that simply presents information and one that actually meets the needs of learners.

What should be evaluated?

Evaluation of online learning should centre on three issues: the learning that has taken place, the learning materials and the learning environment.

The learning that has taken place

When considering whether learning has taken place you may wish first to consider a number of conventional assessment methods. For example, you may wish to have learners demonstrate their ability to do something. This demonstration can be to a panel, an assessor or an audience, and it can be observed in a structured environment or unobtrusively by various means. In this same mode you may want to ask learners to undertake practical work in the workplace and be observed as the work takes place.

Finally, while still in a demonstration mode, learners may be given a product to analyse for errors and problems.

A second conventional assessment methodology you may want to consider is an oral format. Here learners are asked to prepare a presentation and present various findings or evidence to the assessor. A third methodology is the standard written test. This can take the form of a formal or supervised examination or it can be given in an online environment using some form of CML application.

With the exception of CML, these methodologies are not any different from the assessments used in a standard face-to-face learning environment. However, when you are developing an evaluation methodology to be used in an online environment, a number of new factors such as interactivity, navigation, motivational components and the like have to be kept in mind.

The learning materials

Consider the criteria and indicators of success set out in Table 15.2 as a guide to your overall evaluation of online learning materials.

Table 15.2 *Evaluation of online learning materials*

Criteria	Indicators of Success
Materials Content	The learning includes the right amount and quality of information based on the job family or profile map.
Overall Design	The learning is designed in such a way that learners will actually learn. Learners are asked if they would like their pages in a different language.
Interactivity	Learners are engaged throughout the learning.
Navigation	Learners can determine their own course through the learning mateials. There is an exit option available. There is a course map accessible. There is an appropriate use of icons and/or clear labels so that learners don't have to read excessively to determine options.
Motivational Components	The materials engage learners through a variety of game elements, testing and unique content.
Media	The materials effectively employ animation, sound and other special, but appropriate, visual effects. The gratuitous use of media is avoided.

Assessment	Mastery of each section's content is required before proceeding to later sections?
	Topic quizzes are used.
	There is a final exam if appropriate to the needs of the organization and learners.
Look	The materials are attractive and appealing to the eye and ear.
Record Keeping	A computer-managed learning component is included as part of the materials and is responsible for record keeping and the collection of learner data.
	The learner data are automatically forwarded to the course manager.
Tone	The materials are designed in such a way that they avoid being condescending to learners.

Learning event evaluation

As well as evaluating the learning materials from an overall perspective you should conduct a broad-based evaluation of the learning event itself. For this task you need to consider the criteria and indicators of success set out in Table 15.3. These criteria are based on the nine events of instruction, as described by Gagné (1977).

Table 15.3   *Learning event evaluation*

Criteria	Indicators of Success
Getting the learners' attention.	Development of a profile of the topics that have to be learnt and organizing them accordingly.
	Development of an overview for each part of the learning materials.
	Development of an introduction for each segment of learning in the actual event.
	Development of a summary for each part of the learning materials.
Telling learners where they are going and how they are to get there.	Written performance objectives for each part of the learning materials.
Helping learners remember what they have done before and relate it to what is coming up.	Materials are organized into a systematic presentation format.
	Development of an overview of the materials relevant to learners.
	Development of a consistent layout for each screen.

Provide learners with learning materials.	Matching information with the relevant objective.
	Development of a subject heading structure.
	The removal of all non-relevant information.
	The amount of text is reduced to a minimum.
	The text is as simple as possible.
	The reading level is correct for learners.
	Development of a glossary and telling learners where to find it and how to use it.
	Development of font styles and background to make the screen readable.
	Development of materials using colour and/or bold for emphasis.
	Simple visual material.
	Learners are encouraged to make notes, summaries and concept maps.
	Development of a series of questions, where appropriate, to 'test' knowledge acquisition as the learning proceeds.
	Development of worked examples for learners to practise.
	Navigation without confusion.
	Clear, rational thought behind the organization of the material and the way the pages are linked.
Showing learners what they have to be able to do to complete the task.	Development of a series of worked examples for the learners.
	Development of a series of tutorials linked to the learning materials.
	Development of a series of helpful hints linked to the materials.
Having learners practise what they have learnt.	Simulating a new situation and having learners develop a working example.
	Use of activities and questions for learners to complete.
	Use of varied activities and questions.
	Uses of activities that arouse interest and expand the learning materials.
Telling learners how they are doing.	Use of activities that are self-assessing.
	Development of answers for learners to consider.

Helping learners transfer their learning to a new situation.	Use of collaboration activities with other learners to 'discover' the answers to a problem.
	Requiring learners to predict, hypothesize and experiment to find a solution to the problem.
	Requiring learners to work in groups, discuss issues and report findings.

Materials design evaluation

When it comes to the evaluation of actual learning materials you need to consider the criteria and indicators of success set out in Table 15.4.

Table 15.4   *Materials design evaluation*

Criteria: Materials Design	Indicators of Success
Provide learners with new knowledge and skills.	Development of clearly stated learner goals and objectives written in behavioural terms.
Provide learners with the opportunity to view the materials in the languages of their choice.	Use of a translation tool or duplicate files in other languages.
Provide a graphic design to catch the eye and inform and educate learners about the topic.	An eye-catching and informative design A clear conceptual and intuitive path between areas of information.
Provide a graphic design within technology limits.	Use of text and images based on screen quality and monitor size, browser and/or access speed of the client computer.
Provide multimedia files that do not distract learners from the learning objectives.	Graphic files that download in 15 seconds or less.
Provide an overall design that is both effective and clear to learners.	Clear, rational thought behind the organization of the materials and the manner in which the pages are linked. A coherent, consistent layout style. A design that anticipates learner questions and makes the answers easily accessible. Navigation without confusion.

Clear logic behind the way screens are linked and the navigational access learners have to each part of the program.

Use of space to help set up text and images and make it easier for learners to focus.

Use of space to create an open, balanced feeling and to set off text and images.

The overuse of large text, bold style, all capitals and coloured text is avoided.

Use of the whole width of the screen.

Buttons that are easy to use and identify and connected to the indicated item on the screen.

The use of lengthy text that requires scrolling to find buttons at the bottom of the screen is avoided.

Learners are asked if they would like the materials in a different language.

Criterion: Metaphor or Theme	Indicators of Success
Provide learners with an element that catches their attention and immerses them in an environment.	The element is clearly related to 'the suspension of disbelief'. The program is so interesting and appealing or so intellectually stimulating that the learners actually like it!

Criteria: Information Structure	Indicators of Success
Provide a user interface that has several standard menu options present on every screen.	The screen options include home, search, menu and contact the teacher. Learners are just one mouse click away from the main index page. The links to other pages are included in the text of the introduction page. The links include the table of contents or orientation page in addition to having embedded links. Clear, brief explanations for each of the hot links are listed as a resource.

| Provide search utilities that help learners browse for specific information. | Use of a title or map at the head of each screen to keep learners clear as to where they are. |
| | Use of a search engine. |

The learning environment

This final section of the chapter considers the online environment, its design and structure. Evaluation issues you need to consider include the criteria and indicators of success set out in Table 15.5.

Table 15.5   *Online environment evaluation*

Criteria: Hardware and Software	Indicators of Success
Operating system	The operating system supports a variety of different capabilities needed for different types of learning events.
Hardware	Characteristics of the learner hardware are compliant with the system hardware.
Software	Appropriate learner software is available including Web browsers, plug-ins, mail programs, word processing and spreadsheets.
Available peripherals	Appropriate learner peripherals are available including a printer, CD ROM (with sound card), scanner and video camera.
Access	Learners have access to the network at times appropriate to their learning needs.
Competency	The hardware and software used are familiar to learner and little or no training is needed.
Training	Learners and other support staff are able to use the system beyond the completion of basic tasks.

Criteria: Client Server	Indicators of Success
Operating system	The server operating system supports all learner and learning event required software.
Hardware	The server hardware is appropriate to the required speed of the server and the system.

Software	The server software supports all learning needs and services.
	The server software provides the required functionality and performance needed by learners.
Realiability	The server is available during the times appropriate to the needs of learners.
Access	The service can be accessed and modified directly by the appropriate personnel.

Criteria: Distribution	Indicators of Success
Method	Factors that influence the decision to provide online, offline or a combination of distribution methods have been considered and are appropriated to the needs of learners.
Speed of access	Learners are able to access the required learning via modem, ISDN, cable and local area networks.
Cost	Set-up costs are appropriate to the requirements of the learning event, the needs of learners and the requirements of the organization.
Communication	Learners, tutors and facilitators as well as other appropriate parties communicate on a regular basis.
	Learners can communicate simultaneously.

Criteria: Technical Support	Indicators of Success
Level	The level of support is able to maintain the current system and add new elements as required.
Quality	The support is able to understand and appreciate what the system is set up to achieve.
Availability	The support is available at appropriate times during the day, night and weekends to support fully the needs of learners.

Developing your online learning evaluation

Using the previous criteria as a guide to your evaluation methodology development, you will first need to determine the goal(s) of your evaluation. For example, ask yourself how you are going to determine each of the following:

- the learning gains of the learners;
- how effective learners found the online environment;
- the changes you may have to make to the learning materials;
- how effective learners found the learning support;
- the advantages and disadvantages of online delivery;
- if the site architecture is adequate to support learners;
- which were the most effective learning processes in the online environment;
- how the online environment compares with the traditional environment.

Once you have determined your evaluation goals you need to consider the form the evaluation will take. Your first consideration is whether you use a questionnaire format, oral format or both to collect the data.

If you decide on a questionnaire format you need to consider the following:

- When to send out the questionnaires or put them online for completion. If you put the questionnaires online too soon, learners may forget and not complete them; if you send them too late, you won't get the reaction that you need or want because the moment has passed for learners.
- Whether to provide both mid- and end-of-event questionnaires, and what is the best timing.
- How long to give learners to respond and when to send out reminders to those who did not respond.
- How to analyse the information you get and, once analysed, how to use it.

Once you have the goals and the form of the evaluation completed, the actual questions can then be developed. Figure 15.1 is an example of a Web-based Level 1 evaluation questionnaire (adapted with permission from Jolliffe (1997)). This questionnaire is useful for the evaluation of a Web-based environment at the tertiary level. The criteria used included user interface features, design and content, comparison to traditional classes and academic support. This tool uses both a five-point Likert scale and a semantic differential scale for respondents to make a judgement regarding the question posed.

Figure 15.1 *The Virtual College evaluation*

Your Evaluation of the Virtual College

Participant's Profile:

Name: _____ Date: _____

Department:

Year of study:

Section A: User Interface
These questions are designed to inform us of the quality of the user interface of the Virtual College. To what extent do you agree or disagree with each of the following statements? Click on the statement that best indicates how 'user friendly' you find accessing the material in the Virtual College.

SD = Strongly Disagree D = Disagree N = Neither agree nor disagree A = Agree SA = Strongly Agree

Access Response Time   SD D N A SA
The speed of response of the Virtual College is acceptable

Navigating in the Virtual College   SD D N A SA
I find accessing materials in the Virtual College easy

Audio Files   SD D N A SA
The wait time to play an audio file is acceptable

Video Files   SD D N A SA
The wait time to play a video file is acceptable

Audio Files   SD D N A SA
The speed of response of the Virtual College is acceptable

Technical Problems   SD D N A SA
In general, there were very few technical problems, such as
system hangs, and crashes, with the Virtual College

Section B: Virtual College Features
The following questions are designed to inform us as to how useful you found each of the features or capabilities of the Virtual College.

Instructional plan   Useful 1 2 3 4 5 Useless

Lectures   Useful 1 2 3 4 5 Useless

Tutorials   Useful 1 2 3 4 5 Useless

Student database	Useful **1 2 3 4 5** Useless
Bulletin board	Useful **1 2 3 4 5** Useless
Assignments	Useful **1 2 3 4 5** Useless
Virtual laboratory (if applicable)	Useful **1 2 3 4 5** Useless
Digital resources – Library	Useful **1 2 3 4 5** Useless
Digital resources – Course notes	Useful **1 2 3 4 5** Useless
Digital resources – Reference text	Useful **1 2 3 4 5** Useless
Digital resources – Web sites	Useful **1 2 3 4 5** Useless
Digital resources – Past years' questions	Useful **1 2 3 4 5** Useless
Assessment Centre	Useful **1 2 3 4 5** Useless
FAQs (Frequently Asked Questions)	Useful **1 2 3 4 5** Useless
Glossary	Useful **1 2 3 4 5** Useless

What other features or capabilities in the Virtual College would you like to see? Please list them below

Section C: Module Design and Content

These questions are designed to inform us regarding the effectiveness of the instructional method used to deliver the learning materials.

SD = Strongly Disagree D = Disagree N = Neither agree nor disagree A = Agree SA = Strongly Agree

Organization of Module Content   SD D N A SA
The material in the module was well organized and easy to find

Text   SD D N A SA
The text was easy to read and understand

Graphics   SD D N A SA
The graphics were helpful to my learning the materials

Audio   SD D N A SA
The audio was helpful to my learning the material

Video   SD D N A SA
The video was helpful to my learning the material

Subject Matter Coverage   SD D N A SA
The materials contain a lot of information about the topics covered

Interesting/Engaging   SD D N A SA
The materials are both interesting and engaging

Use of Examples   SD D N A SA
There are many examples and illustrations used in the module

Understanding   SD D N A SA
I gained a good understanding of the topics covered in the module

Application of Knowledge Gained   SD D N ASA
I will be able to apply the knowledge I have learnt to new situations

Section D: Comparison of the Virtual College to Face-to-Face Teaching
These questions are designed to inform us regarding the effectiveness of the
Virtual College compared to your regular classes.

SD = Strongly Disagree D = Disagree N = Neither agree nor disagree A = Agree SA = Strongly Agree

Convenience   SD D N A SA
The Virtual College is more convenient than attending
regular lectures and tutorials

Communication between Students   SD D N A SA
I communicated more, using e-mail and bulletin boards,
with other students than I normally do

Communication with the Lecturer   SD D N A SA
I communicated more, using e-mail and bulletin boards,
with the lecturer than I normally do

Enjoyed More   SD D N A SA
I enjoyed more and felt more motivated to learn compared
to regular lectures

Learned More   SD D N A SA
I learnt more from the Virtual College compared to regular
lectures

Supplement to Traditional Lectures/Tutorials   SD D N A SA
The Virtual College is an effective supplement to the
traditional lectures and tutorials

Effective Replacement for Missed Lectures/Tutorials   SD D N A SA
The Virtual College is an effective replacement for missed
lectures and tutorials

Choose to Take Another VC Module   SD D N A SA
I would choose to take another Virtual College module

Method of Study   SD D N A SA
Given the choice between studying by the traditional
lecture/tutorial method and the Virtual College, I prefer
the Virtual College

Section E: Academic Support
These questions are designed to inform us regarding the effectiveness of the Virtual College compared to your regular classes.

SD = Strongly Disagree D = Disagree N = Neither agree nor disagree A = Agree SA = Strongly Agree

E-mail Support   SD D N A SA
When I e-mail my tutor I get a reply within one week

Bulletin Board Support   SD D N A SA
When I post a question on the bullet in board I get a reply
within one week

Assignment Marking   SD D N A SA
The tutor marked and returned my assignments within a
two-week period

General Tutor   SD D N A SA
The tutor support with respect to the Virtual College was
very good

Section F: Overall Comments and Suggestions
What did you like best about your Virtual College experience?

- Learning by computer
- Learning at own rate
- Interesting way to learn
- Access to the Internet
- Use of the bulletin board

- Quick response time by the lecturer to the test taken
- Electronic course notes
- Availability of past year exam papers
- Other

If other, please give details:

What did you like least about your Virtual College experience?

- Learning by computer
- Reduced access to the lecturer
- Too much material covered
- Content boring

- Delivery method boring
- No or little discussion of problems
- Other

If other, please give details:

Have you any suggestions for improving the Virtual College?

- Improve the ease of access to the course materials
- Make the delivery more interesting

- Include more review exercises/tests
- Access from home

- Make the content more interesting
- Other

If other, please give details:

As a final guide to development of a Web-based learning Level 1 evaluation questionnaire, you may want to consider reviewing the following resources:

Caywood, C, Library Selection Criteria for WWW Resources, www.pilot.infi.net/~carolyn/criteria.html. This tool is useful for assessing the value of a Web site to library users. The criteria it uses include access, design and content, and it includes a number of additional resources.

McLachlan, K, WWW CyberGuide Ratings for Content Evaluation, www.cyberbee.com/guide1.html. This tool uses speed, general appearances, navigation, graphics, content, currency, availability and further information as the review criteria.

Finally you may want to consider the following evaluation tool:

McLachlan, K, WWW CyberGuide Ratings for Web Site Design, www.cyberbee.com/guide2.html. This tool uses the same criteria as for guide 1 above. However, the focus here is on Web site design.

CONCLUSION

An evaluation can be carried out using a number of techniques in a variety of settings. For any evaluation to be successful it is important that you see its context as one of both improvement and effectiveness, depending upon the level being carried out. It is also important that your evaluation questions should not be developed in isolation. Data collection can take place using standardized collection instruments or you can develop your own, and any subsequent data analysis should accurately describe and summarize all the information gathered. Finally the evaluation report should detail all the features of the learning event that appear to promote or hinder progress.

Chapter 16
Getting people orientated to the Web-based environment

INTRODUCTION

If you are delivering a learning event via the Web then you will be communicating with your learners via electronic means. An essential component of a Web-based learning event is that learners must have the support of a facilitator to assist them in their studies. It does not matter how effective your learning materials are; the learners will still want to ask questions. Effective facilitator support can overcome one of the major problems of Web learning events, that of learners' feelings of isolation. With communication technology, the facilitator can communicate with the learners in many different ways.

The facilitator role is not just one of answering questions; facilitators have to be involved in formative and summative assessment, counselling, the conducting of traditional tutorials, administration and learner motivation. This means that facilitator time must be used efficiently.

If you are conducting a traditional face-to-face learning event and you use the Web for Web-based support, then Web-based facilitation may not be essential.

Before starting a Web-based learning event, both facilitators and learners will need to be orientated on the structure of the learning event and how it will work for them. Learners will also need to be taught how to study effectively in a self study learning environment.

FACILITATOR ORIENTATION
Using the Web-based learning programme

Facilitators may or may not have been involved in developing the Web-based learning event. One of the first things that must be done therefore is to orientate them in the way the event has been designed. If they are not competent in the use of the Web as a tool to deliver learning they can never effectively support learners. Facilitator orientation can take the form of group-based training in a computer laboratory, where facilitators can practise using the learning event. The orientation can also be conducted individually, where facilitators are taught, perhaps on their own computers, how to work in a Web-based learning environment. In either case, ongoing support should be provided, such as a discussion forum where the facilitators can ask questions and report problems that they or the learners are having.

It is essential that facilitators have access to technical support during the learning event, possibly by the staff who originally programmed the event. Not only is this necessary for the facilitator's support, but also for learners' support, since they will usually contact the facilitator when they are having problems. It is preferable however that learners have access directly to technical support, but in small organizations this is not always possible because of limitations in staff. Research has shown that one of the main reasons learners become frustrated with a Web-based learning event is because of technical difficulties.

Who are the learners?

Facilitators supporting a Web-based learning event may never meet their learners face to face. This is one of the problems of delivering a Web-based learning event; learners often feel isolated and alone in their studies, to the extent that they drop out. Using communication features of the Web, the facilitator can overcome some of the isolation problems. To communicate effectively with learners, the facilitator should know more about them than their name, so as to personalize the communication.

One effective way this can be done is by profiling the learners so that they know the learners' personal details. This is done by using an online questionnaire, sent to learners as soon as or before the learning event commences. Here is an example of some of the questions facilitators can ask:

- What is your preferred name?
- What are your reasons for studying this learning event?
- Why are you studying this learning event via the Web?
- What type of computer do you have?
- What type of Internet connection do you have?
- What type of browser are you using?
- How much experience do you have with computers and the Internet?
- Have you studied using Web-based learning before?
- Do you think that by studying this learning event will have any impact on your personal and employment situation?

- What sort of learning support do you expect from me?
- What type of technical assistance do you expect?
- Do you have any friends or colleagues who will be able to help you with this learning event?
- Do you have any questions for me?

With this information, facilitators can build a class profile so that they know the general level at which to pitch their assistance. They should attempt to answer any questions the learners have and introduce themselves to the learners. Attaching an audio file to an e-mail document is a good way of doing this. A good design feature of a Web-based learning event is that it should have a section where the facilitators outline their background and how they can help learners. This information can be personalized by using photographs and audio. The learners will find it easier to communicate with someone they know something about.

How can a facilitator assist learners?

There are many ways a facilitator can assist learners, although the methods depend very much on the type of instructional support that has been built into the Web-based learning event. For example, the ways the facilitator can assist learners differ with e-mail communication and discussion forums. The form of support the learners need will vary depending on the stage they are at in studying the learning event.

Before they begin the learning event, learners will need to know:

- what to study, the content of the materials and whether that content is relevant to their needs;
- how to study, what study techniques to use and something about goal setting and time management;
- what type of computer equipment they will require;
- how much time they will need to access the Internet;
- how to set up their computer to receive the learning event;
- how to use the various components of the learning event;
- how technical personnel will assist them if they have technical problems.

During the learning event, learners may experience the following:

- They may have some problems with the content no matter how well designed they are.
- They may have questions about assessment and could need assistance preparing for the final assessment requirements.
- They may have problems coping with stress, or have study problems.

- They may need support in relation to their jobs, if they work, perhaps to arrange for time off for study purposes.
- They may need technical support.
- They may be worried about their progress on the assessments.

After the learning event, learners will want to know:

- what subjects they should study next;
- the results of their efforts;
- how they can improve in the future.

The facilitator is expected to answer the above questions and assist learners in terms of their study skills and motivation, encouraging communication, answering questions, helping with assignments and determining learner progress.

Study skills

- Provide general advice on learning.
- Give advice on study and time management skills.
- Plan a study timetable for learners for a particular learning event.
- Develop individual learning plans for learners.

Motivation

- E-mail learners to introduce him or herself, perhaps using an attached audio file.
- Make learners feel at ease when communicating with them.
- Remind learners they are not studying alone.
- Remind learners of the rewards of completing the learning event.
- Encourage learners to communicate with and support one another.
- Encourage learners to form study groups.
- Encourage learners to find information outside the learning materials, using Web sites, Usenet groups and discussion forums.

Communication

- Open a number of communication channels, such as e-mail, discussion forums, telephone and traditional tutorials.
- Encourage learners to answer one another's questions on the discussion forum.
- Encourage learners to participate in discussion forums.
- Discourage individuals from monopolizing discussion forums.
- Discourage learners from asking irrelevant questions on discussion forums.

Questions

- Listen to learners; don't treat any of their comments as superficial.
- Answer learners' questions in a reasonable amount of time.
- Give learners advice on where to find the information they need.
- Assist learners with any administrative problems they are having with organization.
- Remind learners that most people have problems at some stage of the learning event.
- Relate the content of the learning event to the learner's own experiences.

Assignments

- Assist learners with their assignments.
- Always use constructive comments on their assignments and questions.
- Build learners' confidence by giving encouraging comments.

Progress

- Record learners' progress.
- Monitor electronic assessments.
- Ensure that learners are progressing at an adequate rate.
- If learners are not progressing adequately, contact them to find out the reason.
- Adjust individual learning programmes.
- Help learners prepare for any final assessment.

Methods of supporting learners

The facilitator can support learners with synchronous and asynchronous methods. These may be computer-mediated communication such as e-mail and discussion forums, or they may be the more traditional methods such as telephone and face-to-face tutorials.

The synchronous methods include:

- traditional tutorials;
- telephone;
- audio and video conferencing via the Web;
- MUD (a cyberspace game where users take on an identity in the form of an avatar and interact with one another);
- MOO (a specific implementation of a MUD system);
- MUSH (a text-based MUD system);
- chat systems.

The asynchronous methods include:

- e-mail;
- e-mail management systems;
- Usenet groups;
- discussion forums.

Many of the synchronous methods of communication involving audio and video are still relatively unstable due to bandwidth limitation. They also require the learners to meet at the same time but not in the same location, which may not be convenient for everyone. If the synchronous communication is to be meaningful, all the participants will need to be up to the same section in the learning event, otherwise they may not benefit from the topic under discussion. For this reason, another form of communication may be used.

The following is a description of five of the most common ways of providing learner support:

1. e-mail;
2. discussion forums;
3. telephone support;
4. face-to-face tutorials;
5. assignments.

E-mail

E-mail is a great way to communicate, easy, rapid and readily available. In fact e-mail can be a little too easy and the facilitator can become flooded with e-mails from learners, many of which are repetitive and take a great deal of time to answer. For this reason, the facilitator must give learners certain guidelines for e-mail. Learners should e-mail the facilitator for administrative, personal and technical problems, and assignment queries. The facilitator should give learners an approximate time by which he or she will reply, perhaps a maximum period of one week. If learners have problems with the content of the learning event, they should be encouraged to review the frequently asked questions section to see if their question has already been asked and answered. Learners can also post questions on the discussion forum, as this has the advantage that other learners may answer the question before the facilitator does.

The facilitator should provide guidelines regarding the expected length of an e-mail and how much time they can expect the facilitator to spend on the answer.

Facilitators should also inform learners if they are not going to be available for a period of time during the learning event. If they are going to be unavailable for a substantial period of time they should arrange for someone else to take over their facilitation duties.

When e-mailing learners, facilitators should follow these guidelines:

- They should use learners' preferred names.
- They should create a friendly atmosphere between themselves and learners by using the appropriate tone.
- They should not write sentences using capital letters, as that is equivalent to shouting.
- They should keep the message short and to the point, and possibly make it non-scrollable.
- They should answer learners' questions.
- If they can't answer learners' questions, they should explain why, for example because it would take too long or because the question will be covered in the learning materials.
- They should ensure that the message is grammatically correct.
- They should try to reply as soon as possible, bearing in mind that learners have been given approximate guidelines of when the facilitator will reply.
- They should be positive to learners even if learners ask irrelevant questions.
- They should try to keep learners on track with the objectives of the learning event.
- They should be patient if learners appear angry.
- If facilitators are not sure what learners want, they should ask for clarification.
- If facilitators attach files, they should ensure that learners' mailboxes are large enough to take those files, as otherwise they may be locked out of their e-mail accounts. They should also ensure that the files download in a reasonable time and that learners have the appropriate viewer.
- They should not send learners' e-mails to the entire class without permission.
- They should give specific subject headings to their e-mails, so learners know exactly what the message is about.

E-mail is a very effective method of communicating with learners, but in many cases it can be used to vent anger or frustration. If learners' e-mails are angry or threatening perhaps the facilitator could telephone and talk to them personally. An effective facilitator will remain calm and give positive replies even if he or she would like to do otherwise.

The discussion forum

One of the common tasks of a Web-based facilitator is to moderate a discussion forum. Whatever format the discussion forum takes, be it a place where learners can ask questions about the content of the learning event or a moderator-led discussion, the characteristics of a good moderator are the same. Effective moderators should:

- be knowledgeable about the subject matter, otherwise they will have trouble leading the discussion;
- have experience as moderators. Some first-time moderators find moderation a difficult task because there is a lack of physical cues to help them understand the mood or feeling of the learners. Moderators should at least have had the experience of participating in a discussion forum before moderating one;
- know how to lead a discussion. They must know how to keep the discussion on track and keep particular individuals from dominating;
- know when to respond to messages. No message should go unanswered in a discussion, but if there are many responses and they seem to be on track then there may be no need for moderators to answer them;
- know how to keep interest in the forum and maintain the interest of the learners in the topics under discussion;
- know how to communicate in the written word, since the discussion is text-based;
- have the time to be able to moderate. Moderating a discussion forum can take a great deal of time, so moderators must allow for it;
- be able to set limits to their involvement. Although it does take a great deal of time to moderate discussion forums, time limits on moderator time must be set, as learners' demands can be quite heavy and unrealistic;
- be very patient. Moderators who show their anger or intolerance in the discussion forum will not be helpful to learners. Moderators must show great patience with even the most intolerant learners;
- know the learners' backgrounds to be effective. A good source of information is the learner profile the facilitator developed at the start of the learning event;
- know when to change their approach. If the discussion is not going the way they want it to, then they should be flexible enough to change it and achieve something out of the discussion even if it is not want they planned at the start;
- know how to increase participation. If the participation rate in the discussion forum is low or slow in coming, moderators should know how to increase the participation rate without becoming authoritarian;
- know what to do or whom to contact if learners are having technical problems.

To start a discussion forum, the facilitator sends a personal e-mail to all learners inviting them to get involved. To start off the discussion, the

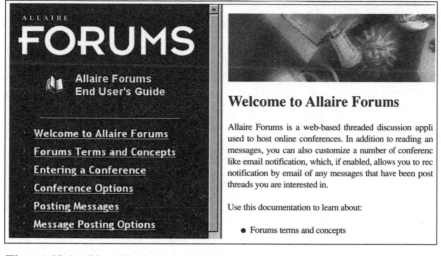

Figure 16.1 *Most discussion forums provide instructions for use,*
http://www.forumspot.org/forums/docs/user/index.htm

(Permission sought)

facilitator will give a question or statement that the learners are expected
to answer or respond to. The design of the question is of critical importance to keep learners on track in the discussion, thus achieving its
learning objectives. Learners should be given guidelines on how to
prepare and take part in the discussion forum (see Figure 16.1).

To stimulate discussion, the facilitator may use a pseudonym and act
as a learner to promote alternative points of view. The facilitator should
comment on each participant's response, but keep stimulating discussion by asking further questions. If the discussion goes off track, the facilitator should reword the original question in an attempt to get the
discussion back on track.

Learners should be asked to justify their positions or opinions, but if
they start to argue the facilitator must stop them. If there are any inappropriate responses the facilitator must delete them and try to keep
things on track. Towards the end of the allotted time the facilitator
should summarize the discussion and draw the appropriate conclusions.
The objectives that have been achieved should also be outlined, so that
learners have a clear understanding of what has been achieved.

For the facilitator, moderating a discussion forum can be a rewarding
task, but it does take some experience to moderate one effectively. It
provides a communication and interaction network that was not
conveniently present before the Web. The discussion forum also person-
alizes learning for learners and lets everyone have an equal footing in the
event.

Telephone support

Telephone support involves the facilitator telephoning learners to check on their progress and find out if they are having any problems with the learning event materials. Alternatively, learners can telephone the facilitator if they are having difficulties with the learning event. If facilitators offer support over the telephone they must be aware that they lose some of their privacy. Facilitators who give learners their office and home numbers can expect telephone calls at any time, to the annoyance of all concerned.

Learners should be given guidelines regarding the use of the telephone. They should only telephone if they have a problem with the content or assessment tasks of the learning event after they have accessed the frequently asked questions. If the answers to their questions are not there, they should post their questions on the discussion forum. If the questions are still not answered to their satisfaction they should e-mail the facilitator to ask the questions and at this stage facilitators may suggest that learners telephone them.

Learners should be told what times are best for contacting their facilitators, and arrangements should be made for an answering machine to be connected to facilitators' telephones if they are unavailable at the appointed times. Facilitators should attempt to return telephone calls to learners as soon as possible. Learners may want to telephone facilitators when they have technical, personal or study problems. Facilitators should make notes about learners' phone calls, so that they don't forget to follow them up or perhaps use them as part of the learning event evaluation.

Facilitators may want to telephone learners regularly to check on their progress and see if they need any assistance. If facilitators do this it is best to find out from the learners the best times to telephone. At the very least, facilitators should telephone learners at the start of the learning event and introduce themselves. They should also try to motivate learners about completing the learning event.

In general, when talking with learners on the telephone, facilitators should be warm, friendly, supportive and helpful. If the problem is one that is applicable to all learners, then facilitators should post the problem and the solution on the discussion forum so that other learners can see the answer. However, facilitators should obtain the permission of learners before doing this.

Face-to-face tutorials

In some Web-based learning events the facilitator and learners are required to meet for face-to-face tutorials or attend an intensive study school, which may be held over several days. These sessions are designed to complement the Web-based learning event by allowing learners to meet other learners and the facilitator involved in the learning event. These sessions can overcome some of the problems of isolation learners may feel and can have a motivational effect on their situation. The tutorial should not be a lecture, where the facilitator is the information-giver and learners are the receivers. The tutorial should be discussion-based with learners encouraged to ask questions and give opinions.

Tutorials should focus on the information given in the learning event, and explore problems, review cases, apply principles, undertake practice exercises, perform calculations and engage in discussions.

There are many elements that make up an effective tutorial, for example, it should:

- have clear goals and objectives;
- not allow the facilitator to talk too much;
- encourage learners to ask questions and discuss problems;
- help learners feel comfortable in a physical sense. The physical environment may need to be changed to facilitate discussion;
- help learners feel relaxed about asking questions;
- be conducted in line with the learning event objectives;
- assist learners to learn;
- establish an effective rapport between the facilitator and learners;
- involve the learners;
- allow for more personal attention than a Web-based learning event.

There are many types of activities that can be used in a tutorial:

- *Buzz groups.* In a buzz group a small number of learners are given a problem or issue to discuss without the assistance of the facilitator and report back to the larger group.
- *Brainstorming.* In brainstorming the facilitator poses a problem and the learners suggest solutions. Members of the group are not expected to comment on the solutions given by others. One member of the group records the solutions.
- *Role-plays.* Role-plays are designed partially to replicate the real world. The larger group will have a discussion and from that a series of problems may be suggested. The smaller groups are asked to prepare a role-play on one of the problems to demonstrate the problem. After the role-play the group should analyse what has happened.
- *Group discussion.* Small group discussions allow the facilitator to introduce ideas, issues, tasks and problems and have learners discuss them. Small groups are formed to discuss the topic. The facilitator can guide the discussion through a series of questions to reach a conclusion.

- *Seminars.* Small groups of learners prepare a paper or presentation on a topic selected by the facilitator or themselves. The presentation is made to the larger group for discussion and analysis. The facilitator plays a less predominant role than in group discussions and attempts to co-ordinate, facilitate and comment on the presentations.
- *Simulation.* Simulation is an attempt to create the illusion of reality when reality cannot be used because of constraints such as time, cost, danger, complexity and location. Simulations are often used in conjunction with games.

Whatever activities are conducted in the tutorial, learners must feel they have gained value from the tutorial and that it was worthwhile.

Assignments

Chapter 9 outlined the importance of facilitator-marked assignments and the need for a consistent marking guide.

The facilitator should assist learners by marking their assignments and conveying advice on further study. By understanding the learners' state of knowledge the facilitator can pass on advice relevant to individual learners. The role of written comments is very important, as they are a personalized method of communication between facilitator and learners. Comments should suggest ways in which learners might improve, therefore, it is important that they be positive, give advice, promote learners' self-esteem, and be constructive and supportive.

To effectively comment on learners' assignments, facilitators should adhere to the following guidelines:

- Use written comments to motivate learners by encouraging them to engage in thinking, reading and other activities related to the topic under study.
- Create a friendly atmosphere by using the right tone and not adopting a threatening tone.
- Comment on learners' work in a number of different ways, for example by using an audio file attached to an e-mail document.
- Start comments from where learners are now rather than offering model answers.
- Point out facts that learners have overlooked or misinterpreted.
- Suggest alternative sources of information.
- Point out errors in learners' reasoning.
- Suggest other ways learners may present their work or ideas.
- Ask for further explanation of confused answers.
- Suggest short cuts learners could have used.
- Respect learners' feelings and give their answers respect, especially when their answers do not agree with the facilitator's answers.
- Put specific comments on assignments where they are required.

- Avoid being too critical of learners' assignments.
- Avoid making ambiguous comments.
- Avoid writing patronizing comments about learners' assignments.
- Ensure comments are informative and helpful.
- Suggest alternative approaches or interpretations learners could use.
- Help learners reflect on how their work might be improved.
- Point out the relation between learners' present and previous work.
- Comment on any special insight learners have given.
- Suggest the good points as well the poor points in learners' work.
- Try to avoid words such as: error, wrong, failed, below standard, unsatisfactory, need to try harder.
- Try to use words such as: good point, I never thought of that point, good example, I like that, I agree, good work, you are right on the topic.
- Keep the turn-round time as short as possible. (Facilitators should set guidelines for assignment turn-round time.)
- Be sympathetic to requests for extensions to assignment submission dates.

Many word processing programs now have editing features, allowing the facilitator to edit learners' work and learners to track the changes the facilitator has made. These programs also have annotation features that allow the facilitator to comment on learners' work in a footnote. Audio files can be added to comment on learners' assignments.

LEARNER ORIENTATION TO THE WEB-BASED ENVIRONMENT

The learner will need orientation to the Web-based learning event and how to study in a learner-centred environment. Both are of equal importance if the Web-based learning event is to be successful. The facilitator is usually the person who orientates learners to the event by providing introduction units and ongoing support.

Using a Web-based learning event

As with the facilitator, learners will need to be orientated in the use of the Web-based learning event. This orientation may take the form of a few hours' training in a computer laboratory, where learners are shown how to use the event or complete an introductory learning unit. The orientation should cover all components of the event and its use. Learners should be told what to do when they have technical problems: whether they should contact the facilitator or whether to contact the Web-based technical support staff.

The learning event should include a help menu explaining how to use the learning event. There should be a frequently asked questions component regarding technical problems, and a discussion forum moderated by technical support staff should be made available. Learners should be able to post questions regarding technical problems and have them answered as soon as possible.

What is a Web-based learning event?

Learners need to be told exactly what a Web-based learning event is and what is expected of them. If the learners are new to Web-based learning, they may think it involves simply browsing or surfing the Web. They need to be told that the Web-based learning event is structured in the way the information is presented, based on detailed learning objectives, and that they will be required to complete various exercises and assessments.

Studying in a Web-based learning environment

One of the major advantages of Web-based learning is that it is learner-centred, meaning that learners have to take more responsibility for their own learning. They cannot rely on the facilitator to motivate them to study the Web-based learning event.

Learners need to complete the following types of activities during the learning event:

- read through their Web-based learning materials;
- play audio, animation and video files;
- interact with computer-based training programs and simulations;
- develop mind maps and summaries;
- complete quizzes and assessments;
- complete assignments;
- make their own notes;
- access external resources, libraries and other Web-based resources;
- access frequently asked questions;
- access a glossary of terms;
- discuss topics and otherwise participate in discussion forums;
- complete formal assessment;
- contact their tutor.

Assisting learners to answer the four questions below will help them take control over their own learning:

1. Where will learners find time to study?
2. Where will learners study?
3. What resources will learners use?
4. How will the facilitator assist the learners?

Where will learners find time to study?

Learners, especially working adults, are already busy people and many wonder where they will find the time to study a Web-based learning event. The advantage of studying via the Web is that the material is available at any time and at any location where there is a computer with Web access. Still, learners need to make time available for study in their already busy schedule. One way of doing this is teaching them how to manage their time well.

One effective way of teaching learners to manage their time well is to ask them to produce a timetable of their existing week. Generally, part-time study requires approximately eight hours of study per week, but this will obviously vary depending on the type of learning event. Learners now need to produce a new timetable and decide what activities they will give up so they can study. This is the difficult part: giving up activities they presumably like and enjoy, and replacing them with study time. This may affect learners' work and family environments, but if they want to study and gain a qualification they have to be prepared to give up something.

Here are some hints the facilitator can give learners about developing their timetables:

- Learners should study in two- or one-hour blocks. Within a two-hour block, they should study for one hour and have a 10- to 15-minute break. Within a one-hour block, they should study for half an hour and have a five-minute break.
- They should schedule four or five two-hour study blocks per week. If they miss a study block, they should try to catch it up within that week.
- If they feel like it or they have time, they can study for more than two hours and they can use this as credit, but they should be careful they do not burn themselves out.
- If they have spare time, they should use it for study. Even 15 minutes can be used to do some study.

Where will learners study?

Learners can study wherever they have access to a computer and the Internet. Most of their study will be done at home, so if possible they should have their own study area with a computer and Web access. Libraries and learning institutes usually allow learners computer and Internet access, so these make ideal places to study at weekends. If learners are employed they can be encouraged to stay after work to complete assignments as long as they have computers with Internet access and the permission of the organization. In many organizations, access to the Internet is restricted to all but a few employees.

What resources will learners use?

Learners have a vast array of resources in their Web-based learning event from which they can study. The facilitator should encourage learners to interact with one another; ideally this is done in small study groups that meet regularly. One of the advantages of using the Web for delivering instruction is that it allows easy communication between learners via e-mail and discussion forums. Learners should be actively encouraged to create electronic learning networks with other learners. They may have a good source of assistance in friends who have themselves completed the learning event. They should be encouraged to joint Usenets and partici-pate in outside discussion forums.

How will the facilitator assist the learners?

Learners should be told what the facilitator role is and how the facilitator can help them study. They must be told when the facilitator will be avail-able to help and how they can contact him or her. Learners must be made aware that although the facilitator grades their assignments he or she is also available to assist with study. They must be made aware that facili-tator comments on facilitator-marked assignments must be taken constructively. Learners take a lot of time and put a lot of effort into their assignments, so the facilitator must ensure that they gain valuable feed-back to enable them to complete their learning event successfully.

CONCLUSION

Facilitators play a critical role in the success of a Web-based learning event, as they are the ones who support learners. The Web provides many methods to communicate with learners and these, together with the more traditional forms of support, must be used to assist learners with problems in their studies. The orientation of facilitators is often given little attention and it is assumed that anyone can act as a facilitator. Facilitators need orientation and assistance not only in the operation of the Web-based learning event but also in how to support learners effec-tively. A Web-based learning event cannot be successful without well-designed learning materials and good facilitator support.

Just as facilitators need orientating, so do learners. Web-based learning is self-based learning and places the responsibility for study directly on the learners themselves. They need to know how to use the Web-based learning environment to be successful.

Chapter 17
The technical infrastructure

INTRODUCTION

Web-based learning programs demand more resources and technical understanding than what is typically required of similarly structured disk-based or CD ROM-based programs. Unlike traditional computer-based training programs, Web-based training programs are built, delivered and maintained as part of a total system.

The system can be divided into software and hardware sub-systems, and includes everything from Internet connectivity and Web, database and e-mail servers to integration with existing groupware applications, Web sites, MIS systems and often much more. Operating and supporting an online learning system requires trained personnel, as well as software and server technologies that can support a flexible, scalable learning environment.

This chapter examines the software and hardware infrastructure needed to support a mid- to large-size online learning environment.

PLANNING FOR SIZE AND SCALABILITY

Most large-scale online learning infrastructures begin by supporting a single course or department, and often extend to other departments or the entire company or institution. The pace of growth, like most developments related to the Internet, can be very rapid, especially if there is a big demand for your courses and they gain widespread popularity. Therefore, it is necessary to consider the long-term resources needed to support properly a virtual campus that offers dozens, or perhaps hundreds, of online courses.

BANDWIDTH ISSUES

When considering the resources needed to support your Web-based learning system, perhaps the most important factor is bandwidth requirements. Bandwidth can be considered as the amount of data that can flow through your network at any given time, and as such it has direct implications on the types of media and features you can realistically include in your Web-based learning event, the number of learners who can simultaneously access your online materials, the speed at which your content is delivered and more. It is therefore important to consider two key questions: 1) how much bandwidth does your current infrastructure support?; and 2) how much bandwidth do you estimate that you will require for future expansion? Establishing these parameters early on can save you from having to deal with frustrated learners complaining of slow access times, as well as countless hours spent reworking your learning content to suit the often-rigid constraints of what your network is truly capable of supporting.

METHODS OF CONNECTING YOUR VIRTUAL CAMPUS TO THE INTERNET

If learners are accessing your virtual campus across the Internet, you have a variety of choices to connect your network to the global Internet. Choosing the type of connection will depend on actual bandwidth requirements, cost, availability and integration with existing systems.

ATM

ATM (Asynchronous Transfer Mode) is a technology being implemented by many major Internet service providers and telephone companies. Table 17.1 shows the various classes of ATM service.

Table 17.1   *Classes of ATM service*

Class	Service	Use
A	real-time guaranteed delivery	two-way audio or video
B	real-time, non guaranteed delivery	one-way audio or video
C	non-real-time, guaranteed delivery	
D	non-real-time, non-guaranteed delivery	

Table 17.2 shows ATM transmission rates.

Table 17.2   *ATM transmission rates*

Designator	Bit Rate	Notes
ATM-T1	1.5 Mbps	ATM over T1 circuit
ATM-25	25 Mbps	designed for LANs using UTP cable
OC-1	51 Mbps	one ATM channel over fibre optic cable
OC-3	155 Mbps	3 ATM channels
OC-12	622 Mbps	12 ATM channels
OC-48	2.4 Gbps	48 ATM channels
OC-192	9.6 Gbps	192 ATM channels

Digital circuits

Connecting a campus LAN to the Internet is commonly done by way of leased-grade lines. In the United States and Canada, these lines are normally indicated by a 'T', while in Europe, South America and Mexico they are normally indicated by an 'E'. Tables 17.3 and 17.4 give the bandwidth capabilities of commonly available North American and European digital circuits.

Table 17.3   *North American digital circuits*

Carrier	Bandwidth	Aggregation
T0	56 Kbps	1 voice circuit
T1	1.544 Mbps	27 T0 circuits
T2	6.312 Mbps	4 T1 circuits
T3	44.736 Mbps	28 T1 circuits
T4	274.176 Mbps	168 T1 circuits

Table 17.4   *European digital circuits*

Carrier	Bandwidth	Aggregation
E0	64 Kbps	1 voice circuit
E1	2.048 Mbps	320 E0 circuits
E3	34 Mbps	16 e1 circuits

Other common methods of connecting a campus LAN to the Internet are by way of ADSL, ISDN and cable modem circuits.

ADSL

ADSL (Asymmetric Digital Subscriber Line) is a technology that operates over normal voice telephone wiring. ADSL implements a low-data-rate up-link and a high-data-rate down-link. An advantage of ADSL is that it can be implemented over conventional telephone lines and does not require you to install (often expensive) coaxial or fibre optical cable to your point of connection. ADSL data rates operate from 1 to 6 Mbps on the down-link channel (depending on distance from the telephone exchange) and between 16 Kbps and 640 Kbps on the up-link channel.

ISDN

ISDN (Integrated Services Digital Network) is a dial-up digital circuit. Unlike leased lines, which are permanently connected to the Internet, an ISDN circuit allows you to make and break the connections between any two ISDN adaptors. ISDN technology has been available for some time now, and is normally available in many areas of the world. ISDN data rates are normally quoted at 64 Kbps and 128 Kbps, and can go as high as 256 Kbps when an ISDN's two 'B' channels are 'fused' together.

Cable modems

A typical cable modem provides a download capability of 10 Mbps and an upload capability of 768 Mbps. Cable modems have become a popular method in many places that offer cable television service. Cable modems are broadband modems, which operate at very high data rates.

CHOOSING YOUR WEB SERVER SOFTWARE

The Web server(s) used to host your online events represent the hardware foundation of your online learning infrastructure. They allow you to send your learning content over the Internet using the HyperText Markup Language (HTML). The Web server accepts page requests from Web browsers like Internet Explorer and Netscape, and then returns the appropriate HTML documents. A number of server-side technologies can be used to increase the power of the server beyond its ability to deliver your online materials as standard HTML pages; these include CGI scripts, COM components, SSL security and Active Server Pages (ASPs).

While a single computer may be sufficient to host perhaps dozens of courses, you will quickly find that its resources become saturated if many thousands of learners begin regularly logging in and accessing courses. Therefore, it is important to consider server technologies that are capable of supporting a scalable learning environment, open development architectures, leveraged content, computer-managed instruction, and automated registration and assessment.

There are many Web server products capable of serving up your learning materials. When evaluating the best product for your institution or company, you need to consider many factors including features, price, performance, scalability, hardware requirements, compatibility with existing hardware/software, administrative overhead, training required, future plans and more. The next section provides a short review of Microsoft's Internet Information Server, one of the many Web server products to choose from when building or expanding your online learning infrastructure. Other products include IBM/Lotu Notes/Domino, Apache Web Server, O'Reilly's Website Pro and Netscape Enterprise Server.

Microsoft Internet Information Server (IIS)

While only available for Windows NT, IIS has transformed the NT operating system into a platform for delivering Web-based learning applications. IIS 4.0/5.0 offers a platform for building a sophisticated online learning infrastructure. Many courseware management systems or Web classroom builders are available for NT/IIS, and developers can use a wide range of tools to build and deploy Web-based training applications for IIS. As a Web server, IIS is relatively easy to set up and maintain, and it is available for the Server edition of Windows NT 4.0 and Windows 2000.

The Web services of IIS are integrated with NT's core system and networking capabilities and the application infrastructure of Microsoft's Transaction Server 2.0. This allows developers and administrators using IIS to share many of NT's core features and to access Microsoft's Component Object Model (COM) technology. IIS's Active Server Pages offer an open, compile-free application environment in which you can combine HTML, scripts and reusable ActiveX server components to create dynamic Web-based learning sites and applications.

In addition to IIS, Option Pack 4.0 includes a collection of server technologies that can enhance the capabilities of your online learning infrastructure. Beyond IIS's core HTTP 1.1 services, these include Transaction Server (for building distributed applications), Index Server (indexing and search capabilities for your learning materials, HTML pages and other documents), Certificate Server (managing digital certificates), Site Analyst (site management and usage), Internet Connection Services for Microsoft Remote Access Service (creation of Virtual Private Networks), SMTP Mail Server, and NNTP News Server.

NNTP only works well for internal newsgroups and does not support Usenet news feeds, making it somewhat impractical as a discussion forum tool for a learning application. Likewise, the SMTP Mail Server is a bit of a lightweight mail server, and probably not the best choice if your learning infrastructure includes large-scale e-mail processing.

IIS features include:

- Crash Protection – a feature that allows you to run multiple applications reliably on the IIS server.
- Transactional Active Server Pages – support for scalable Web-based applications that use scripts and components.
- Integrated Message Queuing – an easy way for applications to send and receive messages reliably over a network.
- Support for Java – IIS 4.0 includes a set of Java classes to build server-side components, and Microsoft's Java 1.1 Virtual Machine, which has been tuned for them. Using ASP pages and Microsoft Transaction Server (MTS), you can build server applications using Java and run them efficiently in a demanding server environment.

For users of Windows 95 and the Windows NT Workstation, the NT 4.0 Option Pack also includes Microsoft's Personal Web Server 4.0 (PWS). PWS is a desktop Web server that allows courseware developers to build and debug applications at their workstations, before deploying them to the main IIS server.

Courseware management systems

Courseware management systems (CMS) or learning management systems (LMS) are off-the-shelf products that can provide much of the software infrastructure needed to operate and maintain a large-scale virtual campus. Several CMS packages are available in the market, and they vary widely in price, features, ease of use and more. Following is a short review of a few of the more popular packages.

Blackboard CourseInfo

Blackboard CourseInfo is a relatively easy-to-use courseware management and creation package that institutions and corporations can install locally to support multiple materials developers interested in creating Web-based classes. CourseInfo is an open, flexible server that provides developers with everything they need to create, deliver and manage a Web-based learning environment. Blackboard's features include:

- asynchronous communication;
- synchronous communication;
- assessment tools and gradebook;
- content creation such as syllabus and event description pages;
- database reporting;
- online assistance;
- collaborative work groups;
- online file exchange;
- messaging system;
- user tracking;
- back-up and restoring;
- online upgrades/patches;
- creation and deletion;
- full course management;
- upcoming Educom IMS specification support.

The Learning Manager

The Learning Manager (TLM) is an integrated collection of Windows-based components for curriculum development, course delivery and the management of distributed learning. Based on Microsoft BackOffice technology, coupled with Microsoft SQL Server for database support, TLM is designed for developing and delivering cohesive online learning solutions.

Curriculum developers use TLM to produce online courseware and tests. TLM delivers these resources over the Internet or Intranet, integrating text, graphics, audio, video and computer-delivered materials with external communications tools such as e-mail, conferencing and shared whiteboard applications. The application manages learner progress through online events, tracking what's been completed, what's outstanding and what should be done next. It tracks learners' activity, storing and reporting details of how long they spend at each course component, and scores on all system-issued tests.

TopClass

TopClass is a family of server products that provides a virtual classroom environment to manage all aspects of content and class management. It is a flexible learning environment built entirely on the open, non-proprietary standards of the Web. The software is well suited to educational institutions, as it enables them to create secure, reusable learning objects for delivery via a Web browser.

RUNNING A HELP DESK

If your institution or company is planning on building and delivering a wide selection of Web-based courseware, you will almost certainly need resources to support and maintain your entire system. This typically will come by way of a help desk, or a group of individuals charged with the responsibility of keeping things running smoothly.

To help reduce the number of calls or e-mails to your help desk, it is wise to publish on your Web site as much information as you can regarding the operation of your courseware, and any related software or systems. This can be done in the form of a frequently asked questions page, a searchable database of problem scenarios, screen captures showing configuration settings, and even small video clips that 'walk' users through a problem resolution. It is equally wise to put in place a problem tracking system, which can help disseminate information pertaining to common problems, as well as ensure they are resolved on a timely basis. In most cases, you should staff your help desk with individuals who are technically literate and can communicate effectively with non-technical people.

CONCLUSION

The viability of Web-based learning events depends on an understanding of and attention to the technical infrastructure. This chapter discussed the various issues that should be addressed.

Chapter 18
Copyright considerations

INTRODUCTION

Copyright is a complex issue, and it is not the function of this chapter to provide a discourse on its legalities. It is important, however, to understand that for the most part everything you use to design, develop and build your Web-based learning materials has some form of copyright encumbrance attached. To help you better understand the issues of copyright, this chapter briefly outlines the copyright basics, including a definition of copyright and what is and is not protected by copyright.

For the most part this discussion is based on copyright law as it is applied in the United States. Generally speaking, US copyright law can be used as a guide to the basic rules of copyright world-wide. However, it would be wise for you to check the specific laws of your country to ensure that the learning materials you produce do not infringe copyright. Following the general principles of copyright is a discussion of the issues you should consider when developing Web-based learning materials.

COPYRIGHT – GENERAL PRINCIPLES

Copyright is a form of protection provided in law to the authors of 'original works of authorship'. This includes literary, dramatic, musical, artistic and certain other intellectual works. In other words, copyright is a person's ownership of the intellectual property he or she has created. Copyright protection is available for both published and unpublished works. The copyright owner has the exclusive right to do, or authorize others to do, a number of things with respect to the work created. These include:

● prepare the work;

- prepare derivative works;
- distribute copies by sale, renting, leasing or lending;
- perform the work in public in the case of musical, dramatic and chore-ographic works, motion pictures and other audio-visual works;
- display the works publicly in the case of pictorial, graphic or sculptural works;
- perform the work publicly in the case of sound recordings.

A copyright does not have to be registered, but to prove ownership the author must have registered the work. Copyrighted materials must be in tangible form, that is written down on paper or contained in a computer program or on a Web page, taped, painted or otherwise expressed so that they can be seen, heard or touched. Copyright protection is granted from the time the work is created in fixed form. The copyright in the work immediately becomes the property of the author who created the work and only those deriving rights through the author can claim copyright.

When a work is made for hire, the employer not the employee is considered to be the author. A work made for hire is a work prepared by an employee as part of the scope of their employment or a work specifically ordered as a contribution to a collective work such as a film, Web page or instructional text, as long as the authors agree that the work is to be considered as a work made for hire.

When there is more than one author of the work, such as is the case with this book, each is co-owner of the copyright unless some other agreement is reached. In the case of a journal or periodical, the collective work is copyrighted, but each contribution is also copyrighted by the author of that contribution. Ownership of a book, manuscript, computer application or program and the like does not give the owner copyright. Typically the law states that when you buy a copyrighted work, the copyright stays with the original copyright holder.

Works that are protected under copyright law include:

- literary works;
- musical works and any words that accompany the work;
- dramatic works and any music that accompanies the work;
- pantomimes and choreographic works;
- pictorial, graphic and sculptural works;
- motion pictures and other audio-visual works;
- sound recordings;
- architectural works.

These are very broad categories and typically computer programs are registered as literary works, while maps and building plans, for example, are registered as pictorial, graphic and sculptural works.

There are four categories of materials that are not protected by copyright. These include:

1. works that have not been fixed in a tangible form – this can include impromptu speeches or performances that have not been written or recorded;
2. titles, names, short phrases, familiar symbols and designs, lettering or colouring;
3. ideas, procedures, methods, systems, processes, concepts, principles, discoveries or devices;
4. works made up entirely of information that is common property and containing no original authorship, for example standard calendars and height and weight charts.

Copyright endures for different time periods depending on when the work was created. For example, a work created on or after 1 January 1978 or a work that was created but not published or registered by that same date is automatically given copyright protection from the moment it is 'fixed in tangible form' until 70 years after the author's death. In the case of joint authorship the term lasts for 70 years after the death of the last surviving author. For works for hire, the duration is 95 years from publication or 120 years from creation, whichever is shorter. For a work created and published or registered before 1 January 1978, typical copyright protection extends for 95 years.

There is no such thing as an international copyright that will protect an author throughout the world. Protection against unauthorized use of a work depends on the laws of a particular country. Most countries do, however, offer some form of copyright protection under certain conditions.

COPYRIGHT – WEB-BASED LEARNING MATERIALS

There are a lot of issues surrounding copyright, and you need to be very careful to ensure that your learning materials do not infringe copyright.

The first issue to deal with is design. Very few designs just happen. They are based consciously or unconsciously on what you have seen previously, what is familiar to you and what is appropriate for you, culturally speaking. To get ideas for design many people review books and magazines, and surf the Web. What this means, however, particularly in the case of the Web, is that it is very easy to 'borrow' and modify ideas to suit what you want or need.

For the purpose of this discussion, consider a Web page to be similar to a magazine or book page in that it might contain text and graphics. In some cases the Web page might also contain video and audio components. Typically a Web page is protected as a whole product. No matter that your browser might display the page differently to someone else's browser or that you might modify your browser to display Web pages differently. The underlying design of a Web page consists of a certain arrangement of various elements and as long as that arrangement is original then the design of the page is protected by copyright.

If you decide to use that page or part of it in your learning materials, two issues arise. The first creates much discussion. When your browser downloads the page you requested from a server, it copies all the information it needs to put up that page on your screen into your hard drive. This includes information regarding graphics, audio files, video files, location of text, links and so on. The question is: are you as the user violating copyright? For the most part the answer is no, the line has not been crossed – yet. But if you go a step further and use your browser save button or some other methodology to save either the page and/or its code to your hard drive, then the line has definitely been crossed and you are in violation of copyright.

In order to determine the true extent of the violation, the fair use test has to be applied. Before 1990, the fair use test was typically only applied in academic circles, where making copies of materials for classroom use and/or copying materials for review and discussion was the order of the day. However, the fair use test is becoming more and more of an issue in a Web-based environment. For the most part the concept of fair use lies in the interpretation by the courts of four issues:

1. *The purpose and character of the use.* Was it for commercial or educational non-profit use? Is the new work for criticism, comment, news reporting, teaching, scholarship or research? Does the new work supplant the original or add something new that alters the meaning or message?
2. *The nature of the copyrighted work.* Is the copyrighted work worthy of copyright protection?
3. *The amount used in proportion to the copyrighted work as a whole.* Is the amount and value of the materials reasonable in relation to the purpose of copying? Was no more taken than was necessary?
4. *The effect of the use on the potential market for, or value of, the copyrighted work.* What harm was done to the market or potential market for the original and any derivative works?

What you have to decide when you consider your learning materials page designs is whether the materials being considered for use in the learning materials will pass the fair use test. If you are developing learning materials for an organization that puts learning materials online for potential users to access as they see fit and pay for that privilege, it's very possible you will not pass the fair use test. If you work in an educational environment, is that environment truly non-profit? Remember that in a 'work for hire' situation it is your responsibility to ensure that the materials you use are free of copyright encumbrances.

In many Web-based learning events, learners are directed to other resources, which are often in the form of links to Web sites or other Web-based learning materials. Quite often the designer provides a list of links for learners to choose from, either in a remedial mode or in order for learners to 'drill down' into hyperlinked text. A link is a URL; it is considered to be a fact and similar to a street address, and is therefore not copyrightable. However, if you research a topic and produce a list of URLs, that list may be copyrightable as it may be deemed to have some originality. This means that if you see a link or URL list, someone else has taken the time to research the topic and produce the list. If you copy it wholesale to your learning materials, it is probably a copyright violation. However, you could use several links from that list without getting into trouble.

Putting direct links from your learning materials to other Web sites may also cause you problems. There is something called a doctrine of implied public access on the Web. This means that if a Web site has been created and is available to the general public, the creator or owner of the site has given implied permission to others to link to their site, and they in turn are able to link to other Web sites. This implied permission is fine and works up to a point, but only if the Web site being linked to is reputable and the so-called 'assets of your learning materials' are not diminished by such an association. Netiquette dictates that you request permission before linking to a site.

One final issue with respect to linking is confusion of authorship. The linking of your learning materials to other sites may lead your learners to become confused as to who actually wrote, designed or developed the materials. This could be interpreted as a violation of the original author's rights. This problem can be overcome in the technical design of your learning materials. A far more simple solution is not to do it in the first place. Make sure that your materials are clearly labelled and links correctly identified in ways that leave no doubt in the minds of your learners as to who is the author.

To make sure that you do not run into problems with copyright you would be advised to get a licence to use the material. Typically you would contact the owner of the work, via the publisher in the case of text used from a book, the film-maker in the case of a film clip and possibly via e-mail to the owner of Web-based materials. When you make your request include the following information:

1. the source of your material;
2. a complete bibliographic citation:
   - for a book, the name of the author or authors, the title of the work, the place of publication, the publisher and the date;

- for an article in a periodical, the author's or authors' name(s), the title of the article, the name of the periodical, the volume and number, the date and the pages of the article;
- for an electronic source
  - reference section: author's last name, first initial, date of publication or 'no date' if unavailable, title of article or section used, number of paragraphs, title of complete work, form (such as http, CD ROM, e-mail), complete URL, date of access
  - Web site: title (year, month, day), title of article (online), complete URL, date of access

  (A number of different electronic style formats are in use at present. For a full listing, search under e-references or e-citations on the World Wide Web);

3. a list of the pages, screens and frames you wish to reproduce;
4. the name of the learning event in which you are going to use the material and how many times a year the event will be presented;
5. how many learners may be using the materials.

You should request non-exclusive rights to the material for a minimum of two years in order to avoid having to request permission every time the event takes place. If you think you will not be revising your materials for a longer period of time (not advisable!) then you may wish to request non-exclusive rights for up to three years (but do not expect to receive it).

It is important that you emphasize in your request how the materials are to be used. For example, is the event offered by a non-profit educational institution, or is it a not-for-profit learning event, or is it a commercial event? Fees are often reduced for work used in a non-profit educational/learning situation.

You should be aware that requests for the use of certain comic-strip characters, comic-book heroes, well-known film characters or clips from sports events will most probably not be granted, or if they are a substantial fee will be requested. This relates to the issue of fair use and the effect of the use on the potential market for or value of the copyrighted work.

As you are researching the various materials you want to use in your learning materials, you will come across materials listed in the public domain or materials that are copyright-free. When you see such materials, you are free to use them as you wish. But there are two things to be careful of here. First, if the public domain item you want to use is part of a larger work, you can only use the item and not the entire work. Second, if you see a compilation of public domain documents, the use of one element is permissible, but the entire collection may be held under compilation copyright.

The public domain contains all works that previously had copyright protection. While it is all but impossible to lose copyright protection under today's laws, under previous copyright laws this was not the case. For example, all works published before 1978 that did not contain a valid copyright notice may be considered to be in the public domain. Owners of works published between 1978 and 1 March 1989 that did not contain a valid copyright notice were given a five-year grace period in which to correct the problem of publication without notice; otherwise the work was placed into the public domain. The public domain also contains all works for which the statutory copyright period has expired, and you are free to copy any work published before 1964 for which the copyright owner failed to renew the copyright. Copyrightable works can also enter the public domain if the copyright owner gives the work to the public domain. However, the copyright owner must specifically grant the work to the public domain.

In many countries, government documents and publications are not copyrighted, and are considered to be in the public domain. This means that if you need such a document and obtain it from the Web, for example, you are free to copy and/or use it. Again, some words of caution should be heeded here. As noted at the beginning of this chapter the discussion centres around copyright laws in the United States. Make sure that the same laws regarding government documents apply to your country of residence. It is also possible that the government agency that published the document hired a private contractor to author the work. If this is the case the work is copyrighted and all copyright laws apply.

As you develop your learning materials you should keep a simple copyright log that notes publication data, requests and reply dates, whether or not permission has been granted, the fee if any, and whether the fee has been paid. If a fee is requested, you will probably have to negotiate with someone in your organization about who pays it and how much is to be paid. Several weeks before the learning materials are put up in an online environment, you should check to make sure that all your materials are ready from a copyright perspective. For those materials where copyright permission is still outstanding, make sure you have a method in place to repeat the request. If or when verbal permission is given to use a particular work, make sure you send a written request as a record. This will complete your files and avoid any problems later.

Once you have received permission to use the materials, it is essential that you indicate the status of this permission on one of the first pages of the work before it is reproduced. The most appropriate source statement is generally the complete bibliographic citation followed by the phrase 'Reproduced by permission'. If the copyright holder specifies a particular credit statement or credit line, this must be reproduced exactly in your learning materials.

CONCLUSION

The many issues of copyright are confusing. However, one way or another copyright must be made part of both your materials planning and development. While the issues of copyright are difficult to grasp, the key to copyright matters is quite simple. Assume everything is either copyrighted or copyrightable and ask permission before you use the materials. Begging forgiveness later in a court of law usually won't work.

References

Dick, W and Carey, L (1978) *The Systematic Design of Instruction*, Harper Collins, New York

Dick, W and Carey, L (1990) *The Systematic Design of Instruction*, 3rd edn, HarperCollins, New York

Gagné, R M (1977) *Conditions of Learning*, 3rd edn, Holt, Rinehart & Wilson, New York

Greer, M (1992) *ID Project Management Tools and Techniques for Instructional Designers and Developers*, Educational Technology Publications, Englewood Cliffs, NJ

Jolliffe, A K (1997) *Evaluation of the Virtual College*, Unpublished document, Educational and Staff Development Department, Singapore Polytechnic

Further reading

BOOKS

Driscoll, M (1998) *Web-based Training: Using technology to design adult learning experiences*, Jossey-Bass Pfeifer, California

Forsyth, I, Jolliffe, A and Stevens, D (1999) *The Complete Guide to Teaching a Course: Practical strategies for teachers, lecturers and instructors*, 2nd edn, Kogan Page, London

Gagné, R M, Briggs, L J and Wager, W W (1992) *Principles of Instructional Design*, Harcourt Brace, New York

Hall, B (1997) *Web-based Training Cookbook*, John Wiley, New York

Hilz, S R (1994) *The Virtual Classroom: Learning without limits via computer networks*, Ablex Publications, New York

Keegan, D (ed) (1993) *Theoretical Principles of Distance Learning*, Routledge, London

McCormack, C and Jones, D (1998) *Building a Web-based Education System*, John Wiley, New York

Porter, L R (1997) *Creating the Virtual Classroom: Distance learning with the Internet*, John Wiley, New York

Race, P (1994) *The Open Learning Handbook: Promoting quality in designing and delivering flexible learning*, 2nd edn, Kogan Page, London

Rowntree, D (1986) *Teaching through Self-instruction: How to develop open learning materials*, rev edn, Kogan Page, London

Rowntree, D and Lockword, F (1994) *Preparing Materials for Open, Distance and Flexible Learning: An action guide for teachers and trainers*, Kogan Page, London

ARTICLES

Almeda, M B (1998) University of California extension online: from concept to reality, *Asynchronous Learning Network Magazine*, **2** (2), September, http://www.aln.org/alnweb/journal/vol2_issue2/almeda. htm (retrieved 30 October 1998)

Andriole, S (1997) Paradigms for on-line learning: requirements-driven ALN course design, development, delivery and evaluation, *Asynchronous Learning Network Magazine*, **1** (2), August, http://www.aln. org/alnweb/journal/issue2/andriole.htm (retrieved 25 August 1997)

Beaudin, B P (1999) Copyright dot com: keeping online asynchronous discussion on topic, *Asynchronous Learning Network Magazine*, **3** (2), November, http://www.aln.org/alnweb/journal/Vol3_issue2/beaudin.htm (retrieved 17 January 2000)

Bonk, C J *et al* (1999) A ten level Web integration continuum for higher education: new resources, partners, courses, and markets, http://www.oise.on.ca/~arojo/Overview.html (retrieved 3 April 2000)

Bourne, J R (1998) Net-learning strategies for on-campus and off-campus network-enabled learning, *Asynchronous Learning Network Magazine*, **2** (2), September, http://www.aln.org/alnweb/journal/vol2_issue2/ bourne2.htm (retrieved 30 October 1998)

Bourne, J R *et al* (1997) Paradigms for on-line learning: a case study in the design and implementation of an asynchronous learning network course, *Asynchronous Learning Network Magazine*, **1** (2), August, http://www. aln.org/alnweb/journal/issue2/assee.htm (retrieved 25 August 1997)

Capper, J M and Freeman, M A (1999) Educational innovation: hype, heresies and hopes, *Asynchronous Learning Network Magazine*, **3** (2), December, http://www.aln.org/alnweb/magazine/Vol3_issue2/freeman. htm (retrieved 2 February 2000)

Comber, T (1995), Building usable web pages: an HCL perspective, AusWeb 95 conference, http://www.scu.edu.au/sponsored/ausweb/ ausweb95/papers/hypertext/comber/ (retrieved 19 May 1997)

Diotalevi, R N (1999) Copyright dot com: the digital millennium in copyright, *Asynchronous Learning Network Magazine*, **3** (2), November, http://www.aln.org/alnweb/journal/Vol3_issue2/diotalevi.htm (retrieved 17 January 2000)

Eaton, M (1996) Interactive for HTML-based tutorials in distance learning programs, AusWeb 95 conference, http://www.scu.edu.au/sponsored/ausweb/ausweb96/educn/eaton/paper.html (retrieved 19 May 1997)

Eklund, J (1996) Integrating the web and the teaching of technology: case across two universities, AusWeb 96 conference, http://www.scu.edu.au/sponsored/ausweb/ausweb96/educn/eklund2/paper.html (retrieved 27 March 1997)

Ellis, R (1997) Effective use of the Web for education: design principles and pedagogy, A workshop given at the professional and organizational development network in higher education conference in Haines City, Florida, http://staff.washington.edu/rells/pod97/ (retrieved 6 July 1999)

Funaro, G M (1999) Pedagogical roles and implementation guidelines for online communication tools, *Asynchronous Learning Network Magazine*, **3** (2), December, http://www.aln.org/alnweb/magazine/Vol3_issue2/funaro.htm (retrieved 2 February 2000)

Hara, N and Kling, R (1999) Learners' frustrations with a course: a taboo topic in the discourse, CSI working paper, http://www.slis.indiana.edu/CSI/wp99_01.html (retrieved 29 October 1999)

Hiltz, S R (1997) Impact of college-level courses via asynchronous learning network: some preliminary results, *Asynchronous Learning Network Magazine*, **1** (2), August, http://www.aln.org/alnweb/journal/issue2/hiltz.htm (retrieved 25 August 1997)

Jaffee, D (1998) Institutionalized resistance to asynchronous learning networks, *Asynchronous Learning Network Magazine*, **2** (2), September, http://www.aln.org/alnweb/journal/vol2_issue2/jaffee.htm (retrieved 30 October 1998)

Martyn, W and Omari, A (1996) Developing educational content for the Web: issues and ideas, AusWeb 96 conference, http://www.scu.edu.au/sponsored/ausweb/ausweb96/educn/wild/paper.html (retrieved 27 March 1997)

McHenry, B A (1999) New features for learning management systems, *Asynchronous Learning Network Magazine*, **3** (2), December, http://www.aln.org/alnweb/magazine/Vol3_issue2/McHenry.htm (retrieved 2 February 2000)

McLean R S (1996) Assessing course assignments submitted as Web pages, Inet proceedings, Chapter 7, http://www.isoc.org/inet96/proceedings/c7/c7_4.htm (retrieved 14 January 2000)

McManus, T F (1996) Delivering instruction on the world wide web, University of Texas, http://www.svsu.edu/~mcmanus/papers/wbi.html (retrieved 24 March 1997)

Moonen, J (1997) The efficiency of telelearning, *Asynchronous Learning Network Magazine*, **1** (2), August, http://www.aln.org/alnweb/journal/issue2/moonen.htm (retrieved 25 August 1997)

Nguyen, A T A, Tan, W and Kezunonvic, L (1996) Interactive multimedia on the world wide web: implementation and implications for the tertiary education sector, AusWeb 96 conference, http://www.scu.edu.au/sponsored/ausweb/ausweb96/educn/nguyen/paper.html (retrieved 27 March 1997)

Oliver, R, Herrington, J and Omari, A (1996) Creating effective instructional material for the world wide web, AusWeb 96 conference, http://www.scu.edu.au/sponsored/ausweb/ausweb96/educn/oliver/ (retrieved 27 March 1997)

Parson, R (1997) An investigation into instruction available on the worldwide Web, Master of Education research project, Ontario Institute in Education, University of Toronto, http://www.oise.utoronto.ca/~rparson/outld.htm (retrieved 27 March 2000)

Paulsen, M F (1995) The online report on pedagogical techniques for computer-mediated communication, http://tecfa.unige.ch/edu-comp/edu-ws94/contrib/schneider/schneide.book.html (retrieved 11 April 2000)

Paulsen, M F (1998) Teaching methods and techniques for computer-mediated communication, http://www.nettskolen.com/alle/forskning/22/icdepenn.htm#opp (retrieved 30 March 2000)

Pennel, R (1996) Managing online learning, AusWeb 96 conference, http://www.scu.edu.au/sponsored/ausweb/ausweb96/educn/pennell/paper.html (retrieved 27 March 1997)

Pimentel, J R (1999) Design of net-learning system based on experiential learning, Asynchronous Learning Network Magazine, 3 (2), November, http://www.aln.org/alnweb/journal/Vol3_issue2/pimentel.htm (retrieved 17 January 2000)

Raineri, D M, Mehrtens, B G and Hubler, A W (1997) CyberProf – an intelligent human-computer interface for interactive instruction on the World Wide Web, *Asynchronous Learning Network Magazine*, 1 (2), August, http://www.aln.org/alnweb/journal/issue2/raineri.htm (retrieved 25 August 1997)

Ritchie, C R and Hoffman, B (1996) Using instructional design principles to amplify learning on the World Wide Web, Paper presented at the Society for Information Technology and Teacher Education seventh world conference, http://edweb.sdsu.edu/clrit/learningtree/DCD/WWWInstrdesign/WWWInstrdesign.html (retrieved 13 December 1999)

Rojo, A (1996) Electronic forums overview, http://www.oise.on.ca/~arojo/Overview.html (retrieved 4 November 1996)

Schneider, D (1994) Teaching and learning with Internet tools: a position paper, Paper presented at the first international conference on the World Wide Web, http://tecfa.unige.ch/edu-comp/edu-ws94/contrib/schneider/schneide.book.html (retrieved 10 March 2000)

Schrock, K (1998) Evaluation of world wide web site: An annotated bibliography, Clearinghouse on Information and Technology, http://ericir.syr.edu/ithome/digests/edoir9802.html (retrieved 15 May 1999)

Thaiupathump, C, Bourne, J R and Campbell, J O (1999) Intelligent agents for online learning, *Asynchronous Learning Network Magazine*, 3 (2), November, http://www.aln.org/alnweb/journal/Vol3_issue2/Choon2.htm (retrieved 17 January 2000)

Thompson, M M and McGrath, J W (1999) Using ALNs to support a complete educational experience, *Asynchronous Learning Network Magazine*, 3 (2), November, http://www.aln.org/alnweb/journal/Vol3_issue2/Thompson.htm (retrieved 17 January 2000)

Web resources

ABOUT WEB-BASED LEARNING

The Web of Asynchronous Learning Networks – a site that focuses on asynchronous learning. It includes publications, online discussions, workshops and detail of conferences.
http://www.aln.org/

Digital Think – a site that offers various courses on different aspects of Web-based programming.
http://www.digitalthink.com/

Dyro's Web-based Training Site – explains how to use the Internet and Web-based training in education.
http://www.dyroweb.com/index.html

EDC111 Web-based Instruction – a course that explains the principles of Web-based training.
http://www.soe.unc.edu/edci111/8-98/intro111.htm

The IEEE Learning Technology Standards Committee (IEEE LTSC) – an open, accredited standards body tasked to develop 'real', *de jure* learning technology standards. Consortia such as IMS and the AICC increasingly acknowledge the IEEE LTSC as the single forum for turning specifications into standards.
http://ltsc.ieee.org/

Just a lot a Bonk – a site with various articles on the educational use of Web-based learning.
http://php.indiana.edu/~cjbonk/

Learning and Teaching in Cyberspace – a site explaining the use of Web-based learning in education.
http://home.sprynet.com/~gkearsley/chapts.htm

Learning to Learning – a site that discusses instructional design and Web-based learning.
http://snow.utoronto.ca/Learn2/design.html#resources

Links for Teachers – a site that presents links that are useful for teachers including lesson plans.
http://mciunix.mciu.k12.pa.us/~spjvweb/tealinks.html

OISEUT – Canada's leading educational institution dedicated to the establishment of a learning society, through immersing itself in the world of applied problem solving and expanding the knowledge and capacities of individuals to lead productive lives.
http://www.oise.on.ca/

Online Education – lists a large number of online learning resource sites.
http://search.msn.com.sg/exploring/category/C3P95T100LP.asp

The Online Report on Pedagogical Techniques for Computer-mediated Communication – a site that explains the pedagogical uses of computer-mediated communication.
http://www.hs.nki.no/~morten/cmcped.htm

Rick Ellis – a home page that has a course on the effective use of the Web for education and other useful information on Web-based learning.
http://staff.washington.edu/rells/

Springfield Township High School – a virtual library for the Springfield High School, which has some useful links for teachers.
http://mciunix.mciu.k12.pa.us/~spjvweb/index.html

TECFA – an academic unit active in the field of educational technology. It belongs to the School of Psychology and Education of the University of Geneva.
http://tecfa.unige.ch/

WAOE – currently being incorporated as a 'non-profit' organization, through procedures in the state of California, USA. On a broader basis, the association may look for official standing in other parts of the world, should this be helpful to promote the professional, educational needs of members. In the meantime, membership in WAOE is open to anyone in the world with an interest in the quality of online education.
http://www.waoe.org/

Web-based Instruction Lessons – a site that has lessons on Web-based training.
http://www.soe.unc.edu/edci111/8-98/index_wbi2.htm

Web-based Training Information Centre – WBTIC is a non-profit resource for those interested in developing and delivering Web-based training, online learning or distance education. The site contains a WBT primer, surveys, discussion forums and resource links.
http://www.filename.com/wbt/

World Association for Online Education – an electronic journal discussing all aspects of online learning and teaching.
http://waoe.org/web/

INSTRUCTIONAL MANAGEMENT TOOLS

Blackboard.com – an instructional management tool that allows you to place your courses online free. The site also includes a large selection of sample courses.
http://www.blackboard.com/

Centra – Web-based software and services for live collaboration, enabling business interaction, collaborative commerce and corporate learning.
http://www.centra.com/

Learning Space – an instructional management tool that is based on Lotus Notes.
http://www.lotus.com/home.nsf/welcome/learnspace

The Learning Manager (TLM) – a scalable software product that facilitates the development, delivery and administration of e-learning using Intranets or the Internet.
http://www.cbts.com.au
http://www.tlmcorp.com

TopClass – a popular instructional management tool.
http://www.wbtsystems.com/products/gallery.html

EXAMPLES OF WEB-BASED LEARNING SITES

Art History 181 B – a course on modern architecture featuring colour photographs.
http://wwwcatsic.ucsc.edu/~arth181b/

A biology site – has a major component of the course on the Web.
http://www.life.uiuc.edu/bio100/

Chemistry Web site -supplements materials for the course.
http://eee.uci.edu/98f/40370/index.html

Computer-mediated Learning – a course on computer-mediated learning.
http://education.indiana.edu/~frick/r547/

Horizon.com – a site that offers Web-based learning courses.
http://horizon.unc.edu/

Interactive Frog Dissection – an online tutorial showing how to dissect a frog. Extensive use of colour photographs and video, which includes an interactive component.
http://curry.edschool.virginia.edu/go/frog/home.html

An Introductory Botany Course from the University of Illinois.
http://www.life.uiuc.edu/plantbio/102/

Nexted – a company that develops Web-based training courses using Blackboard, commercially available software. The site includes examples of different courses developed using Blackboard.
http://www.nexted.com/

Science Courts – The Science Court CD ROM series for schools mixes animated courtroom drama with hands-on science activities and a proven learning process to teach kids fundamental science concepts.
http://www.teachtsp.com/classroom/scicourt/index.htm

Teaching with Internet – examples of courses using different delivery and teaching strategies.
http://www.enmu.edu/~kinleye/teach/Inetch.html

The World Lecture Hall (WLH) – contains links to pages created by faculty world-wide who are using the Web to deliver university-level academic courses in any language.
http://www.utexas.edu/world/lecture/

Writing HTML – a site with many learning materials online.
http://www.mcli.dist.maricopa.edu/tut/

Glossary

ActiveX control A control using ActiveX technologies. An ActiveX control can be automatically downloaded and executed by a Web browser. ActiveX is not a programming language, but rather a set of rules for how applications should share information. Programmers can develop ActiveX controls in a variety of languages, including C, C++, Visual Basic and Java.

ADSL *Asymmetric digital subscriber line*, a communications technology that allows data to be sent over existing copper telephone lines. ADSL supports data rates from 1.5 to 9 megabits per second when receiving data and from 16 to 640 kilobits per second when sending data.

applet A small Java program that can be embedded in an HTML page. Applets differ from full-fledged Java applications in that they are not allowed to access certain resources on the local computer, such as files and serial devices (modems, printers, etc), and are prohibited from communicating with most other computers across a network.

ASF *Advanced Streaming Format*, a streaming multimedia file format developed by Microsoft. ASF has been submitted to ISO and IETF for standardization. It is expected eventually to replace the older AVI format.

AVI *Audio Video Interleave*, the file format for Microsoft's Video for Windows standard.

bandwidth How much data or information you can send through a connection. Usually measured in bits per second. A full page of English text is about 16,000 bits. A fast modem can move about 15,000 bits in one second. Full-motion full-screen video would require roughly 10,000,000 bits per second, depending on compression.

BBS An electronic message centre. Most bulletin boards typically serve a wide variety of specific interest groups. They allow you to dial in with a modem, review messages left by others and leave your own messages.

CGI *(Common Gateway Interface)* A set of rules that describe how a Web server communicates with another piece of software on the same machine, and how the other piece of software (the 'CGI program') talks to the Web server. Any piece of software can be a CGI program if it handles input and output according to the CGI standard. Usually a CGI program is a small program that takes data from a Web server and does something with it, like putting the content of a form into an e-mail message, or turning the data into a database query.

CML *(Computer Managed Learning)*   A software management tool that is primarily designed to assist large groups of learners, teachers and administrators cope with the problems of tracking learners through series of individualized instruction.

cookie   The most common meaning of 'cookie' on the Internet refers to a piece of information sent by a Web server to a Web browser that the browser software is expected to save and to send back to the server whenever the browser makes additional requests from the server. Depending on the type of cookie used, and the browser's settings, the browser may accept or not accept the cookie, and may save the cookie for either a short time or a long time. Cookies might contain information such as log-in or registration information, online 'shopping cart' information and user preferences. When a server receives a request from a browser that includes a cookie, the server is able to use the information stored in the cookie.

Courseware   Software that has been designed for use as an educational program.

FTP   *File Transfer Protocol*, the Internet protocol used for sending and retrieving files.

GIF Pronounced 'jiff' or 'giff' (hard 'g'), stands for *Graphics Interchange Format*, a bit-mapped graphics file format used by the World Wide Web, CompuServe and many BBSs. GIF supports colour and various resolutions. It also includes data compression, making it especially effective for scanned photos.

HTML   *HyperText Markup Language*, a Web page authoring language.
HTTP   *HyperText Transfer Protocol*, the underlying protocol used by the World Wide Web. HTTP defines how messages are formatted and transmitted, and what actions Web servers and Web browsers should take in response to various commands. For example, when you enter a Uniform Resource Locator (URL) in your browser, this sends an HTTP command to the Web server directing it to fetch and transmit the requested Web page.

Java   A high-level programming language developed by Sun Microsystems. Java is a general purpose programming language with a number of features that make the language well suited for use on the World Wide Web. Small Java applications are called Java applets and can be downloaded from a Web server and run on your computer by a Java-compatible Web browser, such as Netscape Navigator or Microsoft Internet Explorer.

JavaScript A scripting language developed by Netscape to enable Web authors to design interactive sites. Although it shares many of the features and structures of the full Java language, it was developed independently. JavaScript can interact with HTML source code, enabling Web authors to spice up their sites with dynamic content. JavaScript is endorsed by a number of software companies and is an open language that anyone can use without purchasing a licence. It is supported by recent browsers from Netscape and Microsoft, though Internet Explorer supports only a subset, which Microsoft calls Jscript.

JPEG *Joint Photographic Experts Group*, pronounced 'jay-peg'. JPEG is a compression technique for colour images. Although it can reduce file sizes to about 5 per cent of their normal size, some detail is lost in the compression.

plug-in A hardware or software module that adds a specific feature or service to a larger system. For example, there are number of plug-ins for Web browsers that enable them to display different types of audio or video messages.

RealVideo A streaming technology developed by RealNetworks for transmitting live video over the Internet. RealVideo uses a variety of data compression techniques and works with both normal IP connections and IP Multicast connections.

TCP/IP *Transmission Control Protocol/Internet Protocol*, the suite of communications protocols used to connect host computers on the Internet. The TCP/IP protocol suite includes several protocols, including TCP and IP.

URL *Uniform Resource Locator*, the standard convention of specifying the location of every resource on the Internet and within a Web application. A typical Web URL takes the form of:
http://www.website.com/a_page.htm

VBScript *Visual Basic Scripting Edition*, a scripting language developed by Microsoft and supported by Microsoft's Internet Explorer Web browser. VBScript is based on the Visual Basic programming language, but is much simpler. In many ways, it is similar to JavaScript. It enables Web authors to include interactive controls, such as buttons and scroll-bars, on their Web pages.

whiteboard   An area on a computer screen that multiple users can write or draw on. Whiteboards are a principal component of online conferencing or multi-user learning applications because they enable visual as well as audio communication.

World Wide Web   A global, interconnected system of Internet servers that support specially formatted documents, commonly known as Web pages. Web pages are formatted in HTML and support links to other documents, as well as graphics, audio and video files. Users accessing a Web page can jump from one page to another by clicking on hyperlinks.

XML   *eXtensible Markup Language*, a specification developed by the World Wide Web Consortium. XML is a pared-down version of SGML, designed especially for Web documents. It allows designers to create their own customized tags, enabling the definition, transmission, validation and interpretation of data between applications and between organizations.

Index

Page references in *italics* indicate figures